T0320914

Patient Capital
The Role of Family Firms in Sustainable Business

Sustainable businesses create economic and social value while simultaneously protecting the natural environment for future generations. This examination of environmental sustainability through the lens of the family business identifies factors that help family and non-family organizations address the dilemma of balancing short-term productivity, efficiency, and profitability objectives, with innovating for long-term sustainable value creation. Exploring the case of the wine industry – an industry characterized by a variety of governance systems – Sanjay and Pramodita Sharma develop fresh insights into influences and drivers for proactive environmental strategies to address major global sustainability challenges. By doing so, the authors are able to demonstrate that family firms with a focus on transgenerational continuity of business, long temporal orientation, shared vision, faster decision-making processes, and the goal of preserving socioemotional wealth are more likely to make patient long-term investments for innovations in products, services, processes, and business models to address environmental sustainability challenges.

DR. SANJAY SHARMA is Dean of the Grossman School of Business, University of Vermont. His previous published books include *Competing for a Sustainable World: Building Capacity for Sustainable Innovation* (2014), *Sustainability, Innovation and Entrepreneurship* (2008), *Environmental Strategy and Competitive Advantage* (2005), *and Research in Corporate Sustainability: The Evolving Theory and Practice of Organizations in the Natural Environment* (2004), as well as numerous articles and book chapters.

DR. PRAMODITA SHARMA is Professor and Daniel Clark Sanders Chair in Entrepreneurship & Family Business at the Grossman School of Business, University of Vermont. Her previously published work includes *Entrepreneurs in Every Generation: How Successful Family Businesses Develop Their Next Leaders* (2016), *SAGE Handbook of Family Business* (2014), *Family Business Studies: Review and Annotated Bibliography* (1996, 2012), as well as numerous articles and book chapters.

Organizations and the Natural Environment

Series editors

Jorge Rivera, *George Washington University*
J. Alberto Aragon-Correa, *University of Surrey*

Editorial board

Nicole Darnall, *Arizona State University*
Magali Delmas, *University of California, Los Angeles*
Ans Kolk, *University of Amsterdam*
Thomas P. Lyon, *University of Michigan*
Alfred Marcus, *University of Minnesota*
Michael Toffel, *Harvard Business School*
Christopher Weible, *University of Colorado*

The increasing attention given to environmental protection issues has resulted in a growing demand for high-quality, actionable research on sustainability and business environmental management. This new series, published in conjunction with the Group for Research on Organizations and the Natural Environment (GRONEN), presents students, academics, managers, and policy makers with the latest thinking on key topics influencing business practice today.

Published titles
Sharma and Sharma, *Patient Capital*
Marcus, *Innovations in Sustainability*
Bowen, *After Greenwashing*

Forthcoming titles
Gouldson and Sullivan, *Governance and the Changing Climate for Business*

Patient Capital

The Role of Family Firms in Sustainable Business

SANJAY SHARMA
Grossman School of Business, University of Vermont
PRAMODITA SHARMA
Grossman School of Business, University of Vermont

CAMBRIDGE
UNIVERSITY PRESS

CAMBRIDGE
UNIVERSITY PRESS

University Printing House, Cambridge CB2 8BS, United Kingdom

One Liberty Plaza, 20th Floor, New York, NY 10006, USA

477 Williamstown Road, Port Melbourne, VIC 3207, Australia

314–321, 3rd Floor, Plot 3, Splendor Forum, Jasola District Centre, New Delhi – 110025, India

79 Anson Road, #06–04/06, Singapore 079906

Cambridge University Press is part of the University of Cambridge.

It furthers the University's mission by disseminating knowledge in the pursuit of education, learning, and research at the highest international levels of excellence.

www.cambridge.org
Information on this title: www.cambridge.org/9781107123663
DOI: 10.1017/9781316402528

© Sanjay Sharma and Pramodita Sharma 2019

First published 2019

Printed and bound in Great Britain by Clays Ltd, Elcograf S.p.A.

A catalogue record for this publication is available from the British Library.

ISBN 978-1-107-12366-3 Hardback

Cambridge University Press has no responsibility for the persistence or accuracy of URLs for external or third-party internet websites referred to in this publication and does not guarantee that any content on such websites is, or will remain, accurate or appropriate.

Contents

Figures

Tables

Preface

Sustainable business is about the creation of economic and social value while simultaneously protecting the natural environment for future generations. Therefore, sustainable businesses not only generate economic, social and environmental value, but they also seek to be long-lived and resilient. Such enterprises face the challenge of balancing their short-term performance objectives while simultaneously making long-term patient investments in the future. A major challenge for the achievement of such a balance is a focus of publicly listed companies on short-term financial performance and quarterly reporting and financial analyst scrutiny in response to the expectations of capital markets. These short-term financial results impact the performance of the firm's share value and executive compensation for the top management team of the firm. While the short-term focus certainly has positive impacts on efficiency and productivity improvement, it is often attributed as a reason for the discouragement of investments in radical innovations in clean technologies and business models. This is because such sustainable investments more often than not require patience and a long-term pay back and competitive advantage in the unknown future while having the potential to affect short-term financial results or cash flows negatively.

An important question that researchers in corporate sustainability and organizations and the natural environment seek to address is *how can organizations address the dilemma of balancing short-term productivity, efficiency, and profitability objectives, with innovating for long-term sustainable value creation?* We address this research question by comparing and contrasting organizations with two different governance systems:

1) Firms with dispersed ownership, public listing in capital markets, and in which the relationship between the top management and the firms' owners is guided by an employment contract and agency; and

2) Family firms with an overlap of ownership and management and closely held control by a group of individuals with kinship ties.

In both types of firms, the controlling shareholders' and investors' goals and preferences guide the strategic orientation and resource allocation decisions of the managers. While institutionalized control dominates the mind-set of contractual managers, personalized control guides family firms (e.g., Carney, 2005). In contractually driven firms, delivering on short-term financial performance objectives is not only critical for an organization's relationship with its shareholders, but is also important for the career progression of its top managers since their quarterly and annual performance evaluation is tied to stock prices and a major portion of their compensation includes stock options. The short-term orientation aligns the preferences of the controlling shareholders and firms' top managers.

In sharp contrast, in family firms guided by a relational contract based on an overlap of ownership and management, the primary organizational goal is often the survival and sustainability of the enterprise *to create value for the future generations of the controlling family*. Although such firms certainly cannot afford to ignore the achievement of short and medium-term economic objectives, investment of resources to build valuable capabilities for future business, entrepreneurship, and long-term value creation by succeeding generations is equally, if not more, important.

These insights are not entirely new. Behavioral researchers have differentiated between contractual and relational contracts (Clark and Mills, 1979; Gagné, Sharma and de Massis, 2014), while strategy scholars have made inroads to understanding the agentic vs. stewardship mind-sets (Schulze et al., 2001). Nevertheless, with some notable exceptions (e.g., Berrone et al., 2010; Gómez-Mejía et al., 2011), most of the research in both literatures is focused on contractual and agentic issues. We argue that this inherent bias in the literature is divorced from the realities of a large majority of enterprises (family owned and controlled firms) that dominate between 70 percent and 90 percent of most global economies in number and also in terms of the share of the GDP. Hence, the literature is incomplete in its usable knowledge to help resolve the dilemma of balancing short-term and long-term performance and investments for business organizations and achieving societal goals of meeting global sustainability challenges such as clean air, clean water, preservation of diversity of life and species, and protecting natural habitats on which mankind relies. Without understanding decision-making processes in a major sector of the world's most developed as well as developing economies, namely, family firms guided by relational and stewardship mind-sets, it is difficult to generate comprehensive knowledge of the factors that enhance or inhibit the development of sustainable businesses that simultaneously create economic, social, and environmental value in the short- and long-term.

In this monograph, we address this gap by comparing and contrasting strategic decision-making for sustainable innovation in family and non-family firms. Family enterprises create the bulk of economic and societal value in most economies and contribute to maintaining sustainable environment and communities (Astrachan and Shanker, 2003; La Porta, Lopez-de-Silanes and Shleifer, 1999). Firms in this major sector of the economy are more often, albeit not always, guided by the relational contracts and stewardship mind-set (Miller and Le Breton-Miller, 2005). Yet, in spite of their ubiquity, depth of impact on the economy or society, and a greater likelihood of community and environmental rootedness, these enterprises are an under-researched context in the sustainability literature (Dyer Jr. and Whetten, 2006; Sharma and Sharma, 2011; 2018).

Just as there are major differences between non-family corporations in their sustainability strategies (Àragon-Correa, 1998; Russo and Fouts, 1997; Sharma and Vredenburg, 1998), not all family firms are equally motivated to build capacity for creating sustainable value by preserving natural capital and contributing to social welfare and their communities (Delmas and Gergaud, 2014; Marques, Preses and Simon, 2014). Family firms are also heterogeneous in their strategies and missions (Ward, 1987; Westhead and Cowling, 1998). In this monograph, we also seek to understand the factors that lead to such differences not only among publicly held corporations with diffused ownership but also among family firms where ownership is concentrated with a kinship group. That is, we identify drivers of patient long-term investments in a proactive environmental sustainability strategy in family firms.

To limit the literature and scope of the phenomenon to be studied, *we focus only on environmental sustainability* since the social sustainability and corporate social responsibility literature is substantial and merits another monograph by itself. We identify factors that help and hinder investments of resources by family and non-family firms to build their capacities for long-term sustainable value creation. For such comparisons, it is important to control for external variation in the industry and the institutional environment. Thus, we supplement our theoretical analysis with data from one setting – the winery industry in three countries. This industry is characterized by a variety of governance systems: multi-generational family firms, first-generation family firms, corporate-owned wineries, and lifestyle wineries. Hence, it allows comparison of sustainability drivers and practices across different governance systems. The theoretical arguments presented are illustrated by multiple research interviews and archival data from over twenty-one wineries in Canada, the United States, France, and Chile, supplemented by secondary data from archival material from eleven other wineries. The data are woven into our review of extant literature and theory development to offer our framework, propositions, and recommendations for the unique characteristics of family firms that can be useful guides for organization design and change for non-family firms seeking to develop an effective proactive environmental strategy via innovations, technologies, and business models based on patient long-term investments.

This monograph fills a gap in the sustainability literature by presenting fresh insights for sustainability scholars, family business scholars, practitioners, and policy makers to better understand drivers that help firms balance their short-term goals with long-term sustainable investments. Simultaneously, it casts new light on why some family firms do better than others in building capacity to pursue long-term orientation and trans-generational sustainable value creation. We have enjoyed the process of researching and writing this monograph and hope that the readers will find ideas that stimulate empirical research projects, organizational and strategic change, and policy changes for unleashing the power of business for a sustainable planet.

August 2018

References

Aragon-Correa, J. A. 1998. Strategic proactivity and firm approach to the natural environment. *Academy of Management Journal*, 41(5): 556–567.
Astrachan, J. H. and Shanker, M. C. 2003. Family businesses' contribution to the US economy: A closer look. *Family Business Review*, 16: 211–219.

Berrone, P., Cruz, C., Gomez-Mejia, L. and Larraza-Kintana, M. 2010. Ownership structure and corporate response to institutional pressures: Do family-controlled firms pollute less? *Administrative Science Quarterly*, 55: 82–113.

Carney, M. 2005. Corporate governance and competitive advantage in family controlled firms. *Entrepreneurship: Theory & Practice*, 29: 249–265.

Clark, M. S. and Mills, J. R. 1979. Interpersonal attraction in exchange and communal relationships. *Journal of Personality and Social Psychology*, 37: 12–24.

Delmas, M. and Gergaud, O. 2014. Sustainable certification for future generations: The case of family business. *Family Business Review*, 27(3): 228–243.

Dyer Jr., G. W. and Whetten D. A. 2006. Family firms and social responsibility. Preliminary evidence from the S&P 500. *Entrepreneurship Theory and Practice*, 30(4): 785–802.

Gagné, M., Sharma, P. and De Massis, A. 2014. The study of organizational behavior in family business. *European Journal of Work and Organizational Psychology*. Advance online publication.

Gómez-Mejía, L. R., Cruz, C., Berrone, P. and De Castro, J. 2011. The bind that ties: Socioemotional wealth preservation in family firms. *The Academy of Management Annals*, 5: 653–707.

LaPorta, R., Lopez-de-Silanes, F. and Shleifer, A. 1999. Corporate ownership around the world. *Journal of Finance*, 54: 471–517.

Marques, P., Preses, P. and Simon, A. 2014. The heterogeneity of family firms in CSR engagement: The role of values. *Family Business Review*, 27 (3): 206–227.

Miller, D. and Le Breton-Miller, I. 2005. *Managing for the Long Run*. Boston, MA: Harvard Business School Press.

Russo, M. V. and Fouts, P. A. 1997. A resource-based perspective on corporate environmental performance and profitability. *Academy of Management Journal*, 40: 534–559.

Schulze, W. S., Lubatkin, M. H., Dino, R. N. and Buchholz, R. A. 2001. Agency relationships in family firms: Theory and evidence. *Organization Science*, 12(2): 99–116.

Sharma, P. and Sharma, S. 2011. Drivers of proactive environmental strategy in family firms. *Business Ethics Quarterly*, 21(2): 309–334.

Sharma, P. and Sharma, S. 2018 (forthcoming). The role of family firms in corporate sustainability. In A. Sturdy, S. Huesinkveld, T. Reay and D. Strang (eds.), *The Oxford Handbook of Management Ideas*. Oxford, UK: Oxford University Press.

Sharma, S. and Vredenburg, H. 1998. Proactive corporate environmental strategy and the development of competitively valuable organizational capabilities. *Strategic Management Journal*, 19: 729–753.

Ward, J. 1987. *Keeping the Family Business Healthy: How to Plan for Continuing Growth, Profitability, and Family Leadership*. San Francisco, CA: Jossey-Bass.

Westhead, P. and Cowling, M. 1998. Family firm research: The need for a methodological rethink. *Entrepreneurship Theory & Practice*, 23(1): 31–56.

1 | Definitions

Introduction

The World Commission on Environment and Development (WCED) was created by the United Nations in 1983 to address growing concern about the accelerating deterioration of the human environment and natural resources and its consequences for economic and social development.[1] In its 1987 report, *Our Common Future,* the WCED coined the most-often-quoted definition of *sustainable development* as the "development that meets the needs of the present without compromising the ability of future generations to meet their own needs." This definition placed equity across generations and over *time* at the core of economic development.

Scholarship inspired by the WCED report focused on unpacking the elements of sustainable development, identifying its drivers and barriers, and ascertaining the role of business in addressing the global social and environmental challenges in this domain. For example, in 1989, Karl-Henrik Robèrt, a Swedish oncologist, translated the WCED definition into four system conditions for sustainability via the Natural Step Framework. These conditions called for eliminating humanity's contribution to (i) the progressive buildup of substances extracted from the Earth's crust, (ii) buildup of chemicals and compounds, (iii) physical degradation and destruction of nature and natural processes, and (iv) conditions that undermine people's capacity to meet their basic human needs (*Natural Step*, n.d.).

The central elements of sustainable development as proposed by WCED and the Natural Step Framework are fairly similar. However, these macro systems concepts are easier to visualize at a global, national, or a societal level, but are much more difficult to operationalize, measure, and implement at the firm level of analysis that is the central focus of most strategy and organizational scholars. Unpacking the elements of

1

the WCED definition, however, provides some guidance for operationalization at the firm level of analysis. The definition calls for businesses to adopt three sustainability related principles: (i) sustainability of resource extraction – should not exceed the capacity of natural systems to regenerate resources such as forests, fisheries, soil, and clean water; (ii) sustainability of waste generation – should not exceed the carrying capacity of natural systems to absorb them; and (iii) sustainability of social equity – business activities should have a positive impact on poverty reduction, distribution of income, and human rights. Hence, this definition is relevant to the role of business in sustainable development, as defined in this monograph.

John Elkington, the founder of the consulting firm SustainAbility, coined the term triple bottom line, arguing that firms needed to measure three separate bottom lines: profits, people, and planet (Elkington, 1997; *The Economist*, 2009). Since then, the term sustainability or corporate sustainability began to distinguish a firm's triple bottom line strategy from its traditional economic performance. The urgency and necessity of firms to consider their performance on triple dimensions of profits, people, and planet is increasingly driven by global reports of climate change, rising seas, and air and water pollution brought to the attention of organizational leadership by extensive news coverage of United Nations Conventions such as the 2015 Paris Agreement, award-winning documentaries such as *An Inconvenient Truth* (2006) and its sequel *An Inconvenient Sequel: Truth to Power* (2017), and increasing number of businesses committing to the UN's Sustainable Development Goals (SDGs). While many business leaders and decision makers are persuaded of the need to do something meaningful to contribute to the conservation of our planet and reversing the negative trends in atmospheric destruction, the impact of such actions on the other two 'p's of organizational profits and people is far from clear. Thus, decision makers wrestle with uncertainty while making decisions for their firms.

In this monograph, *sustainability* refers to a firm's strategy and investments intended to achieve performance on a triple bottom line; that is, generation of financial returns on investment that are satisfactory for shareholders and investors, enhancement of social justice and human welfare, and reduction of negative environmental impacts or generation of positive environmental impacts (refer to Table 1.1 for an overview of terms). Further, in order to narrow the scope of the monograph to a manageable set of literature, we focus mainly on *environmental sustainability*; that is, strategies, actions, and practices undertaken by business with regard to their interface with the natural environment. While we do not completely exclude discussions of social impacts of business since in several contexts (especially the emerging low-income markets) where social and environmental issues are closely intertwined, these are less central to the review and discussion.

In academic literature, the term environmental sustainability is most frequently used in niche journals such as *Business Strategy and the Environment*, *Greener Management International*, *Journal of Industrial Ecology*, *Organization and Environment*, and *Sustainable Development* while the focus of corporate response and strategies on social issues is often the focus of journals such as *Business and Society* where the more commonly used term is corporate social responsibility, or CSR. However, its usage in strategy and management journals is more limited. In the traditional strategy literature, the term sustainable is most commonly used in reference to long-lasting competitive advantage or the "economic performance" element of the triple bottom line. In the domain of financial performance, more recently, scholarship on impact investing and corporate philanthropy has emerged. The bottom lines focused on people and the planet have gained momentum in the management literature starting in the late 1990s. Even so, to avoid empirical complexity, most academic research focuses on only one of these dimensions – people or the planet via either CSR or corporate environmental strategy.

The social and environmental research streams are largely addressed by researchers in the two divisions of the *Academy of Management* – Social Issues in Management (SIM) and Organizations and the Natural Environment (ONE). More recently, scholarship on the social dimension of sustainability is gaining momentum in the Organizational Behavior (OB) division (e.g., El Akremi et al, 2015). While there is a great deal of overlap, each research stream tends to use different terms to refer to the elements that make up the concept of sustainability. For example, terms like CSR or corporate citizenship focus on the social dimension of sustainability; while others like corporate greening or corporate environmental strategy focus on the ecological dimension.

Two terms have been used in the literature to describe the organizational strategies focused on each of the three triple bottom line dimensions. These are Corporate Philanthropy and Impact Investing (for the profit dimension), CSR and Corporate Citizenship (for the people dimension), and Corporate Greening and Corporate Environmental Strategy (for the planet dimension). While our focus in this monograph will be to understand patient investments in proactive environmental strategies (PES) by family and non-family firms, understanding the differences between these terms is helpful in delineating the extant literature that is relevant for embedding the discussions in this monograph. Table 1.1 summarizes various terms used in the literature, sometimes without a clear separation or delineation. Following Table 1.1, we briefly elaborate on the more commonly accepted definitions or usage of each of these terms.

Key Terms in the Sustainability Literature

Corporate Philanthropy

Extant literature uses the term corporate philanthropy to describe a firm's actions to mitigate negative social and environmental impacts. Corporate philanthropy usually refers to corporate giving or donations intended to tackle government failures in addressing social needs, problems, and challenges. A distinct stream of literature uses the term strategic philanthropy (e.g., Porter and Kramer, 2002; Post and Waddock, 1995). This concept argues that firms can engage in philanthropy to further their strategic interests. That is, they develop a strategic plan to give away resources with nothing apparent in return in order to garner intangible benefits such as goodwill or legitimacy or license to operate. Even though strategic philanthropy is undertaken for a strategic business purpose, it does not require the firm to change its core strategy or develop goals to achieve triple bottom line performance.

Impact Investing

Since 2009, a diverse community of investors, business leaders, and researchers have coalesced to form the Global Impact Investing Network (GIIN). This nonprofit organization defines impact investments as "the investments into companies, organizations, and funds with the intention to generate social and environmental impact alongside a financial return" (GIIN, n.d.). This initiative provides an infrastructure to support the activities and research related to impact investing. While

Table 1.1 *Key Terms in the Sustainability Literature*

Macro-level concept		Sustainability	
Triple Bottom Line Dimensions	Profits *Economic*	People *Social*	Planet *Environmental*
Focal Stakeholder of Interest	Shareholders / Investors	Internal Stakeholders – employees External Stakeholders – community, NGOs, suppliers, customers, regulators	Community, NGOs, regulators, customers, suppliers, the Earth and its natural resources (e.g., air, water, minerals)
Success Indicators	Financial Return on Investments	Social justice, fair prices and wages, fair treatment, human welfare	Preservation and enhancement of the natural resources, habitats, species
Disciplinary Focus	BPS Division of the Academy of Management Finance	SIM & OB Divisions of the Academy of Management	ONE Division of the Academy of Management
Commonly Used Strategies / Terms in the Literature	Corporate Philanthropy; Impact Investing	Corporate Social Responsibility (CSR) Corporate Citizenship	Corporate Greening; Corporate Environmental Strategy (proactive vs. reactive)
Firm Level Concept		Sustainable Business	

micro-level impact investing efforts at individual, household, and community levels are gaining momentum, scientific research on this topic is in early stages (e.g., Bugg-Levine and Emerson, 2011). However, with the emergence of a specialized niche journal focused on related research – the *Journal of Sustainable Finance and Investments* – scholarly interest in this topic is expected to grow. Jackson (2013) considers it as one of the most promising and creative areas of development finance.

Our interest in this monograph is to understand the factors that enable or hinder the core thinking of key decision makers regarding environmental strategies of ongoing firms rather than on how and where a business invests or spends its profits. Thus, while we acknowledge the importance of financial profitability dimension of sustainability, building related theory is beyond the scope of this monograph.

Corporate Social Responsibility (CSR)

Carroll (1979: 500), provided an early conceptualization of CSR: "Corporate social responsibility encompasses the economic, legal, ethical, and discretionary (philanthropic) expectations that society has of organizations at a given point in time." Building on this conceptualization and other definitions in the literature, El Akremi, Gond, Swaen, De Roeck and Igalens (2015) developed and validated a thirty-five-item scale to measure employees' CSR perceptions. These authors define CSR as "an organization's context-specific actions and policies that aim to enhance the welfare of stakeholders by accounting for the triple bottom line of economic, social, and environmental performance, with a focus on employees' perceptions" (El Akremi et al., 2015: 623). Notable progress is being made in the CSR literature to assess a firm's legal and ethical responsibilities toward its stakeholders.

Since societal perspectives about negative impacts of business operations are constantly evolving, firms need to address a moving target. For example, from the Industrial Revolution through the thirties, child labor was a norm in a wide variety of occupations not only in the United States but in most developed countries of the time. Today, while over 200 million children are still engaged as laborers in the world, such practices are abhorred by the International Labor Organization of the United Nations. Amidst such changing expectations, the CSR literature aims to understand firm activities directed to mitigate what society deems negative or unacceptable behaviors toward its employees or the community in which it operates. This may involve investments in its own operations and/or via philanthropy. However, CSR does not necessarily imply that a firm will fundamentally change its strategy and operations to generate positive social or environmental impacts.

Corporate Citizenship

Corporate citizenship is used to describe a firm's role in, or responsibility toward, society. Broadly, it refers to "the portfolio of socioeconomic activities that companies often undertake to fulfill perceived duties as members of society" (Gardberg and Fombrun, 2006: 330). Since corporations are granted "the legal and political rights of individual citizens through incorporation," they also are ascribed, explicitly and implicitly, "a set of responsibilities" (Gardberg and Fombrun, 2006: 330). These authors provide examples of corporate citizenship as including "pro-bono activities, corporate volunteerism, charitable contributions, support for community education and health care initiatives, and environmental programs – few of which are legally mandated, but many of which have come to be expected by government hosts and local communities" (Gardberg and Fombrun, 2006: 330). Matten and Crane (2005: 173) argue for a broader definition of corporate citizenship as "the role of the corporation in administering citizenship rights for individuals" indicating that the corporation is not only a citizen itself but administers citizenship for "traditional stakeholders such as employees, customers, or shareholders," and "wider constituencies with no direct transactional relationship to the company." Regardless of a narrower or broader definition, the term corporate citizenship includes elements of corporate action and strategy similar to CSR. It is no surprise therefore that the two terms are often used interchangeably in practice to describe a firm's social and community initiatives. Regardless of how these terms are actually used by firms, or are defined by scholars, CSR or Corporate Citizenship do not imply that the firm will change its core operations or strategies. Usually, these terms are used to describe a firm's practices and actions to mitigate the impacts of its operations that society deems negative.

Corporate Greening

While the terms CSR and corporate citizenship emphasize social actions and impacts, corporate greening is used to describe corporate actions to address environmental impacts of a firm's operations. It refers to actions adopted by a firm for risk reduction, reengineering, and cost-cutting (Hart, 1997). Thus, greening usually refers to organizational practices but rarely refers to corporate strategy, innovation, or technology development (Hart, 1997). Like CSR and corporate citizenship, the term corporate greening describes reduced negative environmental impacts but does not imply a change in core operations or strategy to generate positive impacts. Just as societal expectations of appropriate social practices have evolved, societal expectations of environmental pollution continuously evolve. For example, societal perceptions about emissions of waste from manufacturing facilities have changed substantially over the last five decades. Visual representations such as smokestacks represented economic development in the 1950s, but they now represent air pollution in most societies across the world.

Corporate Environmental Strategy

Corporate environmental strategy refers to a firm's strategy to manage the interface between its business and the natural environment (Aragón-Correa and Sharma, 2003). Since the nineties, a significant stream of literature in ONE has emerged around corporate environmental strategy. For example, based on a comparative case study of seven companies in the oil industry, Sharma and Vredenburg (1998) distinguish between firms following *proactive versus reactive environmental strategies*. Proactive environmental strategy for a firm refers to a "consistent pattern of environmental practices, across all dimensions relevant to their range of activities, not required to be undertaken in fulfillment of environmental regulations or in response to isomorphic pressures within the industry as standard business practice" (Sharma and Vredenburg, 1998: 733). Firms pursuing a reactive environmental strategy may comply with the prevailing laws, lobby against environmental regulation, and even excel in specific areas in reducing environmental impacts, but their focus and consistency in pursuit of environmental strategy is limited (Sharma and Vredenburg, 1998). Proactive environmental strategy, on the other hand, implies changes in a firm's strategy to prevent negative environmental impacts at source rather than just reducing them after the negative impacts such as pollution are generated (Russo and Fouts, 1997).

Sustainable Business

A *sustainable business* is one that has altered or developed, or is in the process of altering or developing, its strategy and operations in accordance with the principles of sustainability. These principles encompass the triple bottom line: above industry average performance on financial, social, and environmental metrics. The sustainable firm's business model and strategy are designed to achieve not only its economic or core objectives (e.g., for a nonprofit organization, the core objective may be the delivery of health care or clean water rather than profits), but also its social and environmental performance. Hence, a sustainable business is significantly different from a firm that does not fundamentally change its business model and strategy but rather acts responsibly by adopting practices to mitigate the negative social and environmental impacts of its existing operations. As compared to the terms already discussed, sustainable business, as used in this monograph, has fundamental implications not only for business strategy but also for the core operational and business model of the firm.

It is unlikely and perhaps impossible for any organization to be completely sustainable by itself. While sustainability is a journey on which an increasing number of organizations have embarked, networks of firms are forming industrial ecosystems to use each other's wastes so as to ensure that no pollution leaves the network. A good example of this is the Danish Klundborg Symbiosis, a partnership between eight public and private companies in Kalundborg (Denmark) that use the circular approach to production. This approach builds on the principle that a residue from one company becomes a resource for another thereby benefiting the local economy, environment, and society (for more details, please see www.symbiosis.dk/en).

Sustainability Strategy

At the firm level, a *sustainability strategy* aims to achieve its short-term financial, social, and environmental performance without compromising its long-term performance on these three dimensions. This means that the firm needs to create value for its stakeholders in the present while investing in strategies and resources to improve the social, environmental, and economic performance desired by its stakeholders (including its shareholders) in the future. In this process, the firm has to manage the uncertainty related to the evolving and changing definition of "value" over time for its various stakeholders (El Akremi et al., 2015). Hence, the temporal orientation of the dominant coalition or the top management team of a firm becomes an important determinant in understanding its environmental strategy. *Temporal orientation* is the distance into the past or future that an individual or a collective considers in their cognitive processes, behaviors, and decision-making (Bluedorn, 2002).

Effectively addressing sustainability challenges by an existing business requires it to effect changes in its strategy, and perhaps also its business model and organizational design and structure. These are deep-rooted changes that may require investments in new technologies, entry into unfamiliar market segments such as lower-income markets in developing countries, and building new capabilities that may yield returns over longer term as compared to investments that firms normally make in incremental product innovations and entry into adjacent new markets. In order to build such capabilities, the strategic decision-making unit of the firm, whether the dominant coalition in family firms or the top management team in non-family firms, needs to be aligned in their vision about the firm's future business, their values toward the role of business in environmental preservation, and need to garner the support of their critical stakeholders.

What drives firms to undertake such investments that are likely to pay back over a longer term? What factors determine the top management team's strategic time horizon and expectations of return on investments? This monograph examines these factors within the context of ongoing businesses. While firms may also undertake investments in social sustainability initiatives, such as fair trade in its supply chain, we narrow our focus in this monograph on investments aimed to address major environmental sustainability challenges such as climate change, clean water, and renewable energy, amongst others, and refer to such investments and initiatives as a *proactive environmental strategy* (PES). We use the term *patient capital* for such long-term investments thereby distinguishing them from short-term investments.

Patient Capital

The term patient has been used in extant literature at different levels of analysis, ranging from the individual level at the perspective of an investor, to the macroeconomic or national level, but rarely at the firm level of analysis. A search of peer reviewed scholarly articles in ABI/Inform using the search terms patient and capital reveals almost no scholarly discussion of the concept. In its limited academic usage, the term is neither defined nor used consistently. The prefix patient is often used as a descriptor in the literature in association with terms other than capital and with varying interpretations. For example, "patient money" refers to research and development expenditures with uncertain outcomes undertaken by firms (Manners and Louderback, 1980). The term patient investor is used in theories of economic equilibrium while referring to individual investors or traders with longer-term return expectations (Grenadier and Wang, 2007; Shive and Yun, 2013).

In practitioner articles, patient capital is used in reference to foreign direct investments with long-term development objectives. However, this literature does not offer a definition. Nor does it embed the term in extant literature (Teece, 1992). Patient capital is also used in reference to the restructuring of financial markets to avoid financial crises similar to the one experienced in 2008 (Mazzucato, 2013), and in the context of long-term orientation of companies with shared employee ownership (Fojt, 1995). In referring to the external sources of capital for financing not-for-profit organizations, Kingston and Bolton (2004: 114) provide a rare definition of patient capital as "the finance provided over an extended period and below market rates. For example, a loan might be given with a ten-year capital repayment holiday. A subset of patient capital is when terms are not set until there is some certainty about the prospects for the venture." However, these authors do not refer to investments made by firms internally with long-term return expectations.

At the level of analysis of the firm, references to patient capital are very limited. Robeson and O'Connor (2013) find in their study that firms exhibit higher innovativeness when their decision makers are engaged and supportive of these projects, and patient with the financial results from investments. In the context of family firms, patient financial capital has been argued to be a positive attribute for innovation because of the lower accountability for short-term financial results and a higher motivation to perpetuate the business for future generations

(Sirmon and Hitt, 2003). Building on this idea, this monograph theorizes the conditions that encourage firms to pursue proactive environmental strategies.

Patient capital is not subject to traditional financial valuation models and challenges traditional economic theories such as the classic agency theory, which require managers to act in the best interests of the owners (which are usually equated with maximization of returns in the short term versus the long term) via transparent results that are continuously exposed to external markets for valuation purposes. For example, *Keiretsus* in Japan, *Chaebols* in Korea, and family conglomerates in India are known to deploy patient capital by cross-subsidizing projects that require longer returns with funds from high-profit-making and cash-generating businesses. In the late 1970s and through the 1980s, the Korean *Chaebols* were able to become serious players in dynamic random access memory (DRAM) technology, eclipsing Taiwan and other Asian powerhouses, through this strategy, even after sustaining tremendous financial pressures (Fuller, Akinwande, and Sodini, 2003).

Some common characteristics of patient capital include (a) willingness to forgo maximum financial returns for achieving social/environmental impact, (b) greater tolerance for risk than traditional investment capital, (c) longer time horizons for return of capital, and (d) intensive support of management to grow the enterprise. The last implies that the top management team of the firm has an objective to seek long-term growth rather than short-term returns. Indeed, there is some evidence that members of family businesses may choose growth and control of business over short-term dividends or cash back and, hence, exhibit patience with investments (Oswald et al., 2013). Hence, *patient capital* is not philanthropy or a grant, but an investment that foregoes short-term return for long-term growth and achievement of nonfinancial objectives such as social and environmental impacts, and control of business over generations (e.g., Meier and Schier, 2016). Thomas Friedman states that patient capital has "all the discipline of venture capital – demanding a return, and therefore rigor in how it is deployed – but expecting a return that is more in the 5 to 10 percent range, rather than the 35 percent that venture capitalists look for" (Friedman, 2007, n.p.). Based on this, we adopt Wikipedia's (n.d.) proposed working definition of *patient capital* as the willingness "to make a financial investment in a business with no expectation of turning a quick profit. Instead, the investor is willing to forgo an immediate return in anticipation of more substantial returns down the road."

In order to examine the factors influencing investment of patient capital by firms, in this monograph, we draw on extant literature and original primary and secondary research to compare strategies and investments in sustainable practices and business models by firms operating under two different corporate governance systems: those with ownership that is concentrated vs. dispersed, and firms controlled by one or few families vs. non-family members.

Corporate Governance

Corporate governance is broadly defined as "the process and structure used to direct and manage the business affairs of the company towards enhancing business prosperity and corporate accountability with the ultimate objective of realizing long-term shareholder value, whilst taking into account the interests of other stakeholder" (Keasey, Thompson, and Wright, 1997: 288). This is only one of the several broad-scope definitions from the literature as the focus of governance varies across disciplines. For example, in the economics and finance literatures, scholars relate corporate governance to capital allocation decisions within and across firms (Morck and Steier, 2005), as their interest is on issues relating to how the suppliers of finance to corporations (owners) get a return on their investment (Shleifer and Vishny, 1997). Hence, of prime importance to this research stream are the mechanisms and controls designed to reduce or eliminate the principal-agent problem (Baker and Anderson, 2010; Villalonga et al., 2015). From this perspective, governance is treated as synonymous with ownership (Carney, 2005; Gersick and Neus, 2014). For researchers in the discipline of law, corporate governance is an organizational mechanism that refers to the monitoring and control over the allocation of a firm's resources, and the structuring and management of such relationships within a firm (McCahery and Vermeulen, 2006). Thus, in each definition, there is varied emphasis on ownership and management dimensions.

In this monograph, our focus lies in understanding factors that enable or hinder the performance of a firm on the environmental dimension of its triple bottom line, not only in the short term, but also in the longer term. As both ownership and managerial decision-making significantly influence adoption of environmental strategies, we adopt Keasey, Thompson, and Wright's (1997) above-mentioned comprehensive definition of corporate governance as it includes both these dimensions.

Ownership vs. Management Control

Ownership may be widely dispersed (as in publicly listed companies) or tightly controlled by a small group of individuals (as in privately held companies). The relative proportion of each of these forms of governance varies across nations. In the United States, about 1 percent of all registered companies are publicly listed. While low in number, their impact on the economy is significant and thus these companies have been subject of a large body of research not only in finance but also in strategy (VanderMey, 2017). Ownership of these publicly listed companies is widely dispersed amongst many shareholders, each usually owning a few hundred to a few thousand shares and expecting short-term returns. Despite shareholder protections, these arm's-length equity investors are largely disorganized and lack a voice in corporate boardrooms where key decisions that impact returns on their investments are made. Only investors that accumulate stakes larger than 3 to 5 percent gain a voice in the boardrooms (Morck and Steier, 2005). These include institutional investors and firms such as Berkshire Hathaway that take major stock positions in a firm. However, such investors, while holding significant blocks of shares, do not have majority voting power in the firms they invest in. Such separation of ownership and management control grants significant power to the Chief Executive Officers (CEOs) and their *top management team* (TMT) to determine the strategic goals of the company (Cyert and March, 1963). As this influential group is well positioned to use (or abuse) their power according to their economic, social, and/or environmental values and beliefs, there has been significant scholarly interest in understanding the agency problems and inefficiencies caused as a consequence of separation of ownership and management roles in publicly listed firms (Chen and Smith, 1987; Jensen and Meckling, 1976). Efforts have been devoted to understanding how best to align the interests of owners and managers via incentive structures such as compensation and/or stock options related to corporate performance or monitoring systems (Jensen and Meckling, 1976).

In the last few years, two significant trends have become evident. First, there has been a steady decline in the number of publicly listed firms in the United States. While there were more than 7,000 such companies in the late 1990s, this number went down to about 4,900 ten years ago, and to 3,603 in 2018. Nevertheless, today's listed companies are larger and more stable than their counterparts in earlier decades. Second, is the important role of kinship groups or families in publicly listed firms. While earlier research had assumed that only institutional investors who could gain significant ownership stakes needed to have a strong voice in the boardrooms of public companies, more recently another important stakeholder group – kinship group i.e., members of one or a few related families – may also own significant numbers of shares to put them in an influential position on the board. In fact, both in the United States and the United Kingdom, a third of the listed companies are family controlled (Villalonga et al., 2015). Such control is particularly dominant in some industries like agricultural production and the livestock industry (holding 100 percent market share), the motion picture industry (with 95 percent share), automotive dealerships and service stations (with 88 percent share), hotels and other lodging businesses (79 percent share), and 60 percent in printing and publishing firms (Villalonga and Amit, 2009).

In contrast to the United States and United Kingdom, in much of the rest of the world, few wealthy families exert concentrated control of large corporations and govern them with the intention of retaining this control over generations (Morck and Steier, 2005). For example, LaPorta, Lopez-de-Silanes, and Shleifer (1999) contrasted the ownership of large and medium-sized publicly listed companies around the world and illustrated that a large majority of corporations in countries like Mexico, Argentina, Hong Kong, Israel, Mexico, and Sweden are family controlled.

Family-controlled firms also dominate the private sector, not only in the United States but around the world, as estimates range from 60 percent to 98 percent of all businesses in most countries (e.g., Fernández-Aráoz, Iqbal, and Ritter, 2015; Shanker and Astrachan, 1996; please refer to Global Data Points @ the Family Firm Institute for the most recent data). While a large majority of small and medium businesses are family controlled, in Germany and Japan, family-controlled conglomerates characterized by long-term debt, financial ownership by large investors, weak corporate control, and rigid labor markets tend to dominate the economy (Aguilera, 2005; LaPorta et al., 1999). And, large private enterprise is on a rise as evidenced by a 2010 McKinsey & Co. study that found 60 percent of private sector companies with revenues of over $1 billion each in emerging economies were owned by founders or families. By 2025, family businesses will represent nearly 40 percent of the world's large enterprises, up from 15 percent in 2010 (Björnberg, Elstrodt, and Pandit, 2014), emphasizing the need to examine, understand, and engage this fast-growing segment of the economy in addressing sustainability challenges.

Family vs. Non-Family Control

Family firms are fundamentally different from non-family firms as the *dominant coalition* (DC) of these firms is formed of individuals with bonds of kinship with the next generation and are thus often managed with an eye toward long-term continuity (Chua, Chrisman, and Sharma, 1999). The US Bureau of Labor Statistics reports a decline in the median number of years a salaried employee works for one organization from 4.6 years in 2014 to 4.2 years in 2016. Regardless of their individual values and attitudes toward sustainability, managers with short stints at different organizations are less likely to leave strategic deep-rooted and long-lasting imprints at any one organization. In contrast, the average managerial tenure in long-lived family firms is at least three times higher and values held by the controlling family influence the strategic decisions of the firm (e.g., McConaughy, 2000; Miller and Le Breton-Miller, 2005).

In family-controlled firms, the ownership and management overlap lowers information asymmetry and the classic or Type I agency costs between owners and managers (Anderson, Mansi, and Reeb, 2003; Anderson and Reeb, 2003; Bartholomeusz and Tanewski, 2006). However, family business researchers point to other forms of agency costs between majority and minority shareholders (Type II), family shareholders and family creditors (Type III), and family shareholders and family non-shareholders (Type IV). In each of these agency dualities, the costs and problems differ, as do management strategies to curtail free riding, opportunism, and entrenchment issues (e.g., Chrisman, Chua, and Litz, 2004; Schulze et al., 2001; Villalonga et al., 2015).

Counterintuitively, some argue that formal corporate governance mechanisms aimed at monitoring non-owner or non-kin agents could have negative effects on mutual trust and intrinsic motivation based on the altruistic and cooperative behavior more common in family firms (Davis, Schoorman, and Donaldson, 1997; Dyer, 2003; Karra, Tracey, and Phillips, 2006). Such altruistic behavior is predicated on the stewardship of the family business to ensure the continuity and/or longevity of the enterprise and its mission, by investing in building the business for the long-run benefit of various family members. Long-term continuation of the business is paramount for the controlling family encouraging the managers and employees to focus on cooperative goals (Gomez-Mejia et al., 2007; Habbershon and MacMillan, 1999; Vallejo, 2009).

A combination of ownership and managerial control and long tenures of employees provides a richer context to pursue environmental strategies, the returns of which are only likely to be accrued over time. While companies governed by widely dispersed shareholders will be driven by market and competitive forces, those controlled by one or a few families through concentrated ownership and transgenerational ambitions for the company will be more likely to set longer-term expectations for profitability and social objectives (Aguilera et al., 2007). While studies show a higher propensity to invest in projects and businesses with long-term payoffs, other studies have found that family-controlled firms may be more hesitant and slow in adoption of new technologies and in making riskier investments with uncertain returns, due to their sunk costs and heavy reliance on the company for financial and socioemotional returns (e.g., Gomez-Mejia et al., 2007).

Although these are likely broad-brush generalizations, they provide a starting point to motivate an examination of deployment of patient capital under different governance systems in order to invest in corporate sustainability strategies and practices. Thus, in this monograph, we distinguish companies with concentrated ownership from those with dispersed ownership, as well as firms whose dominant coalition (DC) is controlled by members of one/few families from others controlled by non-family members as a top management team (TMT).

Figure 1.1 depicts an overview of the main variables that are the focus of this monograph, temporal/time orientation of business, concentration of ownership (concentrated or dispersed) and patient capital investments in long-term initiatives and projects necessary for a proactive environmental strategy (PES). Given the early stage of

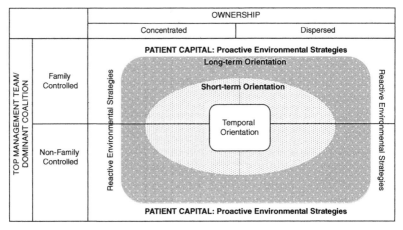

Figure 1.1 An Overview of Time Orientation, Concentration of Ownership, and Patient Capital

research at the interface of corporate environment sustainability and family business, our focus in the monograph is mainly on the two pure cases: non-family firms with dispersed ownership with top management teams of professional managers not related by kinship; and family firms with concentrated ownership with a dominant coalition controlled by family members. While we acknowledge there will be other combinations with less intense influence of professional non-kin managers or family members on ownership and management dimensions of a firm, we leave those categorizations for further finer-grained theory development and empirical analysis.

Layout of the Monograph

In the next chapter, we outline our research design and the data collected to support our theory development. The primary data were collected from family-owned and non-family owned wineries in different institutional contexts: Canada, France, and Chile. The next three chapters review the extant literature on the drivers and barriers to proactive environmental sustainability. These drivers and barriers are broadly classified at three levels: institutional/ stakeholder, organizational, and individual/managerial. Chapter 3 reviews and summarizes the institutional and stakeholder drivers and barriers that influence a firm's adoption of an environmental strategy and examines if family-owned businesses respond differently than companies with dispersed ownership to institutional and stakeholder influences and forces. Chapter 4 focuses on the differences between family owned and non-family firms on corporate governance and ownership, decision-making coalition (DC vs. TMT), organizational drivers and barriers such as organizational structure and design, and market and competitiveness drivers including organizational resources and capabilities. Chapter 5 examines the role of individuals as employees and managers who interpret the business environment (including environmental issues as they evolve), and develop and implement strategy, and the cognitive biases that shape such decision-making. We examine the differences between family firms and non-family firms in motivating employees and managing their cognitive biases by creating opportunity frames that can stimulate and catalyze innovation. During our discussion in Chapters 3 to 5, while we draw upon the literature in corporate sustainability, strategy, organizational behavior, and family business, we illustrate and support our theoretical discussions with primary data from the winery industry and also draw upon other case examples of family-owned businesses. In Chapter 6, we discuss implications of our analysis and our findings in terms of how family firms differ from non-family firms in developing and implementing a proactive environmental strategy in responding to exogenous forces and in their values, organizational design, and capabilities. We conclude with a research agenda for scholars examining environmental sustainability strategy, innovation, and strategic decision-making processes of family and non-family firms. We also discuss what non-family firms can learn from family firms in developing a proactive environmental strategy and vice versa. By bringing research issues of environmental sustainability into family firms, we provide insights for a dominant sector of the economy (family firms), and by bringing insights from family firms into extant sustainability literature, we offer thoughts for finer-grained, process-oriented research studies that account for corporate governance and ownership concentration in the sustainability literature.

Note

1. Also known as the Brundtland Commission after its chair, Gro Harlem Brundtland.

References

Aguilera, R. V. 2005. Corporate governance and director accountability: An institutional comparative perspective. *British Journal of Management*, 16: 1–15.

Aguilera, R. V., Rupp, D. E., Williams, C. E, and Ganapathi, J. 2007. Putting the S back in corporate social responsibility: A multilevel theory of social change in organizations. *Academy of Management Review*, 32(3): 836–863.

Anderson, R. C. and Reeb, D. M. 2003. Founding family ownership and firm performance: Evidence from the S&P 5000. *Journal of Finance*, 58(3): 1301–1328.

Anderson, R. C., Mansi, S. A. and Reeb, D. M. 2003. Founding family ownership and the agency cost of debt. *Journal of Financial Economics*, 68(2): 263–285.

Aragón-Correa, A. A. and Sharma, S. 2003. A contingent resource-based view of proactive environmental strategy. *Academy of Management Review*, 28(1): 71–88.

Baker, H. K. and Anderson, R. 2010. An overview of corporate governance. In *Corporate Governance: A Synthesis of Theory, Research and Practice*, pp. 1–17. Hoboken, NJ: John Wiley.

Bartholomeusz, S. and Tanewski, G. A. 2006. The relationship between family firms and corporate governance. *Journal of Small Business Management*, 44(2): 245–267.

Björnberg, Å., Elstrodt, H. and Pandit, V. 2014. The family-business factor in emerging markets. *McKinsey Quarterly*.

Bluedorn, A. C. 2002. *The Human Organization of Time: Temporal Realities and Experiences*. Stanford, CA: Stanford University Press.

Bugg-Levine, A. and Emerson, J. 2011. *Impact Investing: Transforming How We Make Money While Making a Difference*. San Francisco: Jossey-Bass.

Carney, M. 2005. Corporate governance and competitive advantage in family-controlled firms. *Entrepreneurship Theory and Practice*, 30: 249–265.

Carroll, A. B. 1979. A three dimensional conceptual model of corporate social performance. *Academy of Management Review*, 4: 497–505.

Chen, M. and Smith, K. 1987. Samples used in strategic management research. *Best Paper Proceedings of the 47th Annual Meeting of the Academy of Management*, pp. 7–11. Athens, GA.

Chua, J. H., Chrisman, J. J. and Sharma, P. 1999. Defining the family business by behavior. *Entrepreneurship Theory and Practice*, 23(4): 19–39.

Chrisman, J. J., Chua, J. H. and Litz, R. A. 2004. Comparing the agency costs of family and non-family firms: Conceptual issues and exploratory evidence. *Entrepreneurship Theory & Practice*, 28(4): 335–354.

Cyert, R. M. and March, J. G. 1963. *A Behavioral Theory of the Firm*. New Jersey: Prentice Hall.

Davis, J. H., Schoorman, D. F. and Donaldson, L. 1997. Toward a stewardship theory of management. *Academy of Management Review*, 22(1): 20–47.

Dyer, G. W. Jr. 2003. The family: The missing variable in organizational research. *Entrepreneurship Theory & Practice*, 27(4): 401–416.

El Akremi, A., Gond, J. P., Swaen, V., De Roeck, K. and Igalens, J. 2015. How do employees perceive corporate responsibility? Development and validation of a multidimensional corporate stakeholder responsibility scale. *Journal of Management*, 44(2): 619–657.

Elkington, J. 1997. *Cannibals with Forks: The Triple Bottom Line of 21st Century Business*. Oxford, UK: Capstone Publishing.

Fernández-Aráoz, C., Iqbal, S. and Ritter, J. 2015. Leadership lessons from great family businesses. *Harvard Business Review*, April: 82–88.

Fojt, M. 1995. High flying employee ownership. *Journal of Services Marketing*, 9(3): 49–51.

Freidman, T. L. 2007. Patient capital for an Africa that can't wait. *The New York Times*, 20th April 2007. www.deseretnews.com/article/660214411/African-businesses-need-more-patient-capital.html.

Fuller, D., Akinwande, A. and Sodini, C. 2003. Leading, following or cooked goose? Innovation successes and failure in Taiwan's electronics iIndustry. *Journal of Industry and Innovation*, 10(2): 179–196.

Gardberg, N. A. and Fombrun, C. J. 2006. Corporate citizenship: Creating intangible assets across institutional environments. *Academy of Management Review*, 31(2): 329–346.

Gersick, K. E. and Neus, F. 2014. Governing the family enterprise: Practices, performance, and research. In L. Melin, M. Nordqvist and P. Sharma (eds.), *SAGE Handbook of Family Business*, pp. 196–225. London, UK: Sage Publications.

Global Impact Investing Network (GIIN). n.d. https://thegiin.org/.

Gomez-Mejia, L. R., Haynes, K., Nunez-Nickel, M., Jacobson, K. and Moyano-Fuentes, J. 2007. Family owned firms: Risk loving or risk averse. *Administrative Science Quarterly*, 52(1): 106–138.

Grenadier, S. R. and Wang, N. 2007. Investment under uncertainty and time-inconsistent preferences. *Journal of Financial Economics*, 84 (1): 2–39.

Habbershon, T. G. and Williams, M. L. 1999. A resource-based framework for assessing the strategic advantage of family firms. *Family Business Review*, 12(1): 1–25.

Hart, S. L. 1997. Beyond greening: Strategies for a sustainable world. *Harvard Business Review*, January/February, 66–76.

Jackson, E. T. 2013. Interrogating the theory of change: Evaluating impact investing where it matters most. *Journal of Sustainable Finance & Investment*, 3(2): 95–110.

Jensen, M. C. and Meckling, W. H. 1976. Theory of the firm: Managerial behavior, agency costs and ownership structure. *Journal of Financial Economics*, 3(4): 305–360.

Karra, N., Tracey, P. and Phillips, N. 2006. Altruism and agency in the family firm: Exploring the role of family, kinship and ethnicity. *Entrepreneurship Theory & Practice*, 30(6): 861–877.

Keasey, K., Thompson, S. and Wright, M. 1997. *Corporate Governance: Economic, Management, and Financial issues*. Oxford, UK: Oxford University Press.

Kingston, J. and Bolton, M. 2004. New approaches to funding not-for-profit organisations. *International Journal of Nonprofit and Voluntary Sector Marketing*, 9(2): 112–121.

LaPorta, R., Lopez-de-Silanes, F. and Shleifer, A. 1999. Corporate ownership around the world. *Journal of Finance*, 54: 471–517.

Manners, G. E. Jr. and Louderback, J. G. 1980. Sales potential guidelines for research investment. *Research Management*, 23(2): 25–29.

Matten, D. and Crane, A. 2005. Corporate citizenship: Toward an extended theoretical conceptualization. *Academy of Management Review*, 30(1): 166–179.

Mazzucato, M. 2013. Financing innovation: Creative destruction vs. destructive creation. *Industrial and Corporate Change*, 22(4), 851–867.

McCahery, J. A. and Vermeulen, E. P. M. 2006. Corporate Governance and Innovation – Venture Capital, Joint Ventures, and Family Businesses. ECGI- Law Working Paper # 65/2006.

McConaughy, D. L. 2000. Family CEOs vs. nonfamily CEOs in family-controlled firms: An examination of the level and sensitivity of pay to performance. *Family Business Review*, 13(2): 121–131.

Meier, O. and Schier, G. 2016. The early succession state of a family firm: Exploring the role of agency rationales and stewardship attitudes. *Family Business Review*, 29(3): 256–277.

Miller, D. and Le Breton-Miller, I. 2005. *Managing for the Long-Run: Lessons in Competitive Advantage from Great Family Businesses.* Cambridge, MA: Harvard Business Press.

Morck, R. K. and Steier, L. 2005. The global history of corporate governance: An introduction. In *A History of Corporate Governance around the World*, pp. 1–64. Chicago: National Bureau of Economic Research.

Natural Step. n.d. www.naturalstep.org/en/the-system-conditions (accessed February 8, 2015).

Oswald, J., Ghobadian, A., O'Regan, N. and Antcliff, V. 2013. Dynamic capabilities in a sixth-generation family firm: Entrepreneurship and the Bibby Line. *Business History*, 55(6): 910–941.

Porter, M. E. and Kramer, M. R. 2002. The competitive advantage of corporate philanthropy. *Harvard Business Review*, December.

Post, J. E. and Waddock, S. A. 1995. Strategic philanthropy and partnerships for economic progress. In R. F. America (ed.), *Philanthropy and Economic Development*, pp. 65–84. Westport, CT: Greenwood Press.

Robeson, D. and O'Conner, G. C. 2013. Boards of directors, innovation, and performance: An exploration at multiple levels. *Journal of Product Innovation Management*, 30(4): 608–625.

Russo, M. V. and Fouts, P. A. 1997. A resource-based perspective on corporate environmental performance and profitability. *Academy of Management Journal*, 40(3): 534–559.

Schulze, W. S., Lubatkin, M. H., Dino, R. N. and Buchholtz, A. K. 2001. Agency relationships in family firms: Theory and evidence. *Organization Science*, 12, 99–116.

Shanker, M. C. and Astrachan, J. H. 1996. Myths and realities: Family businesses' contribution to the US economy – A framework for assessing family business statistics. *Family Business Review*, 9(2): 107–123.

Sharma, S. and Vredenburg, H. 1998. Proactive environmental strategy and the development of competitively valuable organizational capabilities. *Strategic Management Journal*, 19: 729–753.

Shive, S. and Yun, H. 2013. Are mutual funds sitting ducks? *Journal of Financial Economics*, 107(1): 220–237.

Shleifer, A. and Vishny, R. W. 1997. A survey of corporate governance. *Journal of Finance*, 52(2): 737–783.

Sirmon, D. G. and Hitt, M. A. 2003. Managing resources: Linking unique resources, management, and wealth creation in family firms. *Entrepreneurship Theory and Practice*, 27(4): 339–358.

Starik, M. and Rands. G. P. 1995. Weaving and integrated web: Multilevel and multisystem perspectives of ecologically sustainable organizations. *Academy of Management Review*, 20(4): 908–935.

Teece, D. J. 1992. Foreign investment and technological development in Silicon Valley. *California Management Review*, 34 (2): 88–106.

The Economist. 2009. Triple bottom line: It consists of three Ps: profit, people and planet. November 17. www.economist.com/node/14301663 (accessed January 6, 2015).

Vallejo, M. C. 2009. The effect of commitment of non-family employees of family firms from the perspective of stewardship theory. *Journal of Business Ethics*, 87(3): 379–390.

VanderMey, A. 2017. IPOs are dwindling, so is the number of public companies. Fortune, Jan 20, 2017. http://fortune.com/2017/01/20/pub lic-companies-ipo-financial-markets/.

Villalonga B. and Amit R. 2009. How are US family firms controlled? *Review of Financial Studies*, 22: 3047–3091.

Villalonga, B., Amit, R., Trujillo, M. and Guzman, A. 2015. Governance of family firms. *Annual Review of Financial Economics*, 7: 635–654.

Wikipedia 1. n.d. https://en.wikipedia.org/wiki/Patient_capital (accessed August 18, 2017).

World Commission on Environment and Development (WCED). 1987. *Our Common Future*. New York: Oxford University Press.

2 | Primary Data: Cases from the Winery Industry in Canada, France, and Chile

The focus of our theorizing is to review extant literature and draw inferences and extrapolate to develop arguments to examine the drivers and barriers influencing patient investments in proactive environmental sustainability strategies in family and non-family firms. In order to build theory on this phenomenon, we supplemented the literature review with empirical case studies to generate a thicker description of the phenomenon and to embed the arguments in practice. In subsequent chapters of this monograph, we illustrate our discussions with examples drawn from these case studies. In order to generate an understanding of the core phenomenon, it was necessary to gather data that allowed us to compare family and non-family controlled firms operating in similar institutional, legal, political, and societal environments. To control for exogenous influences, these firms needed to be fairly similar in their products, services, activities, supply chains, markets, and industry standards, and operating in similar institutional contexts across regions.

The Winery Industry

To generate an understanding of why some firms proactively invest in environmental sustainability strategies while others don't, we decided to focus on a single industry that exhibits a range of firms that are both family and non-family controlled and those that exhibit proactive as well as reactive environmental strategies.[1] For our theory to be applicable beyond a single geographic region, we wanted to focus on an industry where products and processes are relatively similar across locations and over time. Furthermore, we wanted to identify an industry that provided relatively easy access for collecting primary data and an ability to supplement it with secondary data through published articles, informative company websites, and industry associations. For several reasons we will elaborate, we decided to focus on the winery industry.

First, there is empirical evidence that firms in the winery industry demonstrate variation in *governance structures*. For example, research in the Canadian winery industry has revealed three different types of wineries – corporate, traditional family, and lifestyle family wineries (Reay, Jaskiewicz, and Hinings, 2015). These authors found that the different types of governance structures in wineries can be linked to different strategic approaches and decision logics. This within-industry variance made it possible to identify firms and gather data from family and non-family controlled firms, with concentrated or dispersed ownership, to study the drivers and barriers to following reactive versus proactive environmental strategies, while controlling for the institutional environment. While we found the same variation in the wineries in the three countries that we studied, we focused on family owned (and controlled) and corporate (dispersed ownership) wineries. Although we did study founder-run wineries with multiple family members working in the business, we did not study lifestyle wineries since the motivation for founding and running a lifestyle winery can vary from investing in real estate, to engaging in a hobby related to personal interest in drinking wine, to country living, and in some cases to running a business. In many of the lifestyle wineries, economic performance and long-term survival is less important and, hence, it is difficult to compare them with the other two categories.

Second, the winery industry represents a wide range of organizational stages from start-ups to multi-generational family wineries going back several hundred years, to corporate wineries. The history and governance system affects their decision-making processes, path-dependencies, culture and traditions, responses to external pressures, and, thus, environmental strategies. The variance in the *firms' age* provides a nice opportunity to understand whether dominant coalition members of older firms have significantly different temporal orientations than those of younger firms, and whether this in turn influences the environment strategies they adopt.

Third, the winery industry offered the opportunity to examine if tradition and history affected viticulture (i.e., vineyard agriculture) and winemaking practices in different *geographical contexts*, which can be very broadly classified as Old World and New World wineries. The Old World wineries are located in Europe and the Middle East, regions that are considered the birthplaces of wine. In these regions, wineries are subject to guidelines and standards for growing grapes, making wines, and labeling that have been established over centuries. Wines from these regions are named after the specific regions such as Bordeaux, Burgundy, Champagne, or Côtes du Rhone in France, Spain's Priorat or Rioja, or Italy's Abruzzi, Brunello, Chianti, Montefalco, or Montepulciano.

The New World wineries are located in countries like Argentina, Australia, Canada, Chile, New Zealand, South Africa, and the United States; mainly countries that used to be European colonies. Embodying the entrepreneurial spirit, wineries in these regions place less emphasis on tradition while embracing modern advances. New World wines are labeled using grape names. Despite these broad differences, in both the Old and New World wineries there are examples of firms that exhibit reactive versus proactive environmental sustainability strategies (see Table 2.1).

Fourth, wineries have direct *environmental impacts* because land, water, and air are the main source of value creation in this industry. Chemicals, pesticides, and herbicides can be used to a lesser or greater degree in vineyards and winemaking or completely eliminated by using natural ecosystem lifecycles. The environmental footprint of firms varies in their supply chains, their distribution, and their packaging, among other factors. Thus, firms in this industry can choose a wide variety of environmental practices ranging from reactive to proactive strategies.

Reactive vs. Proactive Environmental Strategy in the Winery Industry

Reactive Environmental Strategies: Firms following reactive environmental strategies use legally permitted chemicals, pesticides, and herbicides in their vineyards and/or wine processing, with little conscious focus on the impact of their operations on the environmental ecosystem. Typically, these firms do not examine their value chains for environmental impacts. This does not mean firms following reactive environmental strategies firms never go beyond regulations to reduce material waste or save water or energy. Some do invest in eco-efficiency initiatives and reduce waste, energy, or water usage, and/or curb emission of chemicals or gases. But, such decisions are compelled by a cost-saving or business-profit-enhancement logic, rather than an environmental logic of preserving land or conserving natural resources. These investments are undertaken with a certainty (based on considerable evidence) that these investments will result in cost savings that will recoup the investments in the short term. Hence, we do not consider these investments patient capital.

Proactive Environmental Strategies: Proactive firms not only adopt strategies that go beyond regulatory compliance (such as eco-efficiency via short-term investments) but also undertake investments with long payback or uncertain payback periods in order to preserve the natural environment. In the winery industry, two main forms of proactive environmental practices are organic and biodynamic.

Organic practices eliminate usage of pesticides and herbicides in the vineyards and chemicals in the winery. Organic viticulture is defined as the application of organic agricultural practices such as the use of natural processes wherever possible for nutrient production and recycling, as well as pest, disease, and weed management. These practices are based on the principle of "living soil" that aims to increase the natural soil structure and fertility of the terroir and the unique land habitat on which the vineyard is situated. A good soil structure increases the number and the diversity of terrestrial organisms, reduces the development of harmful ones, and favors the process of nutrient release by organic matter. A living and well-balanced soil composition guarantees the health of the plant and the terroir expression of the wines. Unlike the nonorganic vineyard, which is a monoculture managed by spraying chemicals, an organic vineyard is considered to be an integrated system for converting solar energy, soil nutrients, and water into healthy and natural grape growth. The end product reflects the local terroir that includes hydrology, soil, and micro-climate, as well as the processing practices. In an organic vineyard, grapevines and other plant species grow in harmony, supplementing each other's nutrient needs and hosting beneficial pests. With a functioning natural organic ecosystem, it is much harder for a new pest to infest the vines and score a complete biological victory. The best organic vineyards are micromanaged for crop canopy, soil fertility, and pest and disease control to maximize the quality and the healthiness of the organically produced wine grapes.

Biodynamic farming practices also encompass organic practices such as emphasizing the use of manures and composts and excluding the usage of artificial chemicals on soil and plants. In addition, biodynamic methods also employ soil supplements prepared according to formulas developed by Joseph Steiner at the start of the twentieth century. This approach follows a planting calendar that depends upon astronomical configurations and treats the earth as a living and receptive organism. For example, biodynamic practices include the use of specially pre-pared composts in animal antlers and horns that are buried in the soil according to the phases of the moon, the addition of ingredients such as herbal teas, and the alignment of farming activities with lunar energy. This is a holistic system of integrated ecosystem management. Industry opinion is divided on biodynamic practices. While some experts per-ceive this method as superior to organic practices, others regard it as different but not superior. Still others regard it as esoteric.

Biodynamic and organic practices often require long-term invest-ments with uncertain pay backs since chemicals cannot be eliminated in one cycle without an impact on yield and quality. Converting a vineyard from non-organic to organic practices takes several years as different sections of the vineyard are made chemical free at different times and yield is monitored. Similarly, conversion of a winery requires years of experiments with various natural winemaking methods to eliminate chemicals for processing, filtering, and preserving wine. A major risk factor is the shelf life of the wine since the high-quality heavier red wines increase in quality (aroma, body, flavor, and color) as they age, sometimes over decades. It is more difficult to maintain a long shelf life of wines without any form of preservatives.

After conversion of a vineyard and/or winery to organic/biodynamic, while there are savings in the costs of chemicals, there is a great deal of uncertainty about revenues because the impacts on wine quality and shelf life take time to understand and manage. Thus, pursuit of organic or biodynamic environmental strategies is truly a patient investment since outcomes are uncertain and manifest over time.

Research Design and Case Selection

There are credible third-party certifications for organic and biodynamic practices, such as Agriculture Biologique (AB) certification of France, Vinter Quality Alliance (VQA) in Canada, and the Department of Agriculture's Organic Wine certification in USA. We used such recog-nized classifications to distinguish between firms following proactive environmental strategies from others in the reactive strategy mode.

In an attempt to compare and contrast the impact of varying institutional environments and country factors such as traditional agricultural and wine-making practices, social norms toward sustainability, regulations, and consumer preferences, we gathered data from winery clusters in different countries. Specifically, we compared wineries in one of the world's oldest and most famous region of Bordeaux in France, with two New World clusters in Canada and Chile that are less constrained by centuries of tradition and deep-rooted appellations.[2]

We identified cases that allowed us to compare the environmental strategies of family and non-family firms. Within the family category, we distinguished between the first-generation wineries led by a founder or a non-related founding team, from those controlled by members of multiple generations or by members of later generations of the founding family. First generation or founder-run wineries are different from lifestyle wineries as mentioned above. They bear the strong stamp of the founder(s) who have chosen to own and run a winery. While family members are often an integral part of these wineries, the ultimate decision rests on the founder or the founding team. If the next generation chooses to continue in this business, these wineries evolve into trans-generational family wineries. It was interesting to examine the environmental strategy at the onset of a winery and to understand whether there is a variance in first-generation wineries that founders expect will be continued by next generation family members, from those where such generational continuity is not desired or expected. First-generation wineries are more prominent to the New World winery industry, even though we did visit wineries such as Viña De Martino in Chile that now have third and fourth generation family members working together. Wineries in the Old World often date back several hundred years and several generations of the founder's family have been engaged in the business. Therefore, it is less common to find first-generation family wineries in the Old World winery industry. This is also because the wine growing regions are saturated and a new entrant has a greater possibility of entering the business by buying an existing running winery as compared to the New World where many regions have open land available for the planting of grapes.

The case studies helped strengthen our understanding of a complex social phenomenon in practice. In order to understand the factors that influence the environmental sustainability strategy of family and non-family firms, it was important to retain the holistic and meaningful characterization of real-life events. The phenomena of interest required gathering data from strategic decision makers of firms via narratives and recall. Given the penchant for privacy in family firms, multiple responses were sought from members of the decision-making body, the dominant coalition, via personal interviews (Yin, 2009). As evident from interview questions listed in Appendix A, we made efforts to maintain the conversational tone of the interview and often found ourselves walking around the winery or vineyard with the respondents or spending time in tasting rooms discussing the practices and philosophies behind various wines. We will briefly describe the case selection process and cases in each geographic cluster (see overview in Table 2.1). In terms of winery size by annual production, while industry standards vary by country, in the wine clusters we examined, small (S) = below 15,000 cases, medium (M) = from more than 15,000 to 50,000 cases, and large (L) = above 50,000 cases. Year of founding where available is provided. This table does not show (due to space) the titles or positions of the respondents but through the text in subsequent chapters, we indicate the title or position of the respondent accompanying the quote.

Canadian Wineries

Canada has two major winery clusters – the Okanagan Valley in British Columbia and the Niagara region in Ontario. There are smaller but growing clusters in Nova Scotia and Quebec. Several corporate wineries operate in both the Okanagan Valley and the Niagara regions and often the different divisions/units of a company adopt similar corporate strategies. The Nova Scotia and Quebec clusters are mainly smaller family-owned wineries. To gain a diversity of perspectives in this New World winery region, we chose to conduct case studies in one of the two larger and more established clusters of Okanagan Valley, and one of the two newer, smaller but growing clusters of Nova Scotia where there were no corporate wineries but mainly family-controlled wineries that vary in their environmental strategies.

The Okanagan Valley and Niagara wineries are regulated by Vintners Quality Alliance (VQA), that guarantees the high quality and regional authenticity of these wines. The VQA system allows for sub-appellations, by which the grapes for wines are sourced from very specific geographical

Table 2.1 *Cases Selected*

	Family Firms	Size	Founded	Non-Family Firms	Size	Founded
Reactive Environmental Strategies	*First Generation*					
	Hannibal (Na)	S	1996	**Bird's Nest (Na)**	M	1956
	Mountain (Na)	M	1966	Jackson-Triggs (Na)	L	1993
	Northshore (Na) (2012-Alliance)	S	1978	**Skyline (Na) (Peller)**	M	1997
	Sunset (Na) (2013-Alliance)	S	2009	Château Calon-Segur (O)	L	1625
	Multi-/Later-Generation			Château Lascombes (O)	L	1147
	Europa (Na)	M	1999			
	Andrew Peller (Na)	L	1961			
Proactive Environmental Strategy	*First Generation*					
	Dreamscape (Na)	S	2004	**Viña Indomita (Nb)**	L	2001
	Frogpond (Na)	S	2001	**Viña Santa Rita (Nb)**	L	1880
	Landjoy (Na)	S	2006	**Château Soutard (O)**	L	1513
	Lightfoot & Wolfville (Na)	S	2007			
	SOAHC Estates (Na)	S	2002			
	Tawse (Na)	S	2005			

Vista (Na)	S	2007
Multi- or Later-Generation		
Edge (Na)	M	1998
Nirvana (Na)	S	1986
Southbrook (Na)	M	1991
Sunnyvale (Na)	S	2008
Viña De Martino (Nb)	L	1934
Viña Emiliana (Nb)	L	1986
Château Coutet (O)	S	1643
Château Duvivier (O)	M	1990
Château Fonroque (O)	S	1931
Château Le Puy (O)	M	1610
Château Marguax (O)	L	12th C

Old World Wineries (O); New World Wineries: Canada (Na), Chile (Nb)

Wineries from which primary data was collected are in bold. *Pseudonyms used for wineries from which primary data collected. Real names for wineries for secondary data.*

locations with different soil and climate. This classification follows the concept of terroir that is the unique natural environment in which a particular wine is produced, including factors such as the soil, topography, hydrology, and climate. In order to qualify for these appellations, the wines must be made entirely from grapes grown in a specific region. Other regulatory classifications to assure quality include "*Wines of Distinction*" in British Columbia, "*Wines of Nova Scotia*" in Nova Scotia, and "*Vins du Québec*" in Quebec. Hence, in addition to geography and climate, land use and agricultural regulations, there are industry association requirements in the institutional environment that signal a credible mark of quality for the consumer.

We wanted to gather data from wineries that exhibited a variation on the phenomena of interest – environmental strategies. While we were able to capture this diversity in our sample of cases in one of the two Canadian regions of Okanagan Valley, we found much less diversity in the smaller Nova Scotia region. Nevertheless, we found some interesting perspectives on the industry's understanding of what practices constituted a proactive environmental sustainability strategy. In the final analysis, it was not possible to identify enough cases of family and non-family wineries pursuing reactive and proactive environmental strategies in the regions we focused on. Hence, we supplemented our primary data with secondary research from published materials of wineries.

Our secondary research revealed that in the non-family firm classification, there were no biodynamic or purely organic corporate wineries in any of the industry clusters in Canada including the two clusters we studied as well as the third big cluster in Niagara region. These categories were only reflected in the family owned wineries. This is an interesting finding in itself as it suggests that

In the Canadian winery industry, family-controlled wineries are more likely to adopt proactive environmental strategies as compared to non-family wineries.

We initially identified twenty-two firms in the Okanagan and Nova Scotia based on their websites and published material that indicated some variation in their environmental sustainability practices. Each of these wineries was then contacted over the phone to assess the willingness of one or more members of the ownership team or the dominant coalition to be available for in-depth interviews. The final twelve Canadian cases represent the firms that agreed to participate on a condition that we disguise the names of the wineries. These cases are shown in bold and marked with the legend (Na) in Table 2.1. To expand our data set, we also gathered secondary data from websites and published materials for seven other wineries in Canada. As we relied on published material for these cases, we provide the real names of these wineries in Table 2.1. It is worth repeating that the objective of this data collection was to generate a thicker description of the phenomena (environmental strategy) and strengthen our theoretical discussions based on extant literature and not to develop an entirely new grounded theory. In keeping with this intent, we used the questions listed in Appendix A – based very broadly on categories in the questionnaire developed by Sharma and Vredenburg (1998) and adapted for the winery industry – to assess their environmental strategy, motivating factors/drivers and barriers/inhibitors (including institutional, stakeholder, organizational, dominant coalition, family, and individual), and the benefits and challenges of adoption of a specific strategy. A brief description of the Canadian cases follows.

Reactive Environmental Strategies

Canadian firms following reactive environmental strategies comply with prevailing regulations on use of toxic chemicals, harmful emissions, water or air pollution, greenhouse gases, soil contamination, etc. Most firms achieve such strategies by installing pollution control equipment rather than undertaking long-term investments to reduce pollution at source. In other words, while complying with regulations, the firms follow a reactive environmental strategy rather than going beyond or staying ahead of such regulations. Such firms are often focused on productivity, that is, the ratio of production to resources used. Short-term cost benefit analysis governs decisions of reduction in materials or energy usage. While lower material and energy usage often leads to lower emissions, wastes, and a lower environmental footprint of operations, this is mainly undertaken as a cost savings rather than a core guiding strategy. We briefly describe firms in three categories following reactive environmental strategies during our data collection. These are categorized into (i) first-generation family firms, (ii) multi- or later-generation family firms, and (iii) non-family-controlled corporations.

First-Generation Family Firms

These firms may be either run by one or by more members of a founding team who may or may not be related as family members. In this category, four Canadian wineries, two each from Okanagan and Nova Scotia, were classified as following a reactive environmental strategy category.

Hannibal (pseudonym, Okanagan Valley, BC, primary data): Founded in 1996 by a former Marine engineer, this small-sized winery owned by a married couple has taken a very mechanistic approach in its operations. The winery is mainly run by the founder while his wife runs the business and also works at another profession to supplement income as they struggle to generate consistent profits. As an example of their approach, Hannibal has spent a great deal of money to fence off the entire estate along the slopes of the hill to prevent deer from eating grapes in the vineyard. Most other wineries in the area allow deer to wander into vineyards and factor in a certain percentage of grape loss. Several wineries in the region reduce chemical use by adopting integrated pest management while Hannibal overdoses with chemicals to kill all possible pests. Hannibal has also battled nature by blasting a huge expanse of rock on the hillside to create a wine storage cellar. The founder is also very concerned about the high cost of labor and prefers to hire hitchhikers at low wages to help with the harvest. The winery is located in beautiful natural surroundings but the founder couple do not espouse a philosophy of environmental preservation but rather running the business as a battle to be won against nature.

Mountain (pseudonym, Okanagan Valley, BC, primary data): Mountain winery was founded in 1966 but acquired its first vineyard in 1996. This medium-sized winery is a labor of love for the founder who made his fortune by inventing and marketing a global brand of hard lemonade and invests most of the profits from that business into Mountain. While the winery and its wines are marketed as made at a family estate, the winery is run by the founder and currently no other family member is involved. The estate has one of the most spectacular settings in BC on a hill with gentle slopes and breathtaking architecture built around an old mission. The focus is on producing high quality wines and tourism with compliance of environmental regulations and eco-efficiency. The winery's environmental sustainability strategy is focused on energy savings, recycling, and experimentation with organic viticulture in a small section of the vineyard estate on the mountain.

Northshore (pseudonym, NS, primary data): This small-sized winery founded on the shore of Northumberland in 1978 was the first winery in the province of Nova Scotia. Run by its founder, it is one of the few Nova Scotian wineries not located in the Annapolis Valley. The founder is focused on compliance and keeping the cost of labor low. Subsequent to our data collection in 2010, the founder chose not to pass the winery to his children (who were in high school at the time of data collection). In 2012, it was sold to another family (Alliance – pseudonym) that has acquired four wineries in Nova Scotia to generate economies of scale in marketing and inputs. The new owners are in discussions to experiment with organic practices.

Sunset (pseudonym, NS, primary data): This small founder-run winery was established in 2009 and focused on lowering costs and breaking even. While the winery complies with regulations, it constantly seeks low-cost temporary hourly labor and has not innovated its vineyard or wine-making practices to consider either eco-efficiency or proactive organic practices. Subsequent to our data collection in 2010, this winery too was purchased in 2013 by the same family (Alliance) that purchased Northshore.

Multi- or Later-Generation Family Firms
These firms are either those run by multiple generations of a family who indicate a strong possibility of continuity of the winery beyond the tenure of the incumbent generation members, or those that have been transferred from one generation to another and are being run by descendants of the founding family. While we collected primary data from Europa – a Nova Scotian winery jointly founded by two generations of a family, we supplemented this data by studying a large-sized, third-generation winery – the Andrew Peller winery – that has operations in both Niagara and Okanagan, the latter being the more established region of Canadian winery industry.

Europa (pseudonym, NS, primary data): Europa, a small but growing winery, was founded in 1999 by a Swiss immigrant family. Two generations of the family are engaged in the business. They have partnered with Agriculture Canada to develop grape varietals and vineyard practices designed to thrive in the local soil and the cold oceanic climate of Nova Scotia that is quite different from most other grape growing regions. The strategy of the winery is focused on wine quality. The winery has a well-regarded restaurant, and hosts weddings and events, all designed to generate tourism revenues. The winery is located in a UNESCO World Heritage site but the family did not express any consciousness or strategy for need to preserve the ecosystems and habitats in this very special geographic setting.

Andrew Peller (Ontario and BC, secondary data): This is a large third-generation family business founded in 1961 with several wineries in Ontario and BC. While some of their Ontario wineries exhibit a strategy of compliance, a few others in Ontario and its BC wineries in the Okanagan Valley have recently adopted eco-efficiency practices such as water efficiency and conservation, energy conservation, and lighter packaging. The published materials and websites of the company do not indicate practices indicative of a proactive environmental strategy.

Non-Family or Corporate Wineries

While wineries are often started by one family or a group of entrepreneurs, over time, while some evolve to become later generational family firms, others dilute their ownership by going public or are acquired. These variances are reflected in three Canadian wineries we studied.

Bird's Nest (pseudonym, Okanagan Valley, BC, primary data): Started as a family owned winery in 1956, this medium-sized winery went public as the next generation members of the family were more interested in political careers than running their business. The family members own stock and are on the board of the company but its ownership is dispersed and the winery is professionally managed. The managers we talked to lacked an overall vision of environmental sustainability and were focused on compliance while implementing eco-efficiency practices such as water conservation, energy efficiency, and packaging reduction. Their main focus is on wine quality and wine tourism including their restaurant.

Jackson-Triggs (Ontario and BC, secondary data): This is one of the largest winery groups in Canada with several wineries in Ontario and BC. The company is a part of Vincor, the world's eighth largest producer and marketer of wines with operations in Canada, the United States, Europe, Australia, and New Zealand. The winery was founded by the two partners, Jackson and Triggs in 1993 and incorporated as Vincor. In 2013, Vincor was merged with USA's Constellation Brands, a Fortune 500 company. Constellation Brands and Vincor do not have a proactive corporate environmental sustainability strategy for its wineries, beyond compliance with regulations. Jackson-Triggs adopts a compliance strategy for its wineries that is largely focused on marketing and product quality. This focus is not surprising since Constellation Brands is one of the largest distributors and marketers of wines in the world.

Skyline (pseudonym, Okanagan Valley, BC, primary data): Skyline was a small family-owned winery founded in 1997. In the early 2000s, it was bought by Peller, a third-generation family corporation with multiple wineries but without a proactive environmental strategy. The previous owners (a father-and-daughter team), who still manage the winery, explain that they had begun to implement organic practices that were abandoned when they were bought by the Peller Group. The Peller Group (as discussed) has a strategy of compliance and is focused on product quality and wine tourism.

Proactive Environmental Strategies

In the Canadian context, in order to be recognized as organic, the winery must be certified by a credible third party that conducts an inspection and certifies that the winery is in compliance with the organic standards as per regulations of the federal and provincial governments, the industry association, and internationally accepted organic practices. Organic wine is made from grapes grown without the use of artificial chemical fertilizers, pesticides, fungicides, and herbicides. Chemicals and preservatives such as sulfur dioxide in the fermentation and storage process are avoided. Unless a winery is set up as organic from inception, the conversion process takes between two to three years, and sometimes as long as four or five years, with uncertain outcomes on yields and product quality. This requires patient investment. Often wineries convert into organic over several years as it is done segment by segment of the vineyard.

Biodynamic agriculture is certified by an international body, Demeter. While studying the Canadian winery industry, it became apparent that, while biodynamic encompassed organic, biodynamic practices did not gain momentum for reasons ranging from perceptions of these practices as esoteric or mumbo jumbo, to against religious beliefs (in the case of the founder of Landjoy, an Okanagan Valley based organic winery). Our study is based on data collected from seven first-generation wineries and four wineries being run by multiple members of a family or by descendants of founders. As mentioned earlier, we did not find any Canadian non-family-run corporate winery that followed proactive environmental strategies.

First-Generation Family Firms

Dreamscape (pseudonym, NS, primary data): This is a small first-generation, family-owned winery that was founded in 2004 in the Annapolis Valley of Nova Scotia. From its inception, the vineyards and winery were certified organic by Pro-Cert Organic Systems. Hence, all its wines are inspected and controlled by the Canadian Food Inspection Agency, and could bear the Canadian Organic logo of a rising maple leaf. Other environmental practices include the use of geothermal heating, cooling and hot water, usage of environmentally friendly materials in all construction, solar power, and the location of the winery on a slope to take advantage of natural earth insulation keeping the cellar at constant temperature for optimum aging of its sparkling wines.

Frogpond (Ontario, secondary data): Frogpond is a small winery that was founded in 2001. It is Ontario's first fully certified organic winery. The vineyard and winery are certified by Pro-Cert Organic Systems. It uses plants and animals such as guinea fowl to graze on bugs to control pests. Rainwater is collected in their pond and recirculated for the vineyard. Grapes are handpicked and 100 percent renewable energy is used. As per their website: "Here at Frogpond Farm we believe that creating harmony in nature is the prerequisite for a truly authentic wine. As Ontario's First certified Organic winery we take pride in crafting premium wines using only sustainable practices."

Landjoy (pseudonym, Okanagan Valley BC – primary data): This is a small-sized, first-generation, family-owned certified organic winery founded in 2006. The founder converted another prominent BC winery (Nirvana – see below) in the Okanagan Valley to organic practices as vineyard manager before starting his own winery. Landjoy's owner is an expert in organic agricultural and viticulture practices. He is the hub of related expertise in the Okanagan Valley. Several other wineries (including Vista and Sunnyvale – see below) mentioned Landjoy's founder as a source of great help and expertise in implementing organic practices in the Okanagan Valley. According to the founder, "Organic grape growing is a real labor of love which shows beautifully in the wine, where it really counts." This is evident in the consistency with which Landjoy's ice wines win international first place awards. He cited religious reasons for not engaging in biodynamic practices as one of these practices involves stuffing cow horns with manure compost and burying these in the vineyard through winter for excavation in spring when the compost is spread throughout the vineyard. Moreover, as a trained agriculturist with a Master's degree in agricultural science, the founder is not convinced that biodynamic practices add anything to the terroir and quality of wine that organic does not.

Lightfoot and Wolfville (NS, secondary): This small first-generation family-owned winery was founded in 2007 as an organic and biodynamic winery. Certified organic by Pro-Cert Organic Systems, Lightfoot and Wolfville's practices include 100 percent hand harvesting, traditional basket-press production, indigenous wild yeast fermentation, water recycling, and the use of renewable energy. The name reflects the family's attempt to harmonize the winery's operations with its unique terroir – the family name Lightfoot with the terroir of Wolfville in the Annapolis Valley, Nova Scotia, with its hard soils and cold climate. Located close to Europa in a UNESCO World Heritage site, unlike Europa, this family is very conscious of its stewardship and preservation of this unique ecosystem. Like other family businesses with a proactive environmental strategy, the website of this firm also emphasizes a long-term focus rather than a short-term focus on profit maximization: "For us, wine growing is also a long-term opportunity to indulge, close-up, our fascination with the wonderful complexity of the natural world."

SOAHC Estates (BC, secondary): Established in 2002, this founder-run winery claims that it is one of the first in North America to adopt biodynamic practices from inception. Their ecosystem approach is reflected in the statement on their website: "Every creature and element of the farm plays an important role. From the bees and the spiders to the fruit trees and the thistles, they are all part of the plan." They have animal-friendly fencing around the estate that began fifteen years ago with calculated terroir preparation via farming of specific crops starting with wildflowers and followed by a series of grains and potatoes, before finally moving to grapevines. Their website does not mention any certification for their biodynamic practices.

Tawse (Ontario, secondary): This is a medium-sized, first-generation, family-owned winery that was set up as an organic and biodynamic winery in 2005 on the Niagara Escarpment. With five vineyards, it produces over 30,000 cases a year and its practices are certified by Demeter (Biodynamic), Pro-Cert Organic (Organic), Sustainable Winemaking Ontario, Local Food Plus, and VQA. Tawse uses gravity for movement during the winemaking process, natural geothermal cooling, and renewable energy. It works with local communities on ecosystem preservation and restoration. The firm's website describes their philosophy:

> Biodynamic farming is an approach that sees the vineyard as its own self-sustaining ecological entity and aims to work with the energies that create and maintain life. In the vineyard, this means treating the soil as a living organism and working to bring the grapevine and the soil in balance. Biodynamic farming uses the earth's natural cycles and natural preparations to increase microbial life and nutrients in the soil and to produce balance between the soil and the vines. We strive to create a diversified balanced ecosystem that generates health and fertility from the vineyard itself ... We also get help from our friends from the animal realm. Our chicken feed on bugs, our sheep eat the lower vine leaves to expose the grapes to the ripening sun and using horses instead of tractors whenever we can, helps avoid soil compaction.

Vista (pseudonym, Okanagan Valley, BC, primary data): A couple with young children established this small first-generation winery in 2007. Since the inception, Vista was completely certified organic in its vineyard and winery. Their organic consultant was the founder of Landjoy, who has helped several other wineries either start-up or convert to organic practices. The founders are driven by a passion for human and ecosystem health and providing a safe healthy natural environment for their children. Since early on, their wine quality has been recognized via placement in restaurants. The founders have a vision of growing their business and integrating their children into the business as soon as possible so that it becomes a way of life for them and they can carry it into the future.

Multi- or Later-Generation Family Firms

Edge (pseudonym, BC, primary data): Founded in 1998, this medium-to-large-sized organically certified winery is located at the southern end of the Okanagan Valley. Two generations of family are involved in the business. The southern edge of the Okanagan is the upper boundary of the Sonoran Desert. Hence, this is a drier environment as compared to the western Okanagan Valley and the vines and grapes are less susceptible to mildew that affects the more humid western areas. Edge finds it easier to implement organic practices in the drier climate but nevertheless consults Landjoy's owner on best organic practices.

Nirvana (pseudonym, BC, primary data): Two generations of a family run this biodynamic winery that was founded in 1986. Nirvana is known in the Okanagan Valley for its unusual practices such as storage of wines in a pyramid structure with the family members meditating at the top to radiate calming vibrations that they feel enhance the quality of their wines. Landjoy's founder implemented the organic practices at Nirvana and helped this winery to receive its first organic certification in 2007. Later, he left to start his own winery. Subsequently, Nirvana adopted biodynamic practices and was certified by Demeter in 2012.

Southbrook (Ontario, secondary): This is a third-generation, family-owned organic and biodynamic winery founded in 1991 with certifications from Demeter, Pro-Cert Organic, Sustainable Winemaking Ontario, Local Food Plus, and VQA for its vineyard and wines and LEED certification for its facilities and energy use. Southbrook is also committed to supporting local communities, fostering micro-entrepreneurship, and fair trade. As per their website: "Our pursuit of this ideal has shown us the importance of organic and biodynamic viticulture. It has instilled in us a respect for the soil, water and ecosystems upon which great wine, and our planet, relies."

Sunnyvale (pseudonym, Okanagan Valley BC, primary data): Sunnyvale is a medium-sized, family-owned certified organic winery founded in 2008 with a niche international market. They also make privately branded wine for the Rolling Stones band and organization. Their second generation is now getting engaged in the business. As in the case for Vista, Landjoy's owner is their organic consultant.

Chilean Wineries

As compared to the Old World wineries that have fewer degrees of freedom due to strict appellation guidelines and centuries of tradition, those operating in the New World have greater control over their strategies and influence in shaping institutional environments. But, we were curious if there were significant differences in wineries operating in different countries and regions of the New World. We got an opportunity to visit a few wineries in Chile during a trip to attend a conference unrelated to this project. We were able to obtain interviews with the members of the DC or TMT of four wineries in this region that has added useful data to our primary comparative regions of Canada and France. Hence, the wineries we visited constitute a convenience sample of three wineries that appeared to have different levels of proactivity in their strategies based on their websites and, most importantly, based on availability of the members of the dominant coalition for personal interviews. We also added secondary data from one family-owned winery with a proactive strategy.

It was in the sixteenth century that Spanish conquistadors brought vines from Spain to Chile. In the mid-nineteenth century, French wine varieties such as Cabernet Sauvignon, Merlot, Franc, and Carmenère were introduced as significant numbers of French immigrants moved to Chile. Today, this country is the seventh largest producer and the fifth largest exporter of wines in the world. Chile has nine major grape-growing regions but we focused on the Central Valley region between Santiago and Valparaiso. This is the most productive wine-producing region of Chile and known internationally for its wines. We studied one winery in the Casablanca Valley of the Valparaiso region, and three in the Maipo Valley (two of which we visited) of the Central Valley

Region. As our primary objective was to supplement our data from Canada and France to strengthen our theoretical insights, we collected data from a convenience sample of these four wineries, of which two are corporate wineries and the other two are later generational family firms. All four followed varying levels of proactive environmental strategies.

Proactive Environmental Strategies

Multi- or Later-Generation Family Firms

Viña De Martino (pseudonym, Maipo Valley, primary data): This large winery was founded by the Italian De Martino family in 1934. The third and fourth generations of the family run the winery. De Martino began the process to convert to 100 percent organic farming of their grapes in 1998 and three years later had their first harvest. They were certified organic in 2000. After Emiliana (see below), they are the second largest producer of organic wines in Chile. This winery also has a climate change strategy. In 2007, they were audited by the Carbon Reduction Institute to measure all their carbon emissions and developed a plan to reduce their carbon footprint and have become the first winery in the world to generate carbon bonds (credits). In 2009, they launched the first carbon-neutral wines in Latin America: Nuevo Mundo and Viña De Martino. Interestingly, they are also experimenting with storing and fermenting wines using ancient techniques by using clay amphoras to allow natural settling and aeration.

Viña Emiliana (Maipo Valley, secondary data): Founded in 1986, it is owned by the Guilisasti family. It was in mid 1990s that Emiliana started converting to organic. Their vineyards and wineries are 100 percent organic and they market two wines made in accordance to biodynamic principles. Emiliana claims to be the world's largest organic winery reusing the treated liquid industrial waste from three production wineries for irrigation of their vineyards, using biomass boilers and solar panels for energy, and using recycled materials and lighter bottles for packaging. In 2003, they introduced the vintage Gê as South America's first certified biodynamic wine. The Guilisasti family recruited consulting enologist Alvaro Espinoza to oversee the conversion to organic and biodynamic. Espinoza is regarded as one of the world's premier authorities on organic, biodynamic and eco-balanced wines. As per their website: "The care of nature and the concern for climate change have been and will always be a priority for us ... The commitment and respect with our workers and the community are our main values in Emiliana. To contribute always in improving the quality of life of the local community and society, is essential."

Non-Family or Corporate Wineries

Viña Indomita (pseudonym, Casablanca Valley, primary data): Founded in 2001, this winery is owned by Bethia S. A., a group that owns several vineyards. We visited the winery in the Casablanca Valley. Indomita has a corporate policy of eco-efficiency including waste treatment and reduction, generation of renewable energy, conservation of water and energy, and use of lighter bottles and packaging. In some vineyards, it has conservation programs to protect the native forest, flora, and fauna. Indomita is socially progressive and employs workers only from the communities they are located in, thereby investing in the professional development of employees for career progression. While not all of their production is organic, they have been converting their vineyards in phases to organic viticulture and increasing their organic wine production every year.

Viña Santa Rita (pseudonym, Maipo Valley, primary data): Santa Rita is one of the largest winery companies in Chile with several wineries and vineyards. Founded in 1880 as a family firm, it became a limited liability company when it was acquired by Groupo Claro and the Owens Illinois Company in 1980. The corporate policy across its many wineries is clearly focused on eco-efficiency. However, in 1994, one of its portfolio of wineries, Viña Carmen, re-discovered Carmenere vines that had been assumed as extinct since the mid-nineteenth century, and began growing organic grapes. And, in 1999, released the first line of organic wines from Chile under the brand name Nativa. In 2009, Nativa received its organic certification from the Institute for Marketecology (IMO) – an international certification body based in Switzerland. Santa Rita has also adopted practices of reduced packaging, lightweight bottles, recycled packaging materials, biodegradable inks, and reusing its own organic waste for compost. It is in the process of transforming its various vineyards and wineries into organic.

French Wineries

In France, we collected primary data from the Bordeaux region, which produces some of the most renowned and highest priced wines in the world. We also collected data from one certified biodynamic winery in La Provence in the South of France. With 7,375 chateaux, this is world's largest winery region. Bordeaux wineries and vineyards make more than 10,000 different wines of every vintage (www.thewinecellarinsider.com/ wine-topics/bordeaux-wine-production-facts-figures-grapes-vineyards/, accessed February 3, 2018).

Centered around the city of Bordeaux, this region is densely packed with distinct grape-growing areas that are geographically divided by the Gironde Estuary into a Left and a Right Bank. The Left Bank includes the two regions of Médoc and Graves. The Right Bank includes the three regions of Libournais, Bourg, and Blaye. In turn, each region is sub-divided into sub-regions and each sub-region into appellations. Almost each appellation has its own governing body that dictates the permissible grape varieties, alcohol level, methods of pruning and picking, density of planting, appropriate yields, and winemaking techniques. Thus, as compared to the Canadian and Chilean wineries, there are stricter rules in the Bordeaux regions and fewer degrees of freedom for the vineyard and winery practices. To gain a wider perspective within this region, we studied seven wineries – four on the Left Bank and three on the Right.

At the time of our data collection in 2012, except for a few wineries, there was very little discussion about environmentally sustainable farming in this region. However, since then, there have been rapid institutional changes. In some appellations, there is a move toward 100 percent universal organic or biodynamic practices. For example, the local wine council for four Bordeaux appellations has passed a measure mandating environmentally sustainable farming. Any wine not farmed sustainably may only be bottled as a generic Bordeaux and not from the specific appellation that it is from.

In 2016 (four years after our data collection), the wine council of the St. Émilion region conducted a survey of its growers and found out that 45 percent either had some sort of environmental certification or were working toward one. The council ruled that, starting with the 2019 vintage, every bottle of wine will have to be made from grapes grown with environmentally sustainable farming methods. The impetus is partly because of the attempts being made to recognize this region as a UNESCO World Heritage site. This decision impacts nearly 3.85 million cases of wine made annually by 973 grape growers in this appellation. Wineries can choose between state-approved certifications of organic, biodynamic or the HVE 3 (Haute Valeur Environmentale). St. Émilion is the first Bordeaux appellation to take this bold step toward environmentally sustainable practices. And, the new rules are not legally binding until the national appellations authority has modified the specifications for each appellation. Nevertheless, other appellations have begun to discuss this example and start a movement that may convert the entire country's vineyards into organic or biodynamic.

We were fortunate to collect data before any such discussions had begun to take place so that we could identify variation in environmental sustainability strategies of individual wineries. Our objective was to identify issues that were unique to this Old World institutional context and compare the barriers or drivers for the adoption of proactive environmental strategies with those of the New World industry in Canada and to a lesser extent in Chile. We sampled a few cases of family owned and non-family owned wineries to strengthen our literature review and develop theoretical insights, rather than to conduct a thorough grounded research study to build theory. None of these wineries requested anonymity in reporting data.

Reactive Environmental Strategies

Non-Family or Corporate Wineries

Château Calon-Ségur (Bordeaux, Left Bank, St. Estèphe appellation of the Médoc region, secondary): This winery dates back to the 1100s and has been family owned and run since the early 1800s. At the death of the managing family member in 2012, the younger generation chose not to work in the business and instead sold it to Suravenir Assurances, a large French insurance company. Since then, it has changed hands again to the French bank, Crédit Mutuel Arkéa Bank. In all of their published materials, there is no mention of environmental preservation, eco-efficiency practices, organic/biodynamic practices, or proactive social practices. The website focuses on efforts to increase production, yields, grape quality and density, and improving packaging design and marketing. Of course, with the wave of sustainability in the Bordeaux region, their strategy is likely to evolve in the near future.

Château Lascombes (Bordeaux, Left Bank, Marguax appellation of the Médoc region, primary): This large winery dates back to the seventeenth century when it was founded by the Lascombes family. It had changed hands through several families until 2001, when it was purchased by a US-based corporation, Colony Capital, a real estate investment firm with no experience in the wine industry. In 2011, Colony Capital sold it to a major French insurance company, Mutuelle d'Assurances du Corps de Santé Français (MACSF). These corporate owners invested heavily in modernizing Lascombes, which was an underperformer in relation to its second-growth Grand Cru (or 'great growth' in French) classification. At the time of data collection in 2012, the winery's strategy was compliance with all environmental regulations. However, this is likely to change in the future as a result of the changes in another Bordeaux region of St. Émilion that requires that all wine in the region to be made using organic or biodynamic farming methods. This change is likely to influence other regions as well. During our data collection, however, the interviewees from Lascombes did not exhibit either a philosophy or strategy or a pattern of practices that reflected proactivity on environmental dimensions.

Proactive Environmental Strategies

Multi- or Later-Generation Family Firms

Château Coutet (Bordeaux, Left Bank, Barsac-Sauternes appellation of the Graves Region, primary): The Premier Cru Classé winery located in Barsac in Southern Bordeaux region has been family owned since the 1600s. The winery was certified organic in 2012, but the family members claim that the winery has been organic since much earlier as they have never used herbicides, pesticides, or insecticides at the property, resulting in a unique ecosystem and flora and fauna. However, we got the impression that due to succession issues with the next generation, the winery may be looking for a buyer. This winery needs significant investment and underperforms relative to its classification.

Château Duvivier (La Provence, primary): This winery in the South of France (in the La Provence region) is the only winery that we visited outside the Bordeaux region. It is one of the three wineries owned by a Zurich-based Swiss family (known as the Delinat Group), and the only one they own in France. This family is deeply committed to biodynamic practices and feel that the certifications do not go deep enough to assess true biodynamic and organic operations. As a result, Delinat created its own guidelines for winemaking and viticulture as early as 1983, and these have been continuously improved and developed ever since. They go far beyond EU organic and other organic labels (Ecovin, Demeter, Bio Suisse, etc.) and are the only ones specifically aimed at promoting biodiversity in the eco-system. The goal is for the vineyards to be self-regulating, stable ecosystems that enable above-average wine and terroir quality. The Delinat guidelines are considered to be the most stringent in Europe and have been honored several times as the best Swiss organic label by independent institutions such as WWF Switzerland, Stiftung für Konsumentenschutz and Stiftung Pusch (Swiss Practical Environmental Protection). The family is also passionate about social justice and fair trade in its own operations and contributing to social justice causes across the world. The current managing family members (a couple) exhibit deep commitment to sustainability by visiting their three wineries in different countries on bicycle once a year from Zurich!

Château Fonroque (Bordeaux, Right Bank, St. Émilion appellation of the Libournais region, primary): Chateau Fonroque, a Grand Cru Classé winery has been with the Moueix family since 1931. Grand cru, or great growth in French, is the highest level of wine classification by the Appellation d'origine contrôlée (AOC). This was one of the first wineries in Bordeaux to farm using organic methods. In 2002, they began experimenting with biodynamic farming techniques on select parcels in their vineyards. In 2005, Fonroque became an early member of the Syndicat de Vignerons en Biodynamie, thereby embracing bio-dynamic farming techniques and later earning the related certification. The winery became 100 percent biodynamic in its viticulture practices for their vineyard management techniques in 2008. In 2017, after our visit in 2012, Château Fonroque was sold to the Guillard family that is also associated with founding the insurance company, CHG Participation. The new owners plan to invest substantially and enhance Fonroque's biodynamic practices.

Château Chateau Le Puy (Bordeaux, Right Bank, near St. Émilion appellation of the Libournais region, primary): This château has been owned by the Amoreau family for over 400 years. The family claims that they have always been biodynamic, tending the vines organically for centuries and using biodynamic farming practices. The lunar cycle influences their operations and timing of their decisions. The chateau uses horses on about a third of its vines to maintain the soil's lightness. The winery has global Ecocert and Demeter certifications for their organic and biodynamic operations. According to one Amoreau family member:

My grandfather was influenced by André Birre, a mid-20th-century agronomist, who urged farmers to look after the health of their soils and recommended methods not unlike biodynamics . . . now we are fully biodynamic as per the best global practices where everything that is required for a healthy growing environment is one ecosystem.

Château Marguax (Bordeaux, Left Bank, Marguax appellation of the Médoc region, secondary): Château Margaux is one of four wines to have achieved Premier Cru (first growth in French) status in the Bordeaux Classification of 1855. The estate's best wines are very expensive, with a standard-sized bottle of the Château Margaux *grand vin* retailing at an average price of around US $639. The winery has been family owned since the sixteenth century though it has changed hands between several families, most recently the Agnelli family (of Fiat Motors) in the 1990s, even though the management remained with the Mentzelopoulos family. In 2003, Corinne Mentzelopoulos bought back the majority stake and became the sole shareholder of Château Margaux. Since 2012, the vines used to produce the Grand Vin of Château Margaux have been farmed using 100 percent certified organic farming techniques and some sections are being farmed using biodynamic methods.

Non-Family or Corporate Wineries

Château Soutard (Bordeaux, Right Bank, near St. Émilion appellation of the Libournais region, primary): This is one of the oldest estates in the Right Bank of the Brodeaux region dating back to 1513 when it was a farm and mill. It was in the middle of eighteenth century that Soutard's wine operations began. It remained the property of the

Bogeron family from 1890 to 2006. In 2006, it was sold to a large French insurance company, La Mondiale, which owns two other Bordeaux wineries. Before the corporate takeover, the Bogeron family had a policy of hand-harvesting the grapes and vinifying separately according to variety, age of the vines, and the part of the vineyard. They did not filter the wines, instead, they used egg whites to use natural gravity to filter. However, the adoption of full-scale organic viticulture happened after La Mondiale took over the winery, which led to certification. La Mondiale has a corporate strategy of certifying its three wineries as organic to enhance their market appeal.

Data Collection

As outlined above, we supplemented the case data with secondary data from websites and published materials from wineries in the region. We were prepared to go beyond our cases and add more cases to continue the data collection if we found that the initial cases had not provided us enough insight into the phenomena we were studying. However, we felt that the Canadian cases enabled us to reach theoretical saturation and the convenience samples of cases in France and Chile added richness from two uniquely different institutional contexts. We began to hear the same themes repeatedly and we agreed that additional cases would not provide significant new insights into the phenomena being examined. In essence, we follow Glaser and Strauss's (1967) guidance that once saturation of theoretical concepts and ideas is reached, the phenomena to be studied have been substantially explained. Since our intent was to supplement and enrich insights from our literature review, these cases met our research objectives.

In Canada, data were collected through around forty hours of recorded interviews conducted personally by the authors. The respondents were twenty-two members either of the managing and controlling family, or the single owner, or senior executives who were members of the dominant coalition or top management team, depending on the ownership of the firm as family owned, founder/first-generation owned, and corporate respectively. Interview data were triangulated, via public documents such as websites, annual reports (for corporate wineries), and newspaper items mentioning the included wineries. Our objective was to identify any discrepancies between the interview data and published reports. In addition, we added secondary data from websites and published materials of eight additional wineries to get a richer perspective, especially for corporate wineries.

In France, we added data through twelve hours of interviews from five cases (four in Bordeaux and one in La Provence) and added in-depth secondary data from three wineries. In Chile, we collected data through 8 hours of interviews from three wineries and added secondary data from one winery.

Data Analysis

The interview transcripts were analyzed through the categorization of the data according to the variables in our theoretical framework while remaining open to emergent concepts (Miles and Huberman, 1984). The emergent concepts were identified via a constant comparison of the cases (Glaser and Strauss, 1967) to identify common themes. An interview summary form (Miles and Huberman, 1984) was prepared after each interview to highlight categorization on the variables in the framework as well as the emergent themes, and other issues of interest which would be followed up at subsequent interviews. Each interview was coded in accordance with these emerging themes. Sentences relating to each different theme were entered in separate Microsoft Word text files for each emergent theme. The number of references and intensity of support for each theme were identified within each file before deciding which themes to retain and which to drop as less theoretically significant. Connections between the significant themes were investigated in the data. A number of the themes were dropped at earlier stages of data collection when subsequent interviews revealed them as less theoretically important or part of another theoretical theme. The sifting process continued in tandem with data collection. If theoretical parallels could not be found, then the themes were abstracted into generic descriptive labels. In Chapters 3, 4, and 5 of the monograph, we draw on these cases and use quotes from primary data to illustrate our theoretical discussions. We also discuss findings from the cases as they relate to our theoretical framework and the emergent themes in our data. The results of our analysis are presented in the chapters that follow.

Appendix A: Interview Guide

Questions Related to Family Involvement in Business

1 Can you share a brief history of your firm?
2 What has been the nature of family involvement in business over the years?
3 What type of family involvement do you expect in future generations?
4 Who controls the strategic direction and resource allocation decisions of your business? In other words, who forms the dominant coalition or primary decision-making body of your firm?
5 How does your family feel about the natural environment?
6 Is there unified agreement on the family's attitude toward the natural environment or do some family members feel differently?
7 Describe some activities undertaken by individual members of the dominant coalition toward environmental protection?
8 How does the dominant coalition of your business feel about using the firm as a vehicle for environmental preservation?
9 What resources are devoted toward environmental preservation by your firm?

Questions Related to Family Relationships (Focus on Conflict)

1 How would you describe the relationships between family members?
2 What sort of issues do family members disagree on?
3 How often do such disagreements occur?
4 When there is a disagreement amongst family members, how is it resolved?

Questions Related to Sustainability Strategy

1 Can you explain the different aspects of your business operations such as vineyards, wineries, supply chain, marketing, and retail?
2 What is your understanding of the term "Environmental Sustainability"?
3 To what extent is environmental sustainability important for various aspects of your business operations?

4 What are the environmentally sustainable practices that you have adopted in your (a) vineyards, (b) winery, (c) supply chain and marketing, (d) general operations?

5 How do your practices in each aspect of operations compare with practices operated by other wineries that you are aware of? Are you more advanced, less advanced or about the same as others in your business?

6 What are your goals for environmental sustainability related to your business five years into the future?

7 To what extent do you feel that environmental sustainability is important for the future of the region/country/world?

8 How does environmental sustainability relate to your personal lifestyle? Can you provide an example of how you have adopted environmental sustainability in your personal lifestyle?

9 Do you feel that you have sufficient knowledge and information to adopt advanced environmental practices in your business?

10 What are the obstacles or barriers to adopting such practices?

11 Does the family share your values about environmental sustainability?

12 Does the family believe that it is important to adopt advanced environmental practices in the business?

Notes

1. In this monograph, we mainly draw upon examples from the winery industry based on primary data, and also on examples from other industries that are mostly based on secondary sources.

2. An appellation is a legally defined and protected geographical indication used to identify where the grapes for a wine were grown. To qualify for an appellation, wineries must meet restrictions other than geographical boundaries, such as what grapes may be grown, maximum grape yields, alcohol level, and certain quality factors.

References

Glaser, B. G. and Strauss, A. L. 1967. *The Discovery of Grounded Theory: Strategies for Qualitative Research*. Chicago, IL: Aldine Publishing.

Miles, M. B. and Hunberman, M. 1984. *Qualitative Data Analysis: An Expanded Sourcebook*. Thousand Oaks, CA: Sage.

Reay, T., Jaskiewicz, P. and Hinings, C. R. 2015. How family, business, and community logics shape family firm behaviour and "rules of the game" in an organizational field. *Family Business Review*, 28(4): 292–311.

Sharma, S. and Vredenburg, H. 1998. Proactive corporate environmental strategy and the development of competitively valuable organizational capabilities. *Strategic Management Journal*, 19: 729–753.

Yin, R. K. 2009. *Case study research: Design and methods*. 4th ed. Thousand Oaks, CA: Sage.

3 | Exogenous Drivers of Corporate Environmental Sustainability Strategy

In this chapter, we focus on exogenous forces that influence a firm's environmental sustainability strategy. While a firm's strategy emerges as a result of complex interactions between exogenous and endogenous influences, an analytical examination of each type of driver and its influence on environmental sustainability strategy enables a finer grained analysis of how these influences may be moderated or mediated when applying the family business lens.

The two main exogenous drivers that have been examined in the environmental strategy literature are institutional and stakeholder influences. In the first part of this chapter, we begin by discussing the institutional forces that organizations are subject to. We then draw on the extant literature to examine the institutional forces that influence a firm's environmental strategy, including the impact of different regulatory approaches. Next, we draw insights from the family business literature to discuss institutional influences and logics driving strategy in family firms. Using our primary data from the winery industry, we examine whether or not institutional forces will have a different influence on environmental sustainability strategies of family-owned firms as compared to non-family firms. This part concludes with a discussion of the influence of institutional champions and entrepreneurs in shaping the organizational fields in this domain.

In the second part of this chapter, we focus on the examination of stakeholder influences on a firms' environmental sustainability strategy. We begin with a brief overview of the foundational arguments of stakeholder theory including classification of stakeholders and their influences on a firms' environmental strategy. In reviewing this literature, the salience of several categories of stakeholders (e.g., investors, regulators, media, NGOs) on the environmental sustainability strategy of a firm becomes evident. Noticeably absent from the environmental sustainability strategy literature, however, is a key stakeholder for family firms – the family. For family firms, the family is the controlling principal of a firm, or an influential voice in its dominant coalition, as is the case in a large majority of firms around the world (e.g., Dyer, 2003; LaPorta, Lopez-de-Silanes, Shleifer, 1999) ranging from small firms to many *Fortune 500* firms such as the Ford Motor Company, Wal-Mart, SC Johnson, and Hewlett-Packard. On the other hand, when reviewing family business literature, it becomes evident that the stakeholder lens has not been employed significantly to understand the salience of different stakeholders on family firms or vice versa. Nevertheless, this research confirms that family firms pursue a multiplicity of economic and noneconomic goals in their pursuit for longevity of their enterprises (Kotlar and De Massis, 2013). Based on this literature review and insights from our research, we develop arguments about the influence of different stakeholders on family versus non-family firms, and how these influences are likely to impact the environmental sustainability strategy of these firms.

Institutional Influences on a Firm's Strategy

At a societal level, institutional theory focuses on the deep resilient aspects of social structure and examines the processes by which schemes, rules, norms, and routines are established to guide social behavior (Scott, 1995). At a firm level of analysis, institutional theory views firms as "social structures that have attained a high degree of resilience. [They] are composed of cultural-cognitive, normative, and regulative elements that, together with associated activities and resources, provide stability and meaning to social life" such as acceptable procedures and norms of behavior within the firm (Scott, 1995: 33). In order to survive (Scott, 1995) and to achieve legitimacy (DiMaggio and Powell, 1983), organizations need to conform to the rules and belief systems prevailing in their environment. A firm's organizational structure and strategy, which according to economic rationality should be influenced by rules of efficiency in the marketplace, now are influenced by the constraints imposed by societal-level institutional forces (DiMaggio and Powell, 1983). Revisiting Weber's "iron cage," DiMaggio and Powell argued that as organizations in an industry or a societal field attempted to reconcile their economic performance within conditions of uncertainty and institutional constraints, they tended toward homogeneity of structures and strategy or what these authors called "institutional isomorphism." Isomorphism as an iron cage constrains an individual firm's strategy and influences it so that it increasingly resembles that of other firms within similar environments. As organizations increasingly resemble each other in their strategy, competition for markets and customers is replaced by competition for political power and legitimacy as the intended outcome.

DiMaggio and Powell (1983) proposed that isomorphism is an outcome of three main types of institutional forces: coercive, normative, and mimetic. Coercive forces emanate from societal institutions such as the state, the market or organizations on which a firm is dependent. Examples include governments and regulatory agencies that enforce labor laws, environmental and social legislation, and legal financial reporting requirements. Normative forces emanate from common educational, credentialing and licensing standards and accepted societal norms such as ethical behavior and treatment of employees. While coercive forces are the domain of the state, normative forces are less formalized. Societal-level institutions like the profession, religion, community, or family are conduits that establish expected norms of organizational behaviors considered acceptable and legitimate. It is not surprising therefore that normative forces are especially strong among professional accounting, consulting, or legal services firms. These forces gain momentum particularly when the coercive forces such as the regulatory standards are unclear or evolving, as is the case of changing expectations and perceptions of environmental sustainability driven largely by global-level agreements. Lacking clarity of the relationship between firm-level decisions and planetary-level consequences, and facing a void of regulatory guidance, organizational leaders turn toward normative forces not only to make sense of the exogenous forces but also to draw guidance from individual beliefs, familial values (in the case of family firms), and academic institutions. During such times, empirical studies are also likely to reveal the variant combinations of societal-level logics that particular firms in a field pay more or less attention to and how these hybrids change over time (Ocasio and Radoynovska, 2016). These societal-level logics include the state, market, corporate, professional, community, religion, and family (Thornton, Ocasio, and Lounsbury, 2012). Individual firms make commitments to different combinations of institutional logics as their strategic choices.

Mimetic forces are generated by imitation of other firms within the organizational field (environmental sustainability) that are also coping with similar coercive and/or normative forces. For example, firms may adopt common or best industry practices that may be diffused by normative conduits such as industry associations. Or, they may mimic strategies and standards similar to other firms perceived as industry leaders. Mimetic practices may be diffused via employee migration, religious organizations, community or family networks. These forces may lead to isomorphism (DiMaggio and Powell, 1983). Alternatively, they may lead to heterogeneity in terms of the capabilities of individual firms, dependence on external constituents, ownership structure, managerial values and preferences, geographic proximity to other firms in the same industry, and availability of influential champions of change.

Institutional Influences on a Firm's Environmental Sustainability Strategy

Almost all of the literature on institutional influences on a firm's sustainability strategy is based on research in publicly held or dispersed-ownership firms or without considering firms' dominant coalition as family or non-family controlled. As pointed in Chapter 1, the meaning of environmental sustainability is socially constructed and evolving. How firms in an industry or in a geographic context interpret and understand environmental sustainability and infuse the term with meaning depends on institutional fields within which they are embedded (Jennings and Zandbergen, 1995). Societal and organizational fields are formed around sustainability and enable the diffusion of norms, rules, meanings and practices among organizations in the field (Jennings and Zandbergen, 1995). This is illustrated in Hoffman's (1997) study of how the evolving regulatory environment and the environmental social movement led to the changing meaning, perceptions and practices of environmental sustainability for firms in the chemical and petroleum industry between 1960 and 1993 as the industry sought legitimacy within increasing institutional pressures for its regulation subsequent to high-visibility industrial accidents including the Union Carbide's Bhopal pesticide plant gas leak in 1984 and the *Exxon Valdez* oil spill in Prince William Sound in 1989.

Historically, the most salient institutional force influencing a firm's sustainability strategy has been social and environmental regulation. Social regulations in the form of labor laws including minimum wage, workplace environment, use of child labor, etc. have been in place for a long period in developed countries. While they still lag in many developing countries, the International Labor Organization (ILO) has a mission to establish minimum standards across the world. Environmental regulations are relatively more recent. In the United States, the publication of Rachel Carson's book, *Silent Spring* in 1962, brought environmental concerns to the attention of the public. Even though the chemical industry initially denied the claims made in the book, the book spurred a reversal in national pesticide policy, led to a nationwide ban on DDT for agricultural use, and catalyzed the environmental movement that led to the creation of the US Environmental Protection Agency in 1970. This was followed by the first UN conference on the environment in Stockholm in 1972 and several European countries established environmental regulations and agencies to implement regulations during the next two decades. The environmental regulatory agencies in various countries themselves were an outcome of institutional mimesis undertaken by political and public policy processes in the Western world to ban or regulate thousands of chemicals emitted by industrial operations under clean air and water regulations. These include the safe disposal and storage of radioactive wastes from nuclear power plants that are harmful to human health for thousands of years.

Governments usually regulate industrial emissions of wastes and NGOs document pollution levels on public websites to highlight the extent to which different firms or facilities pollute the air and water in their communities. In the United States, while the list changes yearly, the EPA requires disclosure of 595 individually listed chemicals and 32 chemical categories (including four categories containing 68 specifically listed chemicals) under a toxic release inventory (TRI). These TRI lists are publicly available for each manufacturing facility in the United States. Similar inventories of wastes are required to be disclosed by countries such as Canada (the National Pollution Release Inventory) and several European countries. China introduced reporting requirements for emissions from manufacturing facilities in 2014. Regulations now require Chinese firms to measure, report, and track a lengthening list of wastes that tends to become increasingly similar across the world. The reporting requirements lead firms not only to isomorphic strategies to measure, track, report these very similar wastes but also to install similar equipment to capture and control the pollution. This is because regulators such as the US EPA often prescribe the technologies to be used to control pollution and waste (using the principle of Best Available Control Technology). Many US firms end up buying the same equipment from the same suppliers and using the same processes for pollution control. The European Union is somewhat more flexible in following the principle of BATNEEC or "Best Available Technology Not entailing Excessive Economical Costs" in the European Union directive 96/61/EC.

The institutional coercion exercised via regulation may be direct, based on command and control or rule-based regulations, or it may be indirect based on flexible regulations. The enforcement of regulations can also be sanction-based on litigation and penalties or exercised via industry associations or other bodies in a consultative process. In the United States, the coercion is based mainly on a centralized prescriptive framework with penalties and sanctions. Canada and the Netherlands have adopted a more decentralized regulatory framework based on participatory decision-making, consultation and consensus. This has been reflected in the industry roundtables and public hearings in various Canadian provinces that involve bargaining and negotiation between firms, associations, regulators, communities, and various stakeholders.

Impact of Different Regulatory Approaches on a Firm's Environmental Sustainability Strategy

Extant research on the influence of regulatory approaches on the environmental sustainability strategy of firms has mainly shown that direct sanction-based prescriptive regulations that specify processes and technologies drive firms into less efficient or nonproductive practices and strategies (Jaffe et al., 1995) and short-term investments. In fact, investments in prescribed pollution control technologies and equipment may also be made to the detriment of long-term investments in production and process efficiency (Gray, 1987). It is argued that pollution control regulations by agencies such as the US EPA are designed by engineers with a focus on technological solutions while ignoring business considerations and hence these regulations lead firms to make capital investments that are likely to be inefficient and improperly sited (Wells, 1973). Under pressure from industry associations, many environmental regulations grandfather or exempt older plants, thus discouraging them from making efficient longer-term investments in pollution prevention and unfairly skewing the competitive field for newer plants. Moreover, excessive procedures and a rule-centered culture adopted by most regulatory agencies stifle patient investments for innovation (Eisenhardt, 1989).

Jennings and Zandbergen (1995) argue that intended outcomes of environmental regulations – clean air and clean water – are often forgotten when implemented in a coercive compliance-based command and control framework that mainly looks at chemical emissions at the end-of-pipe at the plant site rather than the intended outcomes in terms of air or water quality in the ecosystem. Jennings and Zandbergen (1995) also argue that in the consultative Canadian system, there is a high level of ambiguity as compared to the US command and control system. They propose that, under ambiguity, normative and mimetic institutional forces are more likely to be stronger as compared to coercive forces. That is, firms in an industry or a geographic jurisdiction are more likely to adopt common practices by looking to, and following, other firms.

In contrast to the institutionalization perspective, the Porter hypothesis (Porter, 1991; Porter and van der Linde, 1995) argues that stringent environmental regulations positively affect firm efficiency as investments and attention to minimizing pollution lead to positive changes throughout a firm. The greater the stringency of environmental regulations in a jurisdiction, it is argued, the greater the likelihood that firms in that jurisdiction will invest for the long-term to innovate and achieve first-mover advantage in a global competitive arena (Porter, 1991).

Others, such as Majumdar and Marcus (2001), argue for more indirect market-oriented well-designed flexible regulations. They propose that regulations that allow discretion for innovation in terms of ample implementation time while at the same time imposing challenging desired performance outcomes can lead to longer-term investments in efficient strategies. Similarly, Marcus (1988) argues that providing firms with choices within a set of constraints leads to more efficient results by encouraging entrepreneurship and risk taking. If firms can determine the value of an innovative approach within flexible regulations (e.g., such as cost savings due to material reduction or energy savings), they will be more likely to make patient investments to adopt such an approach. However, at some stage, even flexible regulations become a mimetic institutional force rather than an individual strategy as other firms in the industry adopt it without a deep analysis of suitability for their context and operations (Jennings and Zandbergen, 1995).

Noncompliance with environmental regulations could lead to penalties and sanctions by regulatory agencies. A history of compliance and good citizenship by a firm may lead to regulatory agencies giving it the benefit of the doubt in the event of an infraction. This usually leads to greater legitimacy and a license to operate (Sharma and Vredenburg, 1998), and lower scrutiny and coercion by regulators. Hence, firms have greater incentives to be in compliance when they face stringent regulations and a high level of monitoring and strong penalties and sanctions for noncompliance. Firms also adopt isomorphic strategies in implementing industry standards and best practices such as ISO 14001 as shown by Delmas's (2002) study.

While drivers for variation in corporate sustainability strategy are mainly discussed in Chapters 4 and 5, some authors counterintuitively argue that institutional pressures may actually drive firms toward heterogeneity or strategic responses that seek competitive advantage or economic benefit rather than legitimacy via isomorphism. Oliver (1991) argued that responses of individual firms to institutional pressures may be strategic and not entirely isomorphic because individual firms are embedded in unique contexts of resource dependence with external constituents.

Some firms may choose to make patient investments that pay back over the longer-term to prevent pollution at source rather than control it at the end of pipe. Pollution prevention allows for discretion in adopting a range of strategies. For example, pollution could be prevented by investments with long-term paybacks such as changing product formulation/components, processes, distribution systems, inputs, or outsourcing activities, or converting some physical activities to online/digital activities (Russo and Fouts, 1997; Sharma and Vredenburg, 1998).

It has also been argued that institutional isomorphism may be moderated by an organization's ownership structure (Goodrick and Salancik, 1996), board of director interlocks between firms in institutional fields, and by geographic proximity to firms within the same industry, for example the spread of poison pill and golden parachute practices amongst firms (Davis and Greve, 1997). Delmas and Toffel (2008) argue organizational structure influences why organizations adopt heterogeneous management practices in response to institutional pressures for environmental responsibility. They find that the organizational structure influences facility managers' awareness of, and receptivity to, institutional pressures. This is because organizational structure determines how the pressures will be channeled to different organizational functions, such as legal affairs and marketing departments, and heighten managers' awareness of pressures from different institutional constituents.

Berrone, Fosfuri, Gelabert, and Gomez-Mejia (2013) showed that both regulatory and normative institutional pressures had differential effects on individual firms' investment horizon for environmental innovation contingent on the gaps and deficiencies of a firm's resources or capabilities required to respond to institutional pressures. These authors argued that institutional pressures may drive firms toward heterogeneity rather than toward isomorphism in polluting industries as individual firms focus research and development in a quest to develop proprietary processes and technologies that can enable them to improve compliance to regulations and other institutional pressures. On the contrary, these authors argued that "when institutional pressures are weak, firms should be less inclined to seek differentiation through an active program of environmental innovation, as these risky investments may not be justified by legitimacy gains" (Berrone et al., 2013: 905). Their study found that the worst performers on environmental practices faced the greatest legitimacy gap and were the most likely to invest in environmental innovation to respond to institutional pressures.

Firms mimic each other in societal and institutional fields in order to gain legitimacy, license to operate, and copy perceived best practices without the need to spend time and resources on deep analysis. There are several examples of cooperative voluntary agreements (VAs) where firms within an industry agree to adopt certain environmental and social standards or practices by mimicking the industry leaders. Delmas and Montes-Sancho (2010) found that firms that enter into VAs at the beginning or closer to the initiation of the agreements are more likely to adopt meaningful and substantive strategies as compared to greater symbolic cooperation adopted by firms that enter late into the VAs. This is because early versus late joiners face different institutional pressures. Early joiners face greater political pressures and are also better connected to the industry association and are more visible as compared to late joiners. Regardless, Delmas and Montes-Sancho's findings were similar to King and Lenox's (2000) findings that there were no significant differences overall between participants and nonparticipants in the VAs in terms of substantive sustainability outcomes. Lenox (2006) suggests, that some members of VAs are willing to tolerate symbolic behavior by late joiners rather than quit because their continued participation is necessary to maintain the institution. Hence, higher participation rates by firms in an industry leads to more widespread change as compared to the participation of a few firms undertaking more substantive action of ISO 14001 certification across Europe and the United States.

Given that adoption of a proactive environmentally sustainable strategy requires long-term patient investments, there is lack of research that shows how exogenous forces influence such investments in publicly listed firms. A recent study begins to address this issue by examining the institutional influence of financial markets. Using a sample of 1,376 firms, Desjardins' (2018) study finds that firms that experience a decrease in financial analyst coverage lengthen their investment horizon. This effect is stronger for firms covered by fewer analysts, when analysts from larger brokerages discontinue coverage, and under Regulation Fair Disclosure (Desjardins, 2018).

While the normal trend of institutional forces is constantly increasing regulation, it is useful to consider whether deregulation in an industry will lead to different investment horizons by family versus non-family firms. Does the removal of regulation reduce coercive forces and lead to greater variation in corporate environmental sustainability strategy in general regardless of ownership? Delmas, Russo, and Montes-Sancho (2007) argued that since regulation is a coercive force that creates path dependencies toward limited resource development and drives firms toward an isomorphic strategy, deregulation will drive firms toward differentiated environmental strategies in contexts where the citizens and communities have greater environmental sensitivity and also depending on their unique organizational resources. For example, these authors found that the nature of utility regulation created a monopoly for the utility firms, suppressed latent market demand for green renewable energy, and blocked the development of a rich variety of product offerings that characterize a nonregulated environment. Hence, incumbent firms in the electric utility industry that relied heavily on coal-fired generation or enjoyed strong productive efficiencies were less likely to diversify to renewable energy investments. It can be argued that the removal of institutional coercion enables some firms to develop innovative sustainable strategies while maintaining an "iron cage" for others due to path dependencies imposed by regulations. Based on our arguments, it would be interesting to examine if family firms, under conditions of deregulation, are more likely to innovate for the long-term due to their focus on long-term horizon for perpetuating the family business.

Family Firms' Response to Institutional Forces

It bears repeating here that most extant research on the influence of institutional forces on corporate environmental sustainability has been conducted among non-family firms or at least without distinguishing between family and non-family controlled firms. Hence, there is a gap in understanding whether family firms respond similarly to institutional forces in their investment horizons to undertake their sustainability strategy as non-family firms do. The influence of institutional forces on family firms has mainly been examined in contexts other than environmental sustainability (see a comprehensive review of this literature by Soleimanof, Rutherford, and Webb, 2018). This research mainly shows that family firms tend to move toward isomorphic practices and strategies under the influence of institutional forces. For example, normative and mimetic forces influence family firms to adopt isomorphic governance structures, processes and policies (Melin and Nordqvist, 2007) and change or redefine their guiding family values toward social issues such as gender equality (Parada, Nordqvist, and Gimeno, 2010). Some scholars argue that family businesses are influenced by multiple institutional logics, such as markets (or business), regulations/state, family (Thornton and Ocasio, 2008), and community (Reay, Jaskiewicz, and Hinings, 2015). One or more institutional logic may be dominant at a particular time or on a particular issue. For example, in studying the winery industry in Canada's Okanagan Valley, Reay et al. (2015) found that family firms tended to be influenced by all three – business, family, and community logic – while non-family firms were mainly influenced by business logic, and first generation/founder firms (referred to by these authors as lifestyle firms) were influenced mainly by family logic. It is worth emphasizing that the founder/first generation firms studied by the authors were run by couples who had given up professional careers to adopt a winery lifestyle. Hence, their focus on their personal family (spouse and young children) rather than "family" in the traditional sense of family business. This research study indicates that in responding to the common institutional environment, family firms behaved differently as compared to non-family firms. In the Okanagan winery industry, family firms tended to work on collective initiatives in marketing, lobbying for change in regulations and developing common quality assurance standards, while non-family firms focused on maximizing individual efficiencies, production, and profitability, and lifestyle firms wanted to maintain the status quo that had attracted them to the winery lifestyle (Reay et al., 2015).

By coincidence, one region for our data collection is also the Okanagan winery industry with a similar set of first generation family/founder, multi-generation family, and non-family firms. However, our focus is on the emergence of and the adoption of proactive environmental sustainability strategies in response to institutional influences. We also had the benefit of comparing data from family and non-family firms in Bordeaux in France and from Chile. While Reay et al. (2015) found collective action by family firms in common marketing efforts, lobbying for regulatory change, and developing common quality standards, we found no evidence of collective action either by family or non-family firms in the adoption of proactive sustainability practices. This indicates the dominance of individual action and heterogeneity in strategy that we will discuss in depth in Chapters 4 and 5.

A factor to explain the lack of isomorphism in proactive environmental strategy may be that the institutional forces in the Okanagan winery industry were at a basic level of environmental protection to prevent run-off of pesticides and herbicides and other chemicals in the lake and water bodies and control of effluents and air emissions. There were few or no normative or mimetic forces driving firms toward proactive sustainability strategies. From the perspective of regulatory (coercive) institutional forces, firms in all three contexts we studied – Canada, Chile, and France – were in compliance. Hence, the institutional forces neither drove nor explained *proactive* investments in long-term sustainability innovations and practices. This is illustrated by the following quotes from the interviews we conducted.

According to the head of the first generation of the multi-family firm, environmentally proactive Nirvana winery in the Okanagan:

No one is asking us to adopt organic or biodynamic practices. The focus of the regulations is on reducing runoff from the most toxic chemicals into the Lake. The tourists who visit the winery rarely ever ask about our environmental practices or what the organic label implies. The VQA standards do not have any elements of sustainability, and the industry association lobbies against environmental standards. Why do we do it? Because we care for the land and what we put into our bodies. The side effect is the higher quality of our wine and the awards we win.

The founder of proactive Landjoy in the Okanagan, head of the first-generation family who has been a pioneer in helping several wineries develop their organic vineyards and wineries (including Nirvana) expressed similar sentiments:

We do not adopt organic practices because someone asks us to do so. Organic practices lead to a living and well-balanced soil composition that guarantees the health of the plant and the terroir expression of the wines. This leads to wine that is in harmony, healthy, and flavorful. Our wines win awards every year. People who drink our wine want to know more about the organic practices that led to the quality rather than the other way around.

The Chief Operating Officer of the mainly reactive Bird's Nest in the Okanagan, a dispersed-ownership winery originally started by a family and with significant shareholding by the fifth generation of the family but now run professionally, had a different perspective:

We follow all regulations on use of chemicals and emissions and runoffs into our beautiful Lake. We have also gone beyond regulations by installing energy efficient motors and reusing our water, resulting in cost savings.

The winemaker of reactive Skyline in the Okanagan, a winery started by a father-and-daughter team and subsequently bought out by the large family-run Peller group with multiple wineries in the Okanagan Valley and the Niagara region, said:

When we started the winery, we began with organic viticulture. When we were acquired by the Peller Group, the focus has been on product quality and production yields as per the group's policy of compliance with regulations and adopting the most efficient production practices. At the scale at which we operate across our several wineries, it is difficult to standardize organic practices across the Niagara and Okanagan regions.

In the different institutional context of the Nova Scotia winery industry with even fewer institutional influences from regulators, customers, and industry associations, the data once again pointed to a heterogeneity of firm strategy rather than isomorphism. The head of the Europa, a multi-generation family-owned winery with a reactive environmental strategy, stated:

We are in a UNESCO World Heritage site and we get a lot of tourists. We want to deliver a world class experience for tourists and visitors, high quality wines, a great tasting room, fine dining in a great restaurant. We meticulously follow all regulations and best farming and winemaking practices.

In contrast, the founder of Dreamscape, a second-generation family-controlled winery that is located in the same institutional context and location in the UNESCO World Heritage site, but pursues a proactive environmental strategy, had a different perspective:

Our family came into the winery business to be close to the land. Being on the land means respecting the terroir and its unique ecosystem. It's a pity that regulations only require wineries to do the minimum to protect the land.

In the French context, we did not visit any family firms adopting reactive environmental sustainability practices. The general manager of Chateau Duvivier in La Provence, a family firm owned by a Swiss family deeply committed to sustainability, said:

There are no regulations of pressures to be biodynamic. I am not sure that most consumers even understand what biodynamic means. For us it is a matter of harmony of the ecosystem and the biodiversity. A biodiverse and biodynamic ecosystem brings joy to the unique terroir and all of us who work here.

To a varying degree, similar sentiments were expressed by family members of the proactive wineries in the Bordeaux region. In contrast, the Marketing Director of Chateau Lascombs, a ten-generation family winery that became a corporate winery in 2011, explained the clear economic rationale:

Several wineries in the Margaux region are adopting organic/biodynamic to varying degrees. We are not sure if it enhances the quality of the wine or brings premium prices. We are not sure if the market is ready or large enough for organic wines.

Similarly, in the Chilean context, the values-driven approach of family firms in contrast to the economic or business-driven approach of corporate wineries was clear. The fourth generation of the proactive DeMartino family wineries illustrated the family values:

We are constantly experimenting with the latest techniques and practices to make wines that are natural for the terroir. Our latest experiment is the fermentation of wine naturally in large clay amphorae as was done thousands of years ago. While this significantly reduces shelf life and adds an earthy flavor, we are producing smaller quantities that will be consumed within two years.

The winery manager of the mainly eco-efficiency-driven proactive Santa Rita, Chile's largest corporate winery, now owned by a US corporation, had a more market-driven approach:

We are one of the world's largest producers and exporters of wine. This requires consistent quality and affordable prices for all segments of the market. While we are gradually converting our vineyards to organic, a complete overnight conversion would affect product quality and consistency. However, we lead the Chilean industry in our water management, waste reduction, minimizing inputs and using ultra-light bottles.

In our data in the winery industry in three countries, it was quite clear that the institutional forces were mainly regulations on chemical emissions and effluents that were easily met by all firms: family owned and non-family owned. There were few mimetic and normative forces that were apparent in the industry in all three contexts at the time of data collection (and we will discuss how such forces emerged in St. Émilion in France starting 2017). The adoption of proactive environmental strategies via investments in longer-term innovation initiatives were much more evident in family firms that appeared to be driven mainly by familial values rather than the more proximal corporate or market forces. In contrast, corporate wineries seem to be primarily driven by these proximal institutional forces.

In 2017 (five years after our data collection), Conseil des Vins de Saint Émilion, the wine council of St. Émilion, the largest producer of wines in the Bordeaux region, mandated that, starting with the 2019 vintage, all of the 3.85 million cases of St. Émilion wine must be produced with grapes grown by the 973 growers using organic/biodynamic viticulture (Mustasich, 2017). While we have not been able to get additional primary data on this change in the institutional environment, the main drivers according to Franck Binard of the St. Émilion wine council were the increasing number of projects starting in 2015 to reduce insecticides, improve biodiversity, preserve the picturesque landscape of the UNESO World Heritage Site, and the increasing demand from markets in the Nordic countries, Canada, Switzerland, Germany, and Japan, and to a limited extent in certain markets in China and the United States (Mustasich, 2017). In a poll by the wine council in 2015, 45 percent of the members indicated that they had adopted sustainable practices in recent years. Given the dominance of family firms in this region, it can be cautiously assumed that the 45 percent had a major share of such firms. The 25 percent who opposed the measure due to concerns of costs and risk were assured that the Council would work with them to obtain the HVE3 (Haute Valeur Environmentale) certification, though wineries are free to obtain any credible organic/biodynamic certification. This move by the most prestigious region with the most expensive and high-quality wines in the world has the potential to generate the normative institutional forces not only in the rest of France but across the world's winemaking regions. This would be an interesting case study of normative forces influencing firms in the winery industry in a region toward proactivity, which is likely to lead to mimetic forces in other regions.

Until the recent changes in St. Émilion, it appears that the regulations and the normative forces set a low bar, which was met by all wineries, and it was only the family firms that chose to invest for the longer-term via organic and biodynamic transformation of the vineyards and organic winemaking techniques in accordance with their values about the terroir, ecosystems, biodiversity, and health.

The Role of Institutional Entrepreneurs

Even within institutional constraints, firms can entrepreneurially attempt to shape the institutional norms and rules and disseminate best practices (Wijen, 2014). The institutional entrepreneurs are more likely to shape the environment when there is lack of field transparency. Institutional entrepreneurs are "actors who have an interest in particular institutional arrangements and who leverage resources to create new institutions or to transform existing ones" (Maguire, Hardy, and Lawrence, 2004: 657). In fact, DiMaggio (1988: 14) anticipated the role of entrepreneurs in institutional fields when he argued that "new institutions arise when organized actors with sufficient resources see in them an opportunity to realize interests that they value highly." What institutional theorists term institutional entrepreneurship, in this book we term strategic choice or variation in strategy by a firm and this will be discussed in depth in Chapters 4 and 5.

In the Okanagan winery context, the shaping of the organizational field for organic viticulture was clearly driven by the founder of Landjoy, an expert in organic agriculture who became a catalyst for organic transformation of several vineyards. The founder of Landjoy had a personal preference for organic over biodynamic partly due to his deep academic education in agricultural engineering and partly due to his religious beliefs. He also is an energetic champion for sustainable agriculture in the Okanagan region and willing to give his time and expertise to others. In the St. Émilion context, it appears to be a group of families who own the world's most prestigious wineries who are concerned about the image of the region's wines in a changing context where the world increasingly values ecosystem preservation and consumption of organic foods.

Many family firms aspire for transgenerational longevity and success (Miller and Le Breton-Miller, 2005). Such firms are especially motivated not only to be economically viable in the short-run but to also be seen as legitimate within their communities and institutional environments. They are, therefore, more likely to exert efforts to stay in tune with changing macro-environmental knowledge and trends. Family business researchers frequently report the active involvement of family business leaders in their professional associations (Parada et al., 2010), community leadership (Reay et al., 2015), and political processes aimed to influence formal institutions (e.g., Craig and Moores, 2010; Dieleman and Sachs, 2008). Many of these efforts are directed toward understanding the latest developments in science and industry, and enable building knowledge that benefits all members of an association or region.

Family business research has also revealed the dark side of oligarchic family control when a large concentration of a country's assets and wealth lies in the hands of a few families who promote political rent seeking through crony capitalism (e.g., Morck and Yeung, 2004; Soleimanof et al., 2018). Such cronyism retards institutional development in a country leading to inefficient resource allocation and low market competition (Carney, 2005; Fogel, 2006). Thus, not only is it interesting for scholars to understand the differential influence of institutional forces on the environmental strategies of family firms and non-family firms, but also the within-group differences in each of these categories.

Innovating for an environmental sustainability strategy requires patient investments in experimental and new untested technologies, processes, products, and business models. These investments are more likely than not to pay back over a longer term. Coercive regulations drive firms toward the adoption of specific technologies and practices and discourage heterogeneous strategies that may involve long-term patient investments. The pressure to respond to regulations is immediate. Similarly, normative and mimetic pressures to respond to industry association norms and industry best practices discourage creativity and investments in innovative new technologies, processes, products, and business models. The relative importance of coercive, normative, and mimetic forces under different conditions of certainty have not yet been studied. Nevertheless, there is evidence that firms that do adopt environmental strategies and investments that pay back over the long term are driven by familial or individual values rather than societal forces of state, market, or corporation. Hence,

P1. *In the presence of weak and unclear coercive forces (regulations and laws), normative forces (familial or individual values and attitudes toward environmental issues) have a higher influence in strategic choices of environmental strategies of firms.*

P2. *Mimetic forces are stronger in the presence of an influential institutional champion shaping organizational fields. The intensity and impact of these champions is higher and more long lasting when they are members of the controlling family.*

(Example: as in the case of the Landjoy founder as a passionate advisor for the diffusion of organic practices in several organic wineries in the Canadian Okanagan region).

P3. *Family firms are more likely to make long-term patient investments in a proactive environmental sustainability strategy as compared to non-family firms in responding to institutional forces due to their central goal of survival of the business for future generation.*

P4. *Leaders of family firms are more likely than leaders of non-family firms to be driven by family values in responding to institutional influences in developing their environmental strategies.*

P5. *Leaders of family firms are more likely than leaders of non-family firms to play the role of institutional champion to shape organizational fields related to corporate environmental strategy due to their longer-term strategic horizons.*

Next, we examine another major exogenous force that drives firms toward proactive sustainable strategies: stakeholders.

Stakeholder Influences on a Firm's Environmental Strategy

The stakeholder literature argues for the engagement of constituents or groups that can affect or are affected by the firm's operations (Freeman, 1984). The stakeholder literature has developed along two main streams that make differing arguments for engagement. One stream argues firms should engage stakeholders for instrumental reasons that benefit the firm (e.g., Donaldson and Preston, 1995; Jones, 1995; Jones and Wicks, 1999), and the other offers normative and moral arguments for engaging all of the firm's constituencies as the right thing to do (e.g., Donaldson and Dunfee, 1994; Evan and Freeman, 1983; Philips, 1997).

In the environmental sustainability literature, most theoretical and empirical research has focused on instrumental arguments for engaging stakeholders. This literature argues that stakeholders influence a firm's sustainability strategy in order to further their agenda, and also that stakeholders channel institutional forces (especially normative) and make them more immediate for the firm. Some institutional theorists argue that the external constituents (stakeholders) specific to a firm moderate and/or mediate the influence of institutional forces on a firm's environmental strategy (Delmas and Toffel, 2008; Jennings and Zandbergen, 1995).

In the family business (FB) literature, research at the interface of stakeholder management and family firms is limited and lacks empirical studies (Cennamo et al., 2012; Sharma, 2001; Zellweger and Nason, 2008). The main differentiating arguments in the FB literature is that not only is the family an important and missing stakeholder in a large majority of business organizations around the world (Sharma, 2001), it is also central to the decision-making dominant coalition that determines which stakeholders to engage based on familial values and economic and noneconomic goal priorities (such as perseveration of socioemotional wealth) of the controlling family principals (Cennamo et al., 2012; Gomez-Mejia et al., 2012). The concept of socioemotional wealth (SEW) of the family is based on the desire of the controlling principal's identity alignment with the firm and the importance of positive family reputation as the most important factor in strategic decision-making (Berrone, Cruz, and Gomez-Mejia, 2012). When family recognition is challenged or threatened, family business owners have been found to sacrifice economic gains in order to maintain or restore their family control and recognition (for a comprehensive review of this literature see Gomez-Mejia et al., 2012). The linkage of

SEW to a family firm's response to stakeholders is discussed later in this section.

Stakeholder Classification, Salience, and Influence

A firm's stakeholders can be broadly classified into those with solely an economic stake in the firm or those with a stake in one or more social or environmental issues. The stakeholder literature generally classifies stakeholders dichotomously as primary or secondary. Clarkson (1995: 106) uses the logic of instrumentalism to define secondary stakeholders as those groups that "are not engaged in transactions with the corporation and are not essential for its survival." Among secondary stakeholders, he includes the media and special interest groups, such as nongovernmental organizations (NGOs) focused on various social and environmental issues. In contrast, he accords considerable instrumental importance to primary stakeholders as those "without whose continuing participation the corporation cannot survive as a going concern." Here he includes shareholders and investors, employees, customers, and suppliers, and public stakeholders such as governments and communities "that provide infrastructures and markets, whose laws and regulations must be obeyed, and to whom taxes and other obligations may be due" (Clarkson, 1995: 106). Thus, according to Clarkson (1995), there is a high level of instrumental interdependence between the firm and its primary stakeholder groups but not so between the firm and its secondary stakeholders.

Some scholars argue for according instrumental importance to secondary stakeholders because such groups are capable of affecting the economic viability and survival of the firm. For example, Freeman (1999: 234) argues that in order to be effective, organizations need to pay attention to "all and only those relationships that can affect or be affected by the achievement of organization's purposes," including attention to secondary stakeholder groups when they have an impact on corporate operations. Frooman (1999) argues that secondary stakeholders can affect the firm indirectly by influencing its primary stakeholders. For example, in the Canadian forestry industry, environmental NGOs focused on sustainable forestry practices were able to influence the sustainability practices of forestry products companies indirectly via primary stakeholders such as customers and government agencies (Sharma and Henriques, 2005). They did so by either influencing the primary stakeholders such as customers and regulators to withhold resources (such as purchasing power from customers and operating licenses from regulators) or to demand that the resources be used in accordance with the adoption of certain practices by the firm (such as the customers demanding specific environmental certification of products by organizations like the Forestry Stewardship Council standards; Sharma and Henriques, 2005).

Arguments are also made to the contrary: that the influence of secondary stakeholders, concerned mainly with a firm's social and environmental performance, to a firm's economic performance is insignificant. That is, firms should not distribute corporate wealth and resources to their secondary stakeholders to motivate them to take favorable decisions vis-à-vis the organization. For example, Hillman and Keim (2001: 125) conclude from their study that "using corporate resources for social issues not related to primary stakeholders may not create value for shareholders."

Some scholars argue that secondary stakeholders have instrumental importance for a firm and affect its economic performance. Jones (1995) argues that relationships that are based on trust and cooperation with all stakeholders will help a firm reflect a sincere manner and reduce the costs of monitoring and controlling opportunism, leading to competitive advantage. Similarly, normative stakeholder approaches advocate for the inherent moral value of all stakeholder claims (e.g., Donaldson and Preston, 1995; Jones and Wicks, 1999). Both arguments are appealing but both are prescriptive and do not offer the resource-constrained firm guidance for managing multiple conflicting demands from large numbers of stakeholder groups.

Mitchell, Agle, and Wood (1997) argue that instrumental importance can be accorded to stakeholders regardless of their primary or secondary classification and based on their salience for the focal firm. A stakeholder's salience is a function of its power and legitimacy and the urgency of its claims. Power can be coercive, financial, or material. That is, a stakeholder may have the ability to affect a firm's sales, and/ or its brand image and reputation. Stakeholders such as regulators, governments, shareholders, investors, customers, and the media possess this power. A stakeholder may possess the legitimacy of its relationship with the firm and the legitimacy of its actions in terms of desirability or appropriateness. For example, shareholders, employees, suppliers, customers, governments, and regulators, all have legitimacy in their interactions with the firm. These stakeholders also have legal rights attached to their relationship with the firm. Finally, a stakeholder may have urgency of its concerns and/or claims in terms of criticality and time sensitivity. For example, the local community or an NGO may stage a highly visible protest at the firm's facilities, or a customer may file a lawsuit against the firm, or a regulatory agency may impose a crippling fine or issue an order for the shutting down of a firm's operations.

However, Mitchell et al. (1997) do not consider the strategic salience of stakeholders to a firm's current and future operations. Further, they do not consider whether stakeholders that possess a single attribute of salience (such as urgency of claim), but lack one or two of the other attributes (e.g., legitimacy and power), can acquire the other attributes by influencing a primary stakeholder who possesses these attributes (e.g., Frooman, 1999). Hart and Sharma (2004) propose an even more radical instrumental argument that firms need to fan out to the fringe of their stakeholder networks to engage even seemingly non-stakeholders (such as the poor at the base of the economic pyramid) to generate competitive imagination and disruptive innovations for future competitive advantage. Regardless, while a firm needs a longer-term focus to develop a long-term sustainability strategy using radical transactiveness techniques developed by Hart and Sharma (2004), it has to respond immediately to stakeholders that are the most salient to its operations in order to avoid disruption of its activities. Hence, stakeholder salience has significant predictive power as a direct driver of a firm's sustainability strategy.

The salience of a stakeholder group for the firm is determined not only by the number of attributes – power, legitimacy, and urgency – that the group possesses, but also the *extent* to which it possesses these attributes. A stakeholder group that is legitimate and has the power and urgency of its claim is the highest priority for the firm. Therefore, if a government agency requires the firm to reduce carbon emissions by a certain amount and by a certain date, it has the legitimacy, power, and urgency to spur corporate action. Therefore, it is important to keep in mind that these three attributes may be gained or lost over time and may strengthen or weaken over time. Moreover, low-priority stakeholders can increase their salience by combining forces with others to boost their power and urgency. For example, an NGO can influence the firm's customers and the media to increase the salience of their claim.

Stakeholder salience analysis requires careful planning, guidelines for selection of stakeholders, and background information on the stakeholders and their claims (Sharma, 2014).

The power of stakeholders to influence the firm's environmental sustainability strategy and practices depends on the resource interdependence between the firm and the specific stakeholders. Stakeholders can influence how a firm uses certain resources. For example, shareholders may demand that their funds be invested only in investments in pollution prevention (long-term) versus pollution control (short-term) projects. Conflicts could be created if certain stakeholders want a firm to divest from fossil fuels and invest in renewable energy projects with long-term payback, and its shareholders demand that it should invest in booming fossil fuel markets to maximize short-term returns. Stakeholders such as shareholders may withhold further investments or demand repayment or sell the company's shares. Customers can withhold purchasing power and refuse to buy a firm's products or services (Frooman, 1999).

Stakeholders can also use direct or indirect strategies to influence a firm's strategy (Sharma and Henriques, 2005). In situations of high resource interdependence between the firm and the stakeholder, it is likely that stakeholders will use direct strategies to influence how a firm makes its investments and uses its resources. For example, in the forestry industry, major customers, such as construction companies and furniture manufacturers, have insisted that the companies obtain certifications based on more sustainable timber harvesting practices such as the Forestry Stewardship Council Certification (Sharma and Henriques, 2005).

When stakeholders control critical resources but are not in turn resource dependent on the firm, they would be more likely to use a direct strategy to withhold resources from the firm unless it adopts certain sustainability practices. For example, Canadian regulators have denied licenses to forestry companies to operate on Crown (government owned) lands unless they adopt sustainable harvesting practices and supply chains that include the aboriginal First Nations with sovereign rights on the land (Sharma and Henriques, 2005).

When the firm and the stakeholders have no resource interdependence on each other, the stakeholders would be likely to exercise indirect pathways of influence through other stakeholders who may hold resources important for the focal firm. The type of strategy adopted would vary depending on the relative power balance between the stakeholders. For example, environmental groups have actively participated in environmental assessment hearings in Canada to influence provincial government agencies to deny renewal of Crown leases on forestry lands to firms – an example of an indirect withholding strategy. Environmental groups have also picketed large buyers such as Home Depot and Lowe's in the United States and forced them to change their procurement practices so that they buy wood products only from companies that adopt sustainable practices – an example of an indirect usage strategy (Sharma and Henriques, 2005).

When the stakeholder group is resource dependent on the firm but the firm has no resource dependence on the stakeholder group (e.g., minor suppliers and unskilled employees), the firm's sustainability practices are unlikely to be influenced by stakeholder pressures (Sharma and Henriques, 2005).

Having identified salient stakeholders based on their power, legitimacy, and urgency, the firm may choose to focus on the elements of its environmental sustainability footprint that are important and critical for the salient stakeholders rather than for the firm (Sharma, 2014). For example, an energy company operating in the Canadian oilsands faces concerns of provincial, national, and international NGOs about its major environmental impacts such as large amounts of carbon dioxide emissions, usage of very large quantities of water, major destruction of habitats, and social issues such as the impacts on traditional livelihoods and quality of life of the Canadian First Nations (aboriginal tribes in the operating area) that constitute the local communities. Even though the operations of the firm are within the provincial and legal regulations in Canada, NGOs and consumers in the United States have such major concerns that these issues have been politicized nationally and the US Federal government and several US state governments have successfully influenced successive US Presidents (Obama and Trump) to delay or change decisions on allowing the Keystone XL Pipeline System to transport synthetic crude oil from the oil sands of Alberta, Canada, to refineries in the Gulf Coast of Texas. Even though the pipeline provides a measure of energy independence for the United States from regimes that sponsor terrorism around the world, the environmental sustainability issues around the pipeline froze permissions by the US administration since the first phase from Alberta to Nebraska was built in 2010. Therefore, a firm operating in the

Canadian oil sands has environmental impacts such as carbon emissions, water usage, water contamination, and habitat destruction and social impacts on First Nation livelihoods that are salient issues for NGOs and consumers in the province of Alberta, in Canada, in the United States, and internationally, and for the current US federal government and several state governments, in addition to the Canadian national, US, and global media. Obviously, such a firm needs a strategy to address these issues that are important for a large number of salient stakeholders (Sharma, 2014).

A garment manufacturer may have to focus on issues on worker living wage, working conditions, and human rights in its supply chain since these are critical issues for international NGOs, its consumers, and the media, especially after the global outrage over the deaths of over a thousand garment workers in a building collapse in Bangladesh (Greenhouse, 2013). A coffee company may have to develop a strategy to address issues of habitat destruction, fair prices to farmers, and use of chemicals and pesticides, all issues that are important for consumers, NGOs, and media. A winery company has to address stakeholder concerns about clean water, biodiversity, and ecosystem preservation.

Individual Stakeholder Influences on a Firm's Environmental Sustainability Strategy

While the discussion in the previous section analyzes the influence of stakeholders on a firm's environmental strategy based on a broad categorization of stakeholders, several empirical studies have examined how and why firms respond on specific environmental and social issues to concerns of a specific stakeholder group.

Institutional Investors

Individual institutional investors have different goals that they seek to achieve via their investments. Activist investors seek to change the governance structure and corporate policy, some seek to enhance shareholder returns, and others seek to improve a firm's ethical, social, and environmental practices. In an examination of institutional investor activism, Johnson and Greening (1999) found that over 91 percent of institutional investor activism involving social issues was initiated by pension funds. Managers of investment funds initiated shareholder amendments focused on governance and performance issues, and not social and environmental ones. Hence, firms significantly represented in funds under the control of investment managers were not influenced to change their social performance. However, firms represented with funds controlled by pension funds were more proactive in their environmental and social practices. These authors argued that pension fund managers were likely to view responsiveness by a firm to women, minorities, and communities as enhancing the legitimacy and reputation of the firm. Johnson and Greening (1999) speculated that their findings may be due to the fact that investment managers make frequent portfolio changes and a firm's social and environmental performance is not perceived as either a short-term cost or a long-term benefit by them. However, institutional investors can affect board composition as well as managerial incentives and could have an indirect long-term impact on social and environmental policies of a firm through influence on corporate governance and the top management composition. Johnson and Greening (1999) also found that the extent to which managers held equity in the firm increased their attention to stakeholder demands. This led to greater attention to product quality and improved environmental practices as a longer-term commitment to sustainability. Similarly, the role of outside perspectives in a firm via increasing the number of outsiders on a board increases the racial, ethnic, and gender diversity of a company and sensitivity to certain social issues (Zahra, Oviatt, and Minyard, 1993).

Media
Henriques and Sadorsky (1999) found that managers of firms with proactive environmental practices perceived all stakeholders except the media as important. In complete contrast, they found that managers of firms with reactive environmental practices perceived no stakeholder as important, except the media; that is, they were more afraid of being highlighted as noncompliant by reporters than by regulators. They argued that this was because in the event of an environmental crisis, reactive firms would have to manage the media while proactive firms would be able to show due diligence in their environmental practices.

Regulators
In examining stakeholder influences on corporate environmental strategies in large polluting firms in Belgium, Buysse and Verbeke

(2003) found that these firms gave the highest importance to regulators. Such regulators included national governments, local public regulatory agencies, and international agreements (since many firms in the sample were multinational enterprises). It was only firms with leadership strategies in proactive environmental practices that accorded importance to the norms and expectations of stakeholders other than regulators. However, most firms accorded greater importance to primary stakeholders such as shareholders and less to customers. The authors argue this is because most large manufacturing operations in Belgium tend to specialize in the production of intermediate goods and have no direct contact with final consumers. Similarly, Murillo-Luna, Garces-Ayerbe, and Rivera-Torres (2008) found that environmental managers in Spanish industrial firms attached the greatest importance to regulators and government stakeholders. Their study concluded that there was indeed a positive relationship between the environmental demands from stakeholders perceived as important by managers and the proactivity of the environmental strategy of firms; that is, the greater the stakeholder pressures for environmental action perceived by managers, the more solutions their firms tended to adopt beyond the mandatory environmental regulations.

Kassinis and Vafeas (2006) found environmental spending by individual states in the United States was positively related to toxic emissions. This may be because states respond to citizens and community concerns about greater pollution and worsening environmental quality by allocating more funds to regulate and monitor manufacturing activities that may generate pollution. They also found that utilities and plants owned by public corporations were greater emitters of pollution. The authors argued that since utilities were highly regulated, such regulations could have reduced the sensitivity of their managers to the pressures from stakeholders seeking improved social and environmental performance.

Boards
In another study, Kassinis and Vafeas (2002) examined the factors that determine why firms incur penalties or are held responsible for environmental violations in spite of the fact that many organizations violate environmental regulations and are not caught. They analyzed the effects of four factors – board size, director affiliation,

director reputation, and inside ownership – on the likelihood of environmental litigation. They found that larger boards have more members with expertise and this increases the likelihood of the firm pursuing an environmentally sound policy. In terms of board composition, they found that directors with backgrounds in academics, military, clergy, or politics are more likely to combat environmental irresponsibility by the firm. In comparison to firms with few or no outside directors, those with higher numbers of outside directors were found to have a lower likelihood of environmental lawsuits. In terms of inside ownership, they found that directors and board members who own stock in a company were more likely to have an incentive to reduce reputational and litigation threat and the likelihood of an environmental lawsuit. This finding parallels family business research that suggests that when the family name or identity is aligned with that of the firm, concerns about image and reputation, along with a desire to protect family assets, leads these firms toward more socially responsible behaviors (Dyer and Whetten, 2006).

Local Community
Kassinis and Vafeas's (2006) study examining the relationship between stakeholder pressures and firm environmental performance found county-level community stakeholder heterogeneity on income was negatively associated with pollution levels. In short, they found that wealthier and politically active segments of the community were able to use superior resources and power to demand and disproportionately pressure firms to reduce their toxic emissions. Therefore, firms may be more dependent on wealthier communities for resources and more likely to respond to their pressures. They also found that since more people were affected by pollution in densely populated areas, there was greater pressure on firms to adopt more proactive environmental practices.

Similarly, Arora, and Cason (1998) also found that socioeconomic factors including race, income levels, and unemployment explained the level of toxicity of TRI emissions between 1990 and 1993 at the zip code level. They concluded that neighborhoods with low incomes, high unemployment, and minority populations in the Southern United States were likely to have greater numbers of manufacturing facilities with higher pollution levels.

NGOs

More proactive firms are more likely to develop collaboration and cooperation strategies with social and environmental NGOs in order to reduce transaction costs (King, 2007). Collaboration and cooperation with NGOs is undertaken for a variety of motivations by the firm (Wassmer, Paquin, and Sharma, 2012). The first motivation is to garner resources and build capabilities. No firm possesses all the necessary resources to exploit every opportunity and neutralize every threat in its external business environment. Firms frequently seek out environmental collaborations to access resources and capabilities required to green their operations and business practices and develop solutions for reducing their environmental footprint (e.g., Rondinelli and London, 2003; Sarkis, 2003; Vermeulen and Ras, 2006) and for radical and disruptive product and business model innovations (Hart and Sharma, 2004). NGOs provide the firm with specialized and localized environmental and social expertise, reputation, and legitimacy, and access to unique networks (Wassmer et al., 2012). Collaboration with a credible NGO also serves to enhance public trust of the firm enhancing its legitimacy and license to operate (Sharma and Vredenburg, 1998), building strategic bridges to other NGOs (Sharma, Vredenburg and Westley, 1994), and addressing existing conflicts by including other stakeholders in the decision-making process (Arts, 2002; Livesey, 1999; Stafford and Hartman, 1996).

NGOs are also increasingly engaged in policy formulation and implementation. For example, in public environmental review processes and in collaborative regulatory contexts such as Canada and the Netherlands, NGOs seek to collaborate with industry to overcome government failures to develop meaningful regulations (Kolk, van Tulder, and Kostwinder, 2008). Firms also enter into collaborations with NGOs in order to proactively develop environmental solutions to influence and/or pre-empt impending regulations (Christmann and Taylor, 2006; Delmas and Montes-Sancho, 2010; Howard-Grenville, 2002; King, Lenox, and Terlaak, 2005; Sharma and Vredenburg, 1998).

In short, the research on individual stakeholder influences on environmental strategy suggests that:

P6. *Firms with significant influence of institutional investors with longer time horizons for returns (family firms with goals of transgenerational continuity or non-family firms with significant influence of pension funds on their operations) are more likely to adopt proactive environmental sustainability strategies.*

P7. *Firms with large and diverse boards that include owners (especially in family firms) are more likely to adopt proactive environmental sustainability strategies.*

P8. *Firms pursuing proactive environmental strategies are less likely to be influenced by either regulators or media as compared to firms with reactive environmental strategies.*

P9. *Firms pursuing proactive environmental strategies are more likely to work collaboratively with NGOs to find pragmatic solutions for environmental challenges being faced in their industry or community.*

Family Firms' Influence on and Response to Stakeholders

There is a major research gap in our understanding of stakeholders that influence the environmental strategies of family firms, or how dominant coalitions or controlling owners of these firms influence key stakeholder perceptions. Nevertheless, family business literature points to a major shortcoming in the sustainability and stakeholder theory literatures: the neglect of controlling family as a critical stakeholder whose goals and concerns need to be balanced with those of other internal and external stakeholders (e.g., Dyer, 2003; Sharma, 2001; Zellweger and Nason, 2008). For example, in firms in which members of a controlling family serve as board members alongside outside directors (Bettinelli, 2011), or in those in which the controlling owners are deeply embedded in the political and economic landscape of their communities (Chirico et al., 2018), the controlling family is in a strategically opportune position not only to influence the environmental strategy pursued by their firms, but also have an impact on related efforts in their communities (Parada et al., 2010).

Cennamo et al. (2012) present a theoretical framework explaining how a family's goal of balancing its economic goals with its goal of preserving socioemotional wealth (SEW) moderates the influence of internal and external stakeholders. Their arguments are based on Berrone et al.'s (2012) proposed dimensions of SEW, which the authors term the FIBER dimensions:

(1) Family control and influence (on strategy, goals, and decision-making)
(2) Identification of the family members with the firm
(3) Binding social ties (of kinship and social capital)
(4) Emotional attachment of family members to the firm
(5) Renewal of family bonds through dynastic succession

Cennamo et al. (2012) argue that the extent to which a family firm will engage proactively with their stakeholders depends on which dimension of SEW is a focus for the family principal or the dominant coalition. When the desire to maintain control and influence over the firm, and/or preserve the dynasty and long-term reputation of the firm is the primary reference point for family owners, they are more likely to proactively engage with the internal stakeholders including the family members and employees. On the other hand, the family firm will be more likely to engage both internal and external stakeholders when the strategy is related to the family's identity and core values, and/or the existence of strong social ties within the family group, and/or the principal owner's emotional attachment to the firm. In instances where principal owner's emotional attachments emerge, the family firm may even engage stakeholders that are less distinct and remote and consider developing business models for markets at the base of the pyramid (Cennamo et al., 2012; Hart and Sharma, 2004). Logically, similar arguments could be developed for how and why family firms would respond to institutional forces based on the dimensions of SEW that are the focus for the family principal or dominant coalition of the family.

These theoretical arguments for a family's engagement with stakeholders present contrasting arguments to the empirical findings of Delmas and Toffel (2008) in a non-family firm context on how institutional pressures are channeled to the firm's managers via a specific functional area/department depending on the type of stakeholder interacting with that department. In examining the adoption of ISO 14001 standards by firms, these authors found that in responding to stakeholders such as regulators, NGOs, local communities, and the media, managers did not see environmental practices as contributing to a firm's

financial bottom line or productivity. Rather they perceived such practices as a source of cost imposition in order to meet institutional
demands. Hence, firms tended to avoid investing in the demands of
these stakeholders unless required to comply by courts or regulatory
agencies, in which case the issues are relegated to the firm's legal department. These authors also found that in such instances firms were more
likely to adopt government-initiated voluntary programs rather than
universal ISO 14001 standards. The authors found that, in contrast,
managers viewed pressures from economic stakeholders such as customers, suppliers, and competitors as closely connected to their business
and, hence, such pressures were managed by the firm's marketing
department in order to grow market share and profits. In such instances,
firms were more likely to adopt proactive sustainability strategies such as
adoption of the ISO 14001 standards that were demanded by economic
stakeholders and implemented by competitors as a legitimate business
strategy. This echoes our findings above and those of Reay et al. (2015)
that non-family firms are driven mainly by business or market logic in
their strategies and response to external issues in contrast to the values-
driven approach that is more likely in family firms. Hence,

P10. *Family firms with a goal to maintain control and influence over
the firm, and/or preserve the dynasty and long-term reputation of the
firm, are more likely to proactively engage with the internal stakeholders – family members and employees.*

P11. *Family firms with a goal of preserving the family's identity and
core values, and/or the existence of strong social ties within the
family group, and/or the principal owner's emotional attachment
to the firm, will be more likely to engage both internal and external
stakeholders.*

P12. *Family firms in which the principal owner's emotional attachments are paramount, are likely to engage stakeholders that are less
distinct and remote and consider developing unique business models,
for example such as markets at the base of the pyramid.*

Stakeholder Engagement in the Winery Industry

Our data in the winery industry indicates that the arguments made
above are more applicable in contexts of polluting industries and those

that have significant and visible environmental impacts. The winery industry has relatively low levels of pollution and the regulations set a low bar that all wineries are able to meet in terms of emissions and effluents. In all these jurisdictions, respondents did not indicate that regulators, NGOs, and/or local communities had demands or influence on their sustainability practices or strategy. Even the role of consumers was not deemed significant since those demanding organic/biodynamic wines were small percentage of the market (albeit growing such as markets in Sweden and Germany as cited by the wine council of St. Émilion, France) and a winery could choose to ignore this small segment and sell its entire production to the much larger, lessenvironmentally sensitive consumer. In the context of the winery industry in Canada, Chile, and France, the main stakeholders were the industry associations, whether those that regulated the appellations in France or the VQA in Canada, or those in the Okanagan that lobbied for the ability of wineries to sell directly from their winery stores or to restaurants rather than only the provincial liquor control board. It only emerged after our data collection that the wine council in the region of St. Émilion lobbied the wineries to adopt organic/biodynamic viticulture for all wine sold from this region by 2019. As we have indicated in Chapter 2 and in the previous section, family-owned wineries were much more likely than non-family wineries to adopt proactive environmental sustainability (PES) strategies. However, the influence of stakeholders on PES of both family firms and non-family firms was not apparent. This does not, in any way, discount the considerable research that shows the significant influence of stakeholders in firms adopting PES for both managing risk and liability and for developing a competitive imagination for future businesses and products (Hart and Sharma, 2004). Our data indicates that external stakeholders may have lower influence in industries that have visibly low pollution or environmental impact levels.

Based on the arguments presented by Cennamo et al. (2012) and based on our primary data in the winery industry, it was apparent that the main drivers for PES were the emotional attachment of family members to the firm and the renewal of family bonds through dynastic succession. This required engaging internal stakeholders, including family members and employees, to effectively implement organic/biodynamic practices. While non-family firms generally indicated a cost savings and efficiency motivation for the adoption of beyond-compliance practices such as waste and packaging reduction, the family firms were motivated by their emotional attachments to the land and the need to build SEW for the long-term survival of the family enterprise. The adoption of organic/ biodynamic practices required long-term horizons and risky outcomes in terms of yields and wine quality. The quotes in the section on institutional influences clearly mention this attachment of the family to the terroir and the land and the fact that they would continue to live on the land. While our principal data collection was in Canada, France, and Chile, we also opportunistically visited a few wineries in others regions, such as the United States and Spain, and, during a conversation, a second-generation family member of the Benziger Family Wineries in Sonoma Valley California explained the adoption of their biodynamic practices:

Our family has run the Benziger Winery for <u>over two decades</u> with a great deal of passion and love for the craft of winemaking. For many years, we followed conventional practices without giving it a second thought. One morning I looked out of the window and saw our family's children headed to school through a cloud of herbicide being sprayed by our low flying crop duster. That is when I had my epiphany. We lived on the land – the winery was our home – <u>our children would continue to live in this community and the land.</u> We owed it to the family and <u>to our future generations</u> and to the land to work toward a sustainable ecosystem that would be healthy and productive forever. The unexpected by-product of a sustainable winery has been a dramatic improvement in our wines which have won many awards for quality and taste. Perhaps the entire farm ecosystem shares the joy of the family in the land and this joy is manifest in wine quality. (underline added)

Summary

While extant literature based on research in non-family or dispersed-ownership firms clearly indicates the influence of institutional and stakeholder forces on a firm's PES, our primary data from the winery industry indicates that in contexts with similar institutional forces and influences, family firms with a long-term orientation and strategic horizon were more likely to adopt PES as compared to non-family firms. Similarly, in the absence of significant external stakeholder pressures to address social and environmental issues, family firms were once again more likely to adopt PES as compared to non-family firms, due to their goal of building SEW by strengthening family ties and focusing on a long-term horizon for the family's survival. Generically, whether institutional forces lead to isomorphic sustainable strategies among firms in an industry or whether mediating influences (e.g. stakeholders) foster strategic choice, and whether stakeholders directly pressure firms to adopt reactive or proactive sustainability strategies or whether some individual stakeholder groups have greater influence versus others, there is considerable theoretical and empirical literature to show that in addition to the exogenous influences discussed above, endogenous (managerial attitudes and values and internal values, organizational capabilities and design) have greater influence on a firm's sustainability strategy and practices. These firm-level and managerial-level factors may act directly on their own or in interaction with exogenous institutional and stakeholder forces. These are the subjects of Chapters 4 and 5.

References

Arora, S. and Cason, T. N. 1998. Do community characteristics influence environmental outcomes? Evidence from the toxics release inventory. *Journal of Applied Economics*, I(2): 413–453.

Arts, B. 2002. "Green alliances" of business and NGOs: New styles of self-regulation or "dead-end roads"? *Corporate Social Responsibility and Environmental Management*, 9: 26–36.

Berrone, P., Cruz, C. and Gomez-Mejia, L. R. 2012. Socioemotional wealth in family firms: Theoretical dimensions, assessment approaches and agenda for future research. *Family Business Review*, doi:10.1177/0894486511435355.

Berrone, P., Fosfuri, A., Gelabert, L. and Gomez-Mejia, L. R. 2013. Necessity as the mother of "green" inventions: Institutional pressures and environmental innovations. *Strategic Management Journal*, 34: 891–909.

Bettinelli, C. 2011. Boards of directors in family firms: An exploratory study of structure and group process. *Family Business Review*, 24(2): 151–169.

Buysse, K. and Verbeke, A. 2003. Proactive environmental strategies: A stakeholder management perspective. *Strategic Management Journal*, 24(5): 453–470.

Carney, M. 2005. Globalization and the renewal of Asian business networks. *Asia Pacific Journal of Management*, 22: 337–354.

Carson, R. 1962. *Silent Spring*. Boston, MA: Houghton Mifflin.

Cennamo, C., Berrone, P., Cruz, C. and Gomez-Mejia, L. R. 2012. Socioemotional wealth and proactive stakeholder engagement: Why family-controlled firms care more about stakeholders. *Entrepreneurship Theory and Practice*, 2012 (November): 1153–1173.

Chirico, F., Backman, M., Bau, Klaesson, J. and Pittino, D. 2018. Local embeddedness and rural-urban contexts for business growth in family versus non-family firms. *Academy of Management Proceedings*.

Christmann, P. and Taylor, G. 2006. Firm self-regulation through international certifiable standards: Determinants of symbolic versus substantive implementation. *Journal of International Business Studies*, 37: 863–878.

Clarkson, M. B. E. 1995. A stakeholder framework for analyzing and evaluating corporate social performance. *Academy of Management Review*, 20(1): 92–117.

Craig, J. and Moores, K. 2010. Strategically aligning family and business systems using the balanced scorecard. *Journal of Family Business Strategy*, 1(2): 78–87.

Davis, G. and Greve, H. 1997. Corporate elite networks and governance changes in the 1980s. *American Journal of Sociology*, 103: 1–37.

Delmas, M. A. and Toffel, M. W. 2008. Organizational responses to environmental demands: Opening the black box. *Strategic Management Journal*, 29: 1027–1055.

Delmas, M., Russo, M. V. and Montes-Sancho, M. J. 2007. Deregulation and environmental differentiation in the electric utility industry. *Strategic Management Journal*, 28: 189–209.

Delmas, M. A. 2002. The diffusion of environmental management standards in Europe and the United States: An institutional perspective. *Policy Sciences*, 35: 91–119.

Delmas, M. A. and Montes-Sancho, M. J. 2010. Voluntary agreements to improve environmental quality: Symbolic and substantive cooperation. *Strategic Management Journal*, 31: 575–601.

Desjardins, M. 2018. Under Pressure or Fairly Valued? The Effects of Security Analyst Coverage on Firm Investment Horizon. Paper presented at the *Eighth Gronen Research Conference*, Almeria, Spain, June 13th to 16th.

Dieleman, M. and Sachs, W. M. 2008. Coevolution of institutions and corporations in emerging economies: How the Salim group morphed into an institution of Suharto's crony regime. *Journal of Management Studies*, 45: 1274–1300.

DiMaggio, P. 1988. Interest and agency in institutional theory. In L. Zucker (ed.), *Institutional Patterns and Culture*, pp. 3–22. Cambridge, MA: Ballinger Publishing Company.

DiMaggio, P. J. and Powell, W. W. 1983. The iron cage revisited: Institutional isomorphism and collective rationality in organizational fields. *American Sociological Review*, 48: 147–160.

Donaldson, T. and Dunfee, T. 1994. Toward a unified conception of business ethics: Integrative social contracts theory. *Academy of Management Review*, 19: 252–284.

Donaldson, T. and Preston, L. E. 1995. The stakeholder theory of the corporation: Concepts, evidence, and implications. *Academy of Management Review*, 20(1): 65–91.

Dyer, G. W. Jr. 2003. The Family: The Missing Variable in Organizational Research. *Entrepreneurship Theory & Practice*, 27(4): 401–416.

Dyer, G. W. Jr. and Whetten, D. 2006. Family firms and social responsibility: Evidence from S&P 500. *Entrepreneurship Theory & Practice*, 30(6): 785–802.

Eisenhardt, K. M. 1989. Agency theory: An assessment and review. *Academy of Management Review*, 14: 57–74.

EPA1. www.epa.gov/tri/tridata/index.html (accessed October 31, 2012).

Evan, W. and Freeman, R. E. 1983. A stakeholder theory of the modern corporation: Kantian capitalism. In T. Beauchamp and N. Bowie (eds.), *Ethical Theory in Business*, pp. 75–93. Englewood Cliffs, NJ: Prentice-Hall.

Fogel, K. 2006. Oligarchic family control, social economic outcomes, and the quality of government. *Journal of International Business Studies*, 37: 603–622.

Freeman, R. E. 1984. *Strategic Management: A Stakeholder Approach*. Boston, MA: Pittman.

Freeman, R. E. 1999. Divergent stakeholder theory. *Academy of Management Review*, 24(2): 233–236.

Frooman, J. 1999. Stakeholder influence strategies. *Academy of Management Review*, 24(2): 191–205.

Goodrick, E. and Salancik, G. R. 1996. Organizational discretion in responding to institutional practices: Hospitals and Cesarean births. *Administrative Science Quarterly*, 41: 1–28.

Gomez-Mejia, L. R., Cruz, C., Berrone, P. and DeCastro, J. 2012. The bind that ties: Socioemotional wealth preservation in family firms. *Academy of Management Annals*, 5(1): 1–79.

Gray, W. 1987. The cost of regulation: OSHA, EPA, and the productivity slowdown. *American Economic Review*, 77: 998–1006.

Greenhouse, S. 2013. Retailers split on contrition after Bangladesh factory collapse. April 30. *The New York Times* online edition.

Hart, S. L. and Sharma, S. 2004. Engaging fringe stakeholders for competitive imagination. *Academy of Management Executive*, 18(1): 7–18.

Henriques, I. and Sadorsky, P. 1999. The relationship between environmental commitment and managerial perceptions of stakeholder importance. *Academy of Management Journal*, 42(1): 89–99.

Hillman, A. J. and Keim, G. D. 2001. Shareholder value, stakeholder management, and social issues: What's the bottom line? *Strategic Management Journal*, 22: 125–139.

Hoffman, A. J. 1997. *From Heresy to Dogma: An Institutional History of Corporate Environmentalism*. San Francisco, CA: New Lexington Press.

Howard-Grenville, J. 2002 Institutional evolution: The case of the semiconductor industry voluntary PFC emission reduction agreements. In A. J. Hoffman and M. J. Ventresca (eds.), *Organizations, Policy, and the Natural Environment: Institutional and Strategic Perspectives*, pp. 291–310. Berkley, CA: Stanford University Press.

Jaffe, A., Peterson, S., Portnoy, P. and Stavin, R. 1995. Environmental regulation and the competitiveness of U.S. manufacturing: What does the evidence tell us? *Journal of Economic Literature*, 33: 132–163.

Jennings, P. D. and Zandbergen, P. A. 1995. Ecologically sustainable organizations: An institutional approach. *Academy of Management Review*, 20(4): 1015–1052.

Johnson, R. A. and Greening D. W. 1999. The effects of corporate governance and institutional ownership types on corporate social performance. *Academy of Management Journal*, 42(5): 564–576.

Jones, T. M. 1995. Instrumental stakeholder theory: A synthesis of ethics and economics. *Academy of Management Review*, 20(2): 404–437.

Jones, T. M. and Wicks, A. C. 1999. Convergent stakeholder theory. *Academy of Management Review*, 24(2): 206–221.

Kassinis, G. and Vafeas, N. 2002. Corporate boards and outside stakeholders as determinants of environmental litigation. *Strategic Management Journal*, 23(5): 399–415.

Kassinis, G. and Vafeas, N. 2006. Stakeholder performance and environmental performance. *Academy of Management Journal*, 49(1): 145–159.

King, A. 2007. Cooperation between corporations and environmental groups: A transaction costs perspective. *Academy of Management Review*, 32(3): 889–900.

King, A. A. and Lenox, M. J. 2000. Industry self-regulation without sanctions: The chemical industry's responsible care program. *Academy of Management Journal*, 43(4): 698–716.

King, A., Lenox, M. and Terlaak, A. 2005. The strategic use of decentralized institutions: Exploring certification with the ISO 14001 management standard. *Academy of Management Journal*, 48: 1091–1106.

Kolk, A., van Tulder, R. and Kostwinder, E. 2008. Business and partnerships for development. *European Management Journal*, 26: 262–273.

Kotlar, J. and De Massis, A. 2013. Goal setting in family firms: Goal diversity, social interactions, and collective commitment to family-centered goals. *Entrepreneurship Theory and Practice*, 37(6): 1263–1288.

LaPorta, R., Lopez-de-Silanes, F. and Shleifer, A. 1999. Corporate ownership around the world. *Journal of Finance*, 54: 471–517.

Lenox, M. J. 2006. The role of private, decentralized institutions in sustaining industry self-regulation. *Organization Science*, 17(6): 677–690.

Livesey, S. M. 1999. McDonald's and the environmental defense fund: A case study of a green alliance. *The Journal of Business Communication*, 36: 5–39.

Maguire, S., Hardy, C. and Lawrence, T. B 2004. Institutional entrepreneurship in emerging fields: HIV/AIDS treatment advocacy in Canada. *Academy of Management Journal*, 47: 657–679.

Majumdar, S. K. and Marcus, A. A. 2001. Rules versus discretion: The productivity consequences of flexible regulation. *Academy of Management Journal*, 44(1): 170–179.

Marcus, A. A. 1988. Implementing externally induced innovations: A comparison of rule-bound and autonomous approaches. *Academy of Management Journal*, 31: 235–256.

Melin, L. and Nordqvist, M. 2007. The reflexive dynamics of institutionalization: The case of family business. *Strategic Organization*, 5: 321–333.

Miller, D. and Le Breton-Miller, I. 2005. *Managing for the Long Run: Lessons in Competitive Advantage from Great Family Businesses.* Boston, MA: Harvard Business School Press.

Mitchell, R. K., Agle, B. R. and Wood, D. J. 1997. Toward a theory of stakeholder identification and salience: Defining the principle of who and what really counts. *Academy of Management Review*, 22(4): 853–886.

Morck, R. and Yeung, B. 2004. Family control and the rent seeking society. *Entrepreneurship Theory & Practice*, 28: 391–409.

Murillo-Luna, J., Garces-Ayerbe, C. and Rivera-Torres, P. 2008. Why do patterns of environmental response differ? A stakeholders' pressure approach. *Strategic Management Journal*, 29: 1225–1240.

Mustasich, S. 2017. Bordeaux's St. Emilion mandates sustainable viticulture. *Wine Spectator*, November 9. www.winespectator.com/webfeature/show/id/St.-Emilion-Mandates-Sustainable-Viticulture.

Ocasio, W. and Radoynovska, N. 2016. Strategy and commitments to institutional logics: Organizational heterogeneity in business models and governance. *Strategic Organization*, 14(4): 287–309.

Oliver, C. 1991. Strategic responses to institutional pressures. *Academy of Management Review*, 16(1): 145–179.

Parada, M. J., Nordqvist, M. and Gimeno, A. 2010. Institutionalizing the family business: The role of professional associations in fostering a change of values. *Family Business Review*, 23(4): 355–372.

Philips, R. A. 1997. Stakeholder theory and principle of fairness. *Business Ethics Quarterly*, 7(1): 55–66.

Porter, M. E. 1991. America's greening strategy. *Scientific American*, 264: 168.

Porter, M. E. and van der Linde, C. 1995. Green and competitive. *Harvard Business Review*, 73: 120–134.

Reay, T., Jaskiewicz, P. and Hinings, C. R. 2015. How family, business and community logics shape family firm behavior and "Rules of the Game" in an organizational field. *Family Business Review*, 28(4): 292–311.

Rondinelli, D. and London, T. 2003. How corporations and environmental groups cooperate: Assessing cross-sector alliances and collaborations. *Academy of Management Executive*, 17: 61–76.

Russo, M. V. and Fouts, P. A. 1997. A resource-based perspective on corporate environmental performance and profitability. *Academy of Management Journal*, 40(3): 534–559.

Sarkis, J. 2003. A strategic decision framework for green supply chain management. *Journal of Cleaner Production*, 11: 397–409.

Scott, W. R. 1995. *Institutions and Organizations: Ideas, Interests, and Identities*. Thousand Oaks, CA: Sage.

Sharma, P. 2001. Stakeholder management concepts in family firms. *Proceedings of the International Association of Business and Society Annual Meetings, Sedona AZ*, 254–259.

Sharma, S. 2014. *Competing for a Sustainable World: Building Capacity for Sustainable Innovation*. UK: Greenleaf Publishing.

Sharma, S. and Henriques, I. 2005. Stakeholder influences on sustainability practices in the Canadian forest products industry. *Strategic Management Journal*, 26: 159–180.

Sharma, S. and Vredenburg, H. 1998. Proactive environmental responsiveness strategy and the development of competitively valuable organizational capabilities. *Strategic Management Journal*, 19(8): 729–53.

Sharma, S., Vredenburg, H. and Westley, F. 1994. Strategic bridging: A role for the multinational corporation in Third World Development. *Journal of Applied Behavioral Science*, 30(4): 458–476.

Soleimanof, S., Rutherford, M. W. and Webb, J. W. 2018. The intersection of family firms and institutional contexts: A review and agenda for future research. *Family Business Review*, 31(1): 32–53.

Stafford, E. R. and Hartman, C. L. 1996. Green alliances: Strategic relations between businesses and environmental groups. *Business Horizons*, 39: 50–59.

Thornton, P. H. and Ocasio, W. 2008. Institutional logics. In R. Greenwood, C. Oliver and R. Suddaby (eds.), *The Sage Handbook of organizational Institutionalism*, pp. 99–128. Thousand Oaks, CA: Sage.

Thornton, P. H., Ocasio, W. and Lounsbury, M. 2012. *The Institutional Logics Perspective*. Cambridge: Oxford University Press.

Vermeulen, W. J. V. and Ras, P. J. 2006. The challenge of greening global product chains: Meeting both ends. *Sustainable Development*, 14: 245–256.

Wassmer, U., Paquin, R. and Sharma, S. 2012. The Engagement of Firms in Environmental Collaborations: Existing Contributions and Future Directions. *Business & Society*, published online on March 28, 2012. Printed November 2014, 53(6): 754–786.

Weber, M. 1994. Weber: Political writings. In P. Lassman (ed.), trans. Ronald Speirs, *Cambridge Texts in the History of Political Thought*. Chapter xvi. Cambridge University Press.

Wells, L. T. 1973. Economic man and engineering man: Choice of technology in a low-wage country. *Public Policy*, 21: 319–342.

Wijen, F. 2014. Means versus ends in opaque institutional fields: Trading off compliance and achievement in sustainability standard adoption. *Academy of Management Journal*, 39(3): 309–323.

Wikipedia. http://en.wikipedia.org/wiki/Keystone_Pipeline (accessed October 27, 2013).

Zahra, S. A., Oviatt, B. M. and Minyard, K. 1993. Effects of corporate ownership and board structure on corporate social responsibility and financial performance. *Academy of Management Best Paper Proceedings*, 336–340.

Zellweger, T. and Nason, R. 2008. A stakeholder perspective on family firm performance. *Family Business Review*, 21: 203–216.

4 | Organizational Drivers of Corporate Environmental Sustainability Strategy

In examining why some firms invest in proactive environmental strategies (PES) and practices that go beyond compliance of regulations, Chapter 3 focused on two main exogenous factors: institutional forces and stakeholder influences. Based on our review of environmental sustainability and family business literatures, combined with insights from our cases of wineries in Canada, France, and Chile, we concluded:

(i) While institutional influences tend to drive firms toward isomorphic strategies in order to seek legitimacy (DiMaggio and Powell, 1983), under conditions of increased awareness of global sustainability challenges, and a lag in coercive regulations, dominant coalitions and controlling owners rely on their values and judgments in making strategic choices regarding investments in environmental sustainability initiatives. Thus, differentiated environmental strategies coexist within similar institutional contexts.

(ii) As compared to non-family firms with dispersed ownership and shorter managerial tenures, family firms with long leadership tenures and transgenerational strategic horizons for their enterprises are more likely to adopt PES strategies. Thus, even in the absence of significant regulatory or other stakeholder pressures to address environmental issues, family-firm-owned wineries were more likely to adopt PES as compared to non-family firms, due to their focus on building socio-emotional wealth (SEW) by strengthening family ties and focusing on a long-term horizon for the family's survival (Cennamo et al., 2012).

This indicates the significant importance of endogenous influences for family firms. In general terms, regardless of the influence of exogenous institutional forces and stakeholder influences, there is considerable theoretical and empirical literature to show that organizational forces such as governance, organizational structure/design, competitive strategy, resources/capabilities, and managerial/individual-level factors such

as leadership and managerial interpretations and attitudes have significant influence on a firm's sustainability strategy and practices in both
non-family firm and family firm (Berrone et al., 2013) literature.

In this chapter, we focus on organizational-level drivers for PES and in
Chapter 5 we discuss managerial/individual-level drivers. While Chapter
3, on institutional drivers, also discusses variations in firms' sustainability
strategies, the focus is based on studies that find endogenous factors
mediate or moderate the institutional or stakeholder influences. These
mediating factors are all organizational-level drivers: a firm's resource
dependence on external constituents (Sharma and Henriques, 2005); a
firm's unique organizational structure that determines the pathway via
which institutional pressures are channeled to different organizational
functions and, hence, determine which managers will develop strategies
to respond to these pressures (Delmas and Toffel, 2008); the gaps and
deficiencies in a firm's resources or capabilities required to respond to
institutional pressures (Berrone et al., 2013); the timing of entering into
voluntary industry agreements that determine intensity of political pressures, visibility of the firm, and its embeddedness in the industry association (Delmas and Montes-Sancho, 2010); and, a family firm's focus on
building SEW for long-term survival (Berrone, Cruz and Gomez-Mejia,
2012).

PES requires innovations in technologies, processes, products, services,
and business models and even the innovative creation of new markets.
Such innovations may involve a re-examination of organizational structure, design, and strategy. While the corporate social responsibility (CSR)
literature has typically urged firms to incorporate social justice and ethics
into their existing operations, it has rarely urged a reexamination of
organizations and their core strategies. On the other hand, early research
on environmental sustainability proposed a re-examination of management and organization theories that had ignored the natural environment
and its interaction with business operations (Gladwin, Kennelly and
Krause, 1995; Shrivastava, 1994; 1995c). For example, an article by
James Post titled "Managing as if the Earth mattered," argued for bringing the environment into core managerial decision-making (Post, 1991).
This research focused on the embeddedness of the firm in ecosystems and
the need to change extant organizational theories to accommodate the
ecological aspects of business management paradigms (Gladwin et al.,
1995; Purser, Park and Montuori, 1995; Shrivastava, 1994; 1995a).

However, these early discussions were normative and prescriptive making it difficult for scholars to translate these frameworks into empirical research designs and for practitioners to implement these frameworks within organizations. Therefore, there was a push for more mid-range research that examined organizational factors that would directly influence the sustainability strategy of a firm. These factors included corporate governance, resources and capabilities, and market and competitive efficiencies.

Even though innovations in sustainable technologies, products, and business models often require long-term investments and patient capital, the corporate sustainability literature is almost silent about the organizational drivers that motivate and enable the inclusion of time into strategic decision-making. Such research has just begun to emerge. A recent study examined how external financial analyst coverage influenced time horizon of investments. Using a sample of 1,376 firms, the study found that firms that experience a decrease in financial analyst coverage lengthen their investment horizon. This effect is stronger for firms covered by fewer analysts, when analysts from larger brokerages discontinue coverage, and under Regulation Fair Disclosure (Desjardins, 2018). A study by Slawinski and Bansal (2012) of the strategies adopted by oil and gas firms to address climate change found that some firms emphasized linear time characterized by a lower tolerance for uncertainty and a tendency to focus on immediate solutions, while others saw time as cyclical and had a higher tolerance for uncertainty, drew on previous experience, and assessed the future to gain insights. While these are interesting findings that point to short- versus long-term patient investment approaches, *they do not explain the drivers for 'why' some firms took a cyclical rather than a linear view of time.*

This chapter is divided into three sections. The first section examines corporate governance influences related to ownership and management. The role of institutional investors, activist shareholders, and boards of directors on a firm's environmental strategy is discussed. An examination of research on top management teams in non-family firms or dominant coalition of family firms signals the importance of two variables on the environmental sustainability strategy of firms. These are the temporal orientation of key decision-makers (owners or individuals), and the extent to which these decision makers identify with the firm. The second section examines firm strategic responses to market forces and regulatory influences. The relationship between firms' generic and sustainability strategies is discussed, followed by findings related to impact of these strategies on a firms' financial performance. Finally, the last section discusses the importance of organizational capabilities that enable firms to achieve a balance between their economic and environmental performance.

In this review, we find that while the literatures of corporate sustainability and family business have grown rapidly since the nineties, there are very few overlaps in these two fields of study. We observe, however, that the nature of governance of family firms by dominant coalitions of family members fosters a long-term orientation and identification of family members with the business and, hence, there is a greater likelihood of patient investments in a PES. Not all family firms are alike, however, and the heterogeneity of these firms in terms of vision, goals, and strategies is the subject of significant interest in the family business literature (Chua et al., 2012). Thus, in the last section of this chapter, we argue that family firms in which the controlling owners strongly identify with their family business and share a vision of corporate sustainability and long-term stewardship, are more likely to develop organizational capabilities needed to undertake a PES. In turn, such family firms will more likely enjoy positive performance on financial as well as socioemotional dimensions important to their dominant coalition.

Corporate Governance Influences on Firms' Environmental Strategies

In terms of the influence of ownership on the environmental strategies of a firm, researchers' attention has been focused on understanding the influence of block/institutional investors, activist shareholders, and boards of directors. With regard to the management influences, the role of the top management team in non-family firms and dominant-coalition-in-family firms has been studied. Below, we share an overview of this research.

Ownership Influences on Firms' Environmental Strategies

Institutional Ownership
When institutions own large blocks of shares, they have a higher representation on the board and can influence major strategic decisions of a firm. However, not all institutional owners share goals of the

business as a vehicle for environmental preservation and a long-term temporal orientation. Although institutional owners control a majority of shares in corporations in several countries, the type of dominant institution differs by country. In the United Kingdom and France, for example, pension funds and insurance companies are the dominant financial institutions. These financial institutions are more likely to have a long-term investment horizon. In contrast, in the United States, the institutional sector is dominated by mutual funds, which are more likely to have a shorter-term (quarterly) outlook on returns. Investors with a longer-term perspective are more likely to see a company's social and environmental behavior as relevant for making investment decisions (Aguilera et al., 2006). As indicated by our data from the winery industry, some wineries in France have been bought by insurance companies and other financial institutions and were able to maintain a long-term strategic perspective and invest in organic/biodynamic practices. This is reflected in the following quote from the vineyard manager of Chateau Soutard in France, which is owned by the French insurance company La Mondiale.

While the Bogeron family adopted some organic techniques, the full-scale adoption of organic viticulture and certification happened only after La Mondiale bought the winery. The company has three wineries and diversified operations across different sectors. They do not rely on this one winery for financial sustenance and can afford to maintain a corporate policy that requires lower returns while full organic conversion takes place.

In contrast, Canadian corporate wineries are marked by dispersed ownership and are publicly listed and traded. Hence, they demonstrate reactive strategies focused on short-term financial results in order to meet quarterly market expectations set by analysts. This is also empirically supported by Desjardin's (2018) study that looks at the link between long-termism and coverage by financial analysts.

There is a great deal of empirical research to support a positive relationship between the temporal orientation of an institutional investor and corporate sustainability strategies of the firms they invest in and support. For example, studies by Coffey and Fryxell (1991) and Graves and Waddock (1994) found that the level of institutional ownership of firms was positively associated with adoption of proactive corporate social sustainability strategies.

Similarly, Neubaum and Zahra (2006) found that long-term institutional ownership is positively associated with corporate social performance. They also found that the frequency and coordination of shareholder activism interacted with long-term institutional holdings to positively affect corporate social performance after a three-year lag. Similarly, Johnson and Greening (1999) found that a firm's exposure to investors with long-term horizons is positively associated with higher corporate social responsibility. Hence,

P13 Family firms whose dominant coalitions have transgenerational continuity intentions are more likely to undertake patient long-term investments in PES as compared to non-family firms.

Shareholder Activists

In contrast to institutional investors who have substantial investments in companies, shareholder activists hold small(er) blocks of shares with an objective to exercise their influence on a company to address certain issues including social and environmental issues such as pollution, use of sweatshops and child labor, and human rights, among others. Neubaum and Zahra (2006) found a positive relationship between the frequency and the level of coordinated activism and the corporate social responsibility of a firm. In contrast, David, Bloom, and Hillman (2007) found shareholder activism drove managerial attention away from corporate sustainable responsibilities of the firm. Walls, Berrone, and Phan's (2012) research helped explain these contradictory findings, as they found varied impact of shareholder activism and concentration of shareholding on a firm's environmental performance. Specifically, they found that when a firm's environmental performance is below par, shareholder activism is high, possibly due to shareholder concerns regarding environmental violations, fines, remediation costs, and exposure to risk. They speculated whether firms with concentrated ownership may have less freedom to pursue proactive environmental strategies that go beyond legal compliance due to perceptions that such strategies would incur costs that would affect earnings. Later in this chapter, we discuss research that investigates the relationship between proactive environmental strategies and financial performance of the firm. However, it is clear that more research is needed to fully understand the antecedents that propel shareholder activism and the performance outcomes of such activities.

Board of Directors

Increasingly, corporate boards have committees overseeing environmental and social impacts, practices, and investments. It is estimated that 25 percent of Fortune 500 companies have such board committees and the number of investor proposals related to environmental practices nearly doubled between 2004 and 2008 (Kell and Lacy, 2010). Wang and Dewhirst (1992) showed that outside directors bring a different perspective and view stakeholder issues differently as compared to the top management team or the CEO. In studies examining board independence, outside directors have been found to be positively associated with the people and product aspects of CSR (Johnson and Greening, 1999), socially responsible behavior of firms (Webb, 2004), and discretionary dimensions of CSR (Ibrahim, Howard and Angelidis, 2003), and negatively related to environmental litigation (Kassinis and Vafeas, 2006). On the other hand, studies have found no impact of having outside directors on corporate philanthropy (Brown, Helland and Smith, 2006; Coffey and Wang, 1998), legal and ethical dimensions of CSR (Ibrahim et al., 2003), and environmental violations (McKendall, Sanchez and Sicilian, 1999).

Walls et al. (2012) provide a comprehensive review of studies on the role of corporate boards and corporate sustainability outcomes. They show that no relationship was found between directors with a stakeholder orientation and CSR (Hillman, Keim and Luce, 2001) or between environmental committees and environmental violations by the firm (McKendall et al., 1999), although environmental committees can encourage extra vigilance (Kassinis and Vafeas, 2006). Berrone and Gomez-Mejia (2009) found that environmental committees did not influence the relationship between environmental performance and chief executive officer pay. Some studies found a positive association between interest group (stakeholder) pressure and an issue-management-oriented board committee (Greening and Gray, 1994), or legal pressure and a stakeholder-oriented board committee (Luoma and Goodstein, 1999).

In terms of the influence of diversity on CSR or sustainability strategy, studies have examined directors' gender, diversity in experience, expertise, and demography. However, in terms of CSR, the positive findings are connected with female directors. A positive association was found between proportion of female directors and socially responsible firms (Webb, 2004) and CSR (Coffey and Fryxell, 1991; Stanwick and Stanwick, 1998). A firm's CSR has been found to mediate the relationship between the number of female directors and the firm's reputation (Bear, Rahman and Post, 2010). Coffey and Wang (1998) did not find any relationship between female directors and corporate philanthropy. In terms of board size, studies have found a positive association with environmental litigation (Kassinis and Vafeas, 2006) and a positive association with corporate philanthropy (Brown et al., 2006).

Most of the empirical studies discussed have examined CSR or a single social issue that does not require the extent of strategic change and innovation and long-term investment that a PES requires. The mixed results of various empirical studies may also point to a need for an examination of the mediating or moderating factors (whether institutional, stakeholder, or organizational and managerial) that affect the relationships between board characteristics and a firm's sustainability strategy. We will examine these further in this chapter and in Chapter 5.

The review by Walls et al. (2012) examines several interactions between governance variables and the environmental performance of a firm. While several interactions need more research to interpret or may need to be interpreted cautiously, the results suggest the following four conditions as being conducive for proactive environmental performance of a firm: (i) patient long-term investors, (ii) larger boards with a higher number of independent outsiders, and (iii) lower investor activism. Interestingly, where shareholder activism was high, firms with fewer independent directors performed better environmentally.

In the context of family firms, Berrone, Cruz, Gomez-Mejia, and Larraza-Kintana (2010) argue that with a long-term investment horizon family firms exhibit better environmental performance than non-family firms. But, Walls et al.'s (2012) review finds that *patient capital* has a positive effect on environmental performance only when accompanied by a larger number of outside board members who would independently monitor the firm's strategy and actions in this regard. This finding resonates well with family business literature that has long endorsed the important role of outside independent directors in maintaining the strategic decision-making environment amidst the possibility of kinship emotions overtaking board discussions (Ward, 1991).

Top Management Influences on Firms' Environmental Strategies

While institutional owners, activist shareholders, and the board of directors of a company certainly have an influence on a firm's strategy, the day-to-day strategic decision-making unit has a disproportional influence. Corporate sustainability scholars have long argued for the important relationship between the values of a firm's strategic decision-making team and its engagement in PES (e.g., Hart, 1995). This decision-making unit is referred to as the top management team (TMT) in publicly listed firms in the strategy literature and the dominant coalition (DC) in the family-firm literature. We will discuss the role of each in turn.

Top Management Team in Non-Family Firms

Top management teams have a major role in formulating a firm's sustainability strategy. Their perspective may or may not be similar to that of the board. The CEO may view stakeholder concerns and demands differently from the directors (Wang and Dewhirst, 1992). Walls et al. (2012) review studies examining linkages between management and a firm's CSR from the perspective of CEO duality, managerial control, and CEO pay. CEO duality refers to both the positions of the chairman of the Board of Directors residing with the CEO. The results of the studies are mixed. Findings range from a negative association between duality and CSR (Webb, 2004), to no relationship between duality and environmental violations and performance (Berrone et al., 2010; McKendall et al., 1999).

In terms of managerial control, the percentage of shares held by the top management team was found to be associated with the product aspects of CSR (Johnson and Greening, 1999) and the percentage of shares held by inside directors was found to be positively associated with corporate philanthropy (Coffey and Wang, 1998). Another factor related to managerial control is the percentage of CEO stock ownership. Walls et al. (2012) report studies that show a negative relationship of ownership in non-family firms with environmental performance (Berrone et al., 2010).

In terms of CEO compensation, Walls et al. (2012) summarize studies that show no relationship between total compensation (salary, bonus, and stock options) and corporate reputation (Stanwick and Stanwick, 2001) with stakeholder management (Coombs and Gilley, 2005). CEO salary alone was found to be negatively associated with corporate reputation (Stanwick and Stanwick, 2001) and also negatively associated with community, diversity, environmental, and product performance (Coombs and Gilley, 2005). The proportion of bonus in a CEO's total compensation was found to be negatively associated with CSR (Deckop, Merriman and Gupta, 2006) and with employee dimensions of CSR (Coombs and Gilley, 2005). The findings on stock options is mixed. Stock options were found to be unrelated to CSR in one study (Coombs and Gilley, 2005) and positively associated in another (Deckop et al., 2006; Mahoney and Thorne, 2005).

Once again, it needs to be noted that the dependent variable in these studies is CSR, which does not require the patient long-term investments, strategic change, and innovations that a PES does. Other than Berrone et al. (2010), the studies do not specifically include environmental performance of a firm as the outcome examined. The range of mixed and conflicting empirical findings may also point to the need for including unexamined variables that may moderate or mediate direct relationships between top management team characteristics such as CEO duality, managerial control, and CEO compensation and corporate social performance.

Dominant Coalition in Family Firms

As pointed out in Chapter 1, the top management decision-making team in family business is the dominant coalition (DC) that comprises individuals with bonds of kinship with the next generation and thus often manages with an eye toward long-term continuity. As compared to non-family firms, the family's values and beliefs are likely to have a more enduring and tenacious influence on the shared vision and strategic direction of a firm. This is due to the long tenures of leaders and members of the dominant coalition in family firms. This influence is accentuated by the significant ties, at times extending over generations, of these individuals with family (Miller and Le Breton-Miller, 2005). These factors create a context in which there is an enduring influence of family values on the firm (Tapies and Ward, 2008).

Hoy and Sharma (2010) argue that the "family-of-origin" into which one is born or adopted at a young age offers unique opportunities, over several years and many instances, to imbue parental values into family members. For example, a dialogue over a meal or during vacations or during a drive to school can guide the beliefs and values of next generation family members. The behavior of senior family members and also family stories help reinforce the values held sacrosanct by the family (Kammerlander et al., 2015; Sharma and Sharma, 2011). As the same family continues to control the business over generations, the unification of family values with the guiding policies of the firm become deep rooted and resilient (Sorenson et al., 2009). The family values also have a significant impact on the nature of relationships of the family business with the community and its key stakeholders (the community and several stakeholders have expectations of social and environmental performance by the firm) and on multiple dimensions of success and performance of family firms (e.g., Basco and Rodriguez, 2009; Danes et al., 2009; Sorenson and Bierman, 2009).

While family beliefs and values are likely to have a significantly stronger influence on the strategy of a family firm as compared to non-family firms, this may not necessarily mean that the family values will always favor environmental preservation. Family business research shows significant variation within family businesses in terms of their beliefs and values regarding the role of family in business and that of business in family (e.g., Ward, 1987). Therefore, one can expect family firms to vary regarding the core beliefs and values that have been suggested to influence the type of environmental sustainability strategy pursued by them (Sharma and Sharma, 2011). In terms of Ward's (1987) conceptualization of three categories of family firms – family-first, business-first, and family enterprise-first firms – empirical studies have confirmed that family firms that emphasize both family (e.g., harmony) and business (e.g., value maximization) objectives perform well on both dimensions, as compared to those that focus on only one dimension (Basco and Rodriguez, 2009). While the focus of these studies was on beliefs regarding the relative importance of family vs. business system goals, the logic can be extended to the role of business in environmental sustainability (Sharma and Sharma, 2011). For example, even when the DC of the business-owning family(ies) believes in the need to be proactive about environmental sustainability, individuals in this coalition may vary significantly in their belief regarding the extent to which their family business should be an instrument to achieve environmental sustainability. Thus, there may be a significant variance in the preferred environmental strategies for their family firm.

One of the widely accepted definitions of family business is "a business governed and/or managed with the intention to shape and pursue the vision of the business held by a dominant coalition controlled by members of the same family or a small number of families in a manner that is potentially sustainable across generations of the family or families" (Chua, Chrisman and Sharma, 1999: 25). This definition includes two relevant dimensions for the development of a sustainable vision (the word "sustainable" is used here to mean uninterrupted survival and continuance over the long term): the vision of the business held by a DC and the desire to ensure the sustainability of this vision across generations. Therefore, if the founder and DC of a family firm believe in the active role of business in the sustainability of the natural environment, they are likely to exhibit a strong desire and influence that the family firm pursue a proactive strategy. On the other hand, if these leaders do not believe in the preservation of the environment, or do not believe that it is the responsibility of business enterprises to take an active role in the protection of the environment, they are more likely to be content with regulatory compliance or reactive environmental strategies. Such firms are less likely to be propelled toward proactive strategies that go beyond regulatory compliance or actions necessary to protect the societal image and reputation of the firm (cf. Dyer and Whetten, 2006).

This still leaves unanswered the question of whether or not DCs of family firms are more likely than TMTs of non-family firms to pursue a PES. That will depend on two factors that are more likely to be dominant in family firms versus non-family firms: temporal orientation and identification of the family with the firm. We will discuss these, including when there might be exceptional circumstances.

Temporal Orientation
In considering the propensity of a firm to engage in a specific strategy, two temporal dimensions need to be considered: directionality (past vs. future focus) and depth (short vs. long time frame). Strategic management research often includes discussions on the temporal orientation of strategies where short-term plans are contrasted with long-term ones, and past focus is contrasted with future focus. Classic strategy works point to firms adopting past vs. future oriented strategies (e.g., Miles and Snow, 1978). The importance of future orientation is highlighted as it enables firms to explore new options rather than being solely

focused on exploiting the benefits of past innovations (Ackoff, 1970; Chandler, 1966). Empirical studies on temporal depth aim to test how far into the past and future an individual or collectivity considers in their decision-making (Bluedorn, 2000). At both individual and organizational levels, this research suggests a positive relationship between past and future temporal depth (Bluedorn, 2002). That is, the longer into the past that individuals or collectives take into account in their thinking, the longer into the future they are able to consider in their decisions. Longer temporal vistas of the past make it easier to detect patterns in actions and consequences. Temporal dimensions are also mirrored in the family business and corporate sustainability literatures, where research has shown that future-focused firms are more likely to be concerned for the welfare of future generations and undertake strategies to preserve the natural environment (e.g., Aragon-Correa, 1998; Hart, 1995; Miller and Le Breton-Miller, 2005).

Family business research shows that the directional focus varies among firms that move beyond the founder's generation. In some generational firms, the DC tends to be past-oriented, that is, living in the founder's shadow and believing that all decisions of the founder are sacrosanct and must be continued forever (Davis and Harveston, 1999). In others, the DC, while respectful of the historical decisions and beliefs, focuses on the future, adopting strategies needed for continuous renewal and entrepreneurship that meet changed circumstances internally and externally (e.g., Hoy and Sharma, 2010; Kellermanns and Eddleston, 2006; Salvato, Chirico and Sharma, 2010). Thus, in terms of directionality, family firms can be either past or future focused.

However, in terms of depth of temporal orientation, in comparison to non-family firms, family firms with transgenerational continuity intentions are more likely to have a long-term orientation. This is because not only can they identify with the family members who founded the firm, their desire to transition this firm to the next generation motivates the dominant coalition to think beyond the tenure of the current leadership. In addition, the DC also focuses on building and maintaining SEW (Gomez-Mejia et al., 2007). Therefore, family firms are more likely to be focused on transgenerational survival rather than short term or quarterly performance. They are more resilient in suffering short-term deprivation for long-term firm survival due to low overheads, flexible decision-making, and minimal bureaucratic process (Carney, 2005; Miller and Le Breton-Miller, 2005). Such firms are also more likely and able to make patient investments with a longer-term outlook (Sirmon and Hitt, 2003). Hence, families have an opportunity to bring a level of commitment, long-range investment and an entrenched historically based love for the company that most non-family businesses cannot (Gersick et al., 1997). Welfare of future generations creates the *strategic bridge* that allows family firms to undertake investments in PES strategies with long-term paybacks. But, what if there is no subsequent generation available to take over the baton of a family firm? In such instances, the incumbent generation may choose to sell the firm at its most opportune moment. Thus, not all family firms will have a long-term orientation but those with transgenerational intentions certainly will. Hence,

P14. Institutional investors with a long-term orientation are more likely to encourage and support the pursuit of environmental sustainability strategies by the firms they invest in.

Business concerns about environmental sustainability are relatively recent. Therefore, it is probable that the founders of many transgenerational firms were not aware of or concerned about the negative environmental impacts of business or the potential role of business in addressing environmental problems. For past-focused firms, holding onto their founder's beliefs is likely to deter their desire to undertake proactive environmental strategies. However, in future-oriented and long-term focused firms, the more recent environmental awareness is more likely to be incorporated into beliefs of the DC, leading to a desire to engage in proactive environmental strategies. Research on long-lived family firms suggests that it is often a combination of family and non-family members who work together to strategically to champion a shift in the mind-set of influential stakeholders from its focus on founder's business to a future-oriented strategic horizon, especially when knowledge of what is beneficial or harmful for humanity undergoes drastic changes, as is the case with environmental sustainability issues (e.g., Salvato, Chrico and Sharma, 2010).

Directionality and the depth of the time horizon of the family firms are not necessarily discrete and separate. They may be combined in the family's value system as represented in the following quotes.

According to the winery manager of Viña De Martino in Chile, a fourth-generation family member, the family has a past focus that carries into the future but also a long-term strategic horizon.

The family moved from Italy and settled on this land in the 1930s. Ever since then, the family has a philosophy of caring for this land and improving it because we live on the land. Everything we do from growing grapes to producing wine is done with that in mind.

As per the general manager of Chateau Fonroque, a member of the Guillard family acquired the winery in 2012 from the Moueix family that owned it since 1931. The Moueix family were pioneers in organic practices in Bordeaux.

The Chateau's leadership and expertise in organic viticulture and winemaking was already well known in Bordeaux. When the winery became available, we were ready to take over and carry forward the momentum to incorporate biodynamic practices and certification. Our family believes strongly that we must become stewards of the ecosystems and communities if we have to survive into the future.

In contrast, the Marketing Director of Chateau Lascombs (a seventeenth century winery that was sold to a US company (Colonial Capital) in 2001 and then to the French insurance company (MACSF) in 2011), in his interview was consistently skeptical about the long-term investment in PES.

Organic or biodynamic practices take several years to implement and require experimentation which makes the quality of wine unpredictable for a long period of time. We cannot afford to risk our financial survival, quality and reputation to undertake these risky unpredictable practices to satisfy a niche market. Moreover, none of the rating systems add any points for organic or biodynamic.

Similarly, the CEO of Bird's Nest, a Canadian corporate winery, stated:

Our focus [is] on quality in order to generate consumer loyalty. We achieve this quality by complying with all regulations and being a responsible company. Producing organic wine is a personal preference that some wine owners have that I am sure they are willing to pay for in low grape yields and unpredictable quality.

Family Identification with the Firm

Corporate identity is the central enduring characteristic of a firm (Albert and Whetten, 1985). It helps to establish a unified view of what the firm stands for and guides key strategic decisions (Dutton and Dukerich, 1991). In comparison to non-family firms, because of the significant and enduring family influence in the business, family firms have a stronger identity that is intricately linked with the family's identity (Dyer and Whetten, 2006). For example, the family name often becomes synonymous with the firm's name leading to the amalgamation of the family's and the firm's identities (Ward, 2005). Social interaction between family members outside work settings (e.g., family gatherings) reinforces the unified identity, leading to a more coherent, consistent, and unified strategic outlook (Arregle et al., 2007). Moreover, it is likely that the family members' DC will select and promote employees and adopt compensation and human resource management practices that align with the family's goals and values (Arregle et al., 2007). This further helps with the development of a unified identity in the firm. Shared identity leads to ease of information exchange, cooperation, and similarity of managerial interpretations of events and circumstances. Within the corporate sustainability literature, managerial interpretations of sustainability issues as opportunities verses threats have been shown to influence the propensity of a firm to embrace proactive environmental strategies (Sharma, 2000).

Such unification of identities triggers the desire to protect and preserve the family name associated with the business and has been shown to influence the propensity of the firm to engage in CSR (Dyer and Whetten, 2006). However, such unification of identity in family firms is contingent upon the extent to which family members, who form the DC of the firm, themselves identify with the family. It has been argued that the extent of identification of individual family members with the family (or by extension, with their firm) can vary significantly (Lumpkin, Martin and Vaughn, 2008). Research suggests that later-generation family members tend to identify less closely with the values of the founding generation than the first or subsequent generations (Kellermanns and Eddleston, 2004). Family conflicts and disagreement on core values and beliefs emerge as emotional and physical distance between family members increases over generations (Gersick et al., 1997). This could also be a positive factor for the firm adopting a PES. For example, if the founding generation was not in favor of environmental preservation (as is likely the case for most firms founded before the environmental movement started four decades ago), the

later generations that do not identify with the values of the founding generation may be more likely to develop family values and
identity that favors a PES since this does not require a change of the
core business philosophy but rather the addition of a sustainability
mindset to the business. A move in the other direction – that is from
a PES to a compliance strategy – within the family is unlikely since
it would require a drastic change in embedded family values that
care for the environment. This was evident in the case of Benziger
Family winery in Sonoma, California, from which we provide a
quote from the third-generation family member in Chapter 3. While
the founding generation adopted conventional winemaking practices, the second generation was concerned not only about the
harmful impact of chemicals but also the future of the next generations that would continue to live on the land. We repeat a part of
the quote from Chapter 3 here. The quote also indicates the identification of the family name with the name of the winery and the
long-term time horizon of the family on future generations continuing in the business.

*Our family has run the Benziger Winery for over two decades with a great
deal of passion and love for the craft of winemaking. For many years, we
followed conventional practices without giving it a second thought. One
morning I looked out of the window and saw our family's children headed
to school through a cloud of herbicide being sprayed by our low flying crop
duster. That is when I had my epiphany. We lived on the land – the winery
was our home – our children would continue to live in this community and
the land. We owed it to the family and to our future generations and to the
land to work toward a sustainable ecosystem that would be healthy and
productive forever.* (emphasis added)

A fourth-generation family member of Viña De Martino in Chile
expressed similar sentiments.

*The DeMartino name has been on all our wineries for seven decades. The
consumer who buys and consumes our wine is not just drinking our wine, he
is sharing in the DeMartino family passion for quality wine and ecosystem
stewardship.*

Needless to add, the managers of the corporate wineries did not
express any identification with the name of their winery in any of the
contexts. None of them saw themselves as lifelong employees. Hence,

P15. Family firms are more likely to adopt a PES strategy as compared to non-family firms when the family members in the dominant coalition identify with the family business.

Summary. The discussion above indicates that, as compared to the governance system in non-family firms – institutional ownership, shareholder activist, and top management teams of professional executives – the governance system of family firms comprises dominant coalitions of family members bound by kinship ties and value systems and professional executives who are hired and retained based on such shared values. Therefore, family firms are *more likely* to adopt a PES strategy because of time orientations that are forward looking and long term and due to the family members' identification with the family business.

Firm Level Market and Competitive Strategies

Five years after the publication of the *Our Common Future* report by the World Commission on Environment and Development that brought sustainability issues to the attention of the world, the 1992 Rio Summit focused on possible collaborations among member states to make progress on economic development and sustainability initiatives. Stephen Schmidheiny, a fourth-generation member of a major industrial Swiss family, served as the commerce and industry adviser at the Rio Summit. He gathered a group of forty-eight global business leaders to create the Business Council for Sustainable Development (BCSD) (Schmidheiny, 1992). The BCSD urged for corporate action and knowledge creation on win-win situations where proactive environmental sustainability strategies could simultaneously lead to improved firm performance and competitive advantage. This catalyzed practitioner interest and scholarship aimed at reconciling economic development and social equity with environmental preservation by attention to issues of environmental impacts of economic development including growth and sustainable development, the costs of pollution, energy efficiency, consumer preferences for green products, and the efficiencies emerging from environmental innovation and technical diagnostic tools for environmental strategy and management (Kolluru, 1994).

Early research examining the relationship between environmental management and firm performance was generic and prescriptive. It drew broad linkages between consumer preference, employee morale, lower costs of compliance, societal support, amongst other factors, on the one hand, and the environmental practices of firms to discuss impact on economic performance, on the other (Balderjahn, 1988; Bhat, 1992; Buzzelli, 1991; Roome, 1992). An important influence was Porter's (1991) one-page article in the *Scientific American* that became known as the "Porter hypothesis." This article argued that stringent environmental regulations would drive firms toward improved efficiency and international competitiveness. Similarly, Porter and van der Linde (1995) suggested that firms adopting proactive environmental practices could achieve competitive advantage via lower costs and differentiation benefits.

Moving beyond anecdotal evidence, theoretical explanations for linkages between ecological sustainability and competitive advantage were developed by Hart in his "natural resource-based view of the firm" where he introduced the notion of linkages between environmental strategies and organizational capabilities that contributed to competitive advantage (Hart, 1995). Hart developed the theoretical notion that environmental strategies of pollution prevention, product stewardship, and sustainable development would require the development of organizational capabilities that would also contribute to competitive advantage via the reduction of emissions and costs, and the development of new clean technologies. Similarly, Shrivastava (1995c) suggested four ways in which organizations could be competitive and simultaneously contribute to ecological sustainability: total quality environmental sustainability, ecologically sustainable competitive strategy, swap technology, and reduction of the impact of towns on ecosystems.

These articles stimulated a stream of literature to unpack and test the theoretical arguments proposed. The main motivation underlying this stream of research was understanding the business case for the adoption of a sustainability strategy; that is, how variations in a firm's sustainability strategy affected its economic performance. This research evolved around three perspectives: the outcomes of strategies undertaken in response to environmental regulations, the relationship between generic business strategies and environmental strategy, and the link between environmental strategy and firm performance and competitive advantage. We discuss each in turn in the following section before we focus the lens of family firms to see if they would be more or less likely to undertake such strategies in response to market and competitiveness drivers.

Strategies Undertaken as Regulatory Responses

While institutional perspectives presented in Chapter 3 argue mainly for firms adopting isomorphic reactive strategies in response to regulations, there is empirical evidence to show that some firms do indeed adopt variable strategies for a variety of reasons related to their organizational factors and resources/capabilities. Porter (1991) proposed that firms that adopted the most stringent regulations would be forced to innovate and become efficient and thus be able to compete internationally. An early stream of research examining corporate responses to environmental legislation supported this hypothesis. Dean and Brown (1995) examined entry of new firms in industry sectors with stringent environmental legislation and found such regulations favored incumbents and created entry barriers for new firms. In analyzing over a hundred empirical studies examining linkages between environmental regulations and competitiveness of US manufacturing firms, Jaffe, Peterson, Portney, and Stavins (1995) found neutral results or overall little impact on country-specific advantages or firm-specific advantages. It is worth noting here that these studies did not discriminate between family and non-family firms, and it may be interesting to see if there were any family firms (publicly listed) in the data for these studies. In their review of the literature, Rugman and Verbeke (1998) also concluded that stringency of environmental regulations did not disadvantage multinational enterprises (MNEs); that is, firms facing stringent regulatory environments did not attempt to relocate to pollution havens or countries with less stringent regulations. Levy (1995) also found that MNEs that operated in the most stringent environmental regulation jurisdictions and adopted the most proactive environmental practices, exhibited superior environmental performance. In an interview, Robert Shapiro, the CEO of Monsanto – which was a family firm for two generations but later passed into non-family control – confirmed that the firm's philosophy based on self-regulation and going beyond compliance led to innovation and efficiencies (Magretta, 1997).

Nehrt (1996) showed that when firms could see that investment in an innovation led to reduced costs and increase in sales, national differences in environmental regulations were irrelevant: they would invest in innovative technologies regardless of whether or not regulations required the investment. Unpacking this relationship further, Nehrt (1996) found a positive relationship between *timing* of investments and profit growth. He argued that more intense investment patterns, when not tempered by sufficient *time* to absorb the investments, could lead to lower profit growth due to time-compression diseconomies. In his 1998 study, Nehrt found that early movers in implementing pollution control technology had economic advantage over later movers, regardless of national differences in intensity of environmental regulations.

Madsen (2009), in examining the auto industry, also found that firms adopted heterogeneous strategies in response to differences in environmental regulations depending on their individual capabilities. He argued that heterogeneity in a firm's institutional experience and capabilities led to heterogeneity in their preferences for environmental regulation and, hence, heterogeneity in their environmental strategies. He found that the institutional distances (in terms of environmental regulations) between a focal country and both an automaker's home country and the set of countries in which the automaker had previously invested decreased the likelihood that the automaker would invest in the focal country. He did find that the automaker's environmental capabilities moderated the effect of the stringency of a country's environmental regulation and the likelihood and magnitude of the automaker's investment in that country. He concluded that while environmental regulations do indeed have a significant effect on investment, the relationship resides at the firm level rather than at the industry (or institutional) level.

The family business literature does not offer us insights on this issue. While there are no theoretical or empirical arguments for different behavior by family firms in response to regulations as compared to non-family firms, our discussion in Chapter 3 leads us to argue that, for the reasons outlined, family firms would be even more likely to adopt heterogeneous strategies based on internal or exogenous factors in response to regulations rather than isomorphic strategies. Our research in the winery industry in three different regulatory contexts (Canada, France, and Chile) also indicated that compliance with regulations was a very low bar for the wineries and, while many wineries were easily able to achieve this bar, most exceeded these requirements to varying degrees based on internal values (mainly in family firms), resources/capabilities, temporal orientation, and an expectation of family's involvement in business beyond the current generation of leadership.

The Link between Sustainability Strategy and Generic Business Strategy

In the early 1990s, the literature on organizations and the natural environment focused on typologies and classifications of environmental strategies (e.g., Hunt and Auster, 1990; Post and Altman, 1992). Even though these classifications and typologies became increasingly sophisticated conceptually, empirical research tended to collapse these into simpler dichotomous categorizations such as "proactive vs. reactive" (Sharma and Vredenburg, 1998; Sharma, Pablo and Vredenburg, 1999) or "pollution prevention vs. pollution control" (Hart and Ahuja, 1996; Russo and Fouts, 1997) or "compliance vs. voluntary beyond-compliance" (Sharma, 2000). The conceptual typologies helped guide descriptive and empirical research that identified more fine-grained sustainability strategy variations. The focus shifted to a better understanding of factors that helped organizations evolve from reactive or pollution control strategies to proactive or pollution prevention strategies such as adoption of clean technologies, designing products and services for the environment, and product stewardship in terms of reducing material impact from cradle to grave of the product life cycle.

In examining these strategies, scholars also looked at whether there was any linkage between environmental strategies and generic business strategies of a firm (e.g., low cost or differentiation). Shrivastava (1995b) proposed a direct linkage and Hart (1995) proposed an indirect linkage via organizational capabilities, between a firm's sustainability strategy and its generic business strategy of low cost, greater efficiencies, consumer preferences and differentiation as proposed by Porter (1980). Judge and Douglas's (1998) study found evidence that the level of integration of environmental management concerns into the strategic planning process was positively related to financial and environmental performance. They also found that the greater the functional coverage and the more resources provided to environmental issues, the greater the integration of environmental issues in the planning process. Aragón-Correa (1998) found that firms with a prospector strategy (Miles and Snow, 1978) that continually developed entrepreneurial, engineering and administrative processes to search for new technologies were more likely to be proactive in their environmental strategy. Since then, a stream of research has linked corporate sustainability strategies to generic business strategies and, hence, indirectly to improved economic and financial performance or a win-win (Elkington, 1994).

In family business literature, while theoretical and empirical research in this domain is still in its infancy, there is preliminary evidence that family firms with an entrepreneurial orientation tend to successfully overcome market challenges to thrive in the long run (Cohen and Sharma, 2016; Miller and Le Breton-Miller, 2005). Thus, based on the arguments we have developed in Chapter 3 and in this chapter, we can argue that family firms would not differ in terms of the linkage between generic business strategies and their sustainability strategy. Hence,

P16. Both family and non-family firms that continually search for product and market opportunities and engage in regular experimentation are better positioned to respond opportunistically to environmentally sustainability challenges.

Sustainability Strategy and Financial Performance

The early research on the economic outcomes of a sustainability strategy ranged from arguments that any investment in complying with environmental legislation led to increased costs and loss of competitiveness (e.g., Walley and Whitehead, 1994) to arguments that stringent environmental regulations would drive firms toward improved efficiency and international competitiveness (e.g. Porter, 1991). In examining major positive and negative environmental events, such as environmental awards and/or crises and accidents, Klassen and McLaughlin (1996) found a positive relationship between financial performance (as measured by stock market performance) and positive environmental events. Nehrt (1996) found a positive relationship between early environmental investments and profit growth in chemical bleached paper pulp manufacturers. Russo and Fouts (1997) found a positive relationship between pollution prevention investments and financial performance across a multi-sector sample, showing that the relationship was stronger in high growth industries.

However, the studies examining the direct connection between environmental strategies and financial performance had two important limitations that muddied their conclusions. First, the direct effects could conceal the latent relationships that may be the real explanations of the improved performance. For example, production efficiencies associated with environmental strategies could be a factor in improved profitability rather than the environmental practices themselves. Unpacking the black box, Klassen and Whybark (1999) showed that environmental investments may generate competitive benefits if accompanied by managerial changes and efficiencies. Similarly, Sharfman and Fernando (2008) found that firms that develop a strategy that improves their total risk management through better environmental risk management were rewarded by the financial markets via a reduction in the cost of equity, specifically through the reduction in the volatility of the firm's stock. Their results suggested that an environmental strategy benefited the firm in two ways: via improved resource utilization that accompanies improved environmental risk management and via reduced cost of capital in equity and bond markets.

Second, direct linkages could not predict whether the relationship (positive or negative) was sustainable over time. Most studies were cross-sectional and the longitudinal perspective was needed to include the lagged effects of investments in environmental/social practices and strategies and impact on financial performance. Hence, the natural-resource-based research that unpacked these relationships by looking inside the black box of organizational performance, linked to valuable and rare organizational capabilities, and resources became more dominant in corporate sustainability research.

The Natural-Resource-Based View

Research adopting the resource-based view (Barney 1991; Wernerfelt, 1984) addressed the limitations of trying to establish the direct sustainability strategy-financial performance link. This research opened the black box of the organization to examine the organizational capabilities that were associated with developing sustainability strategies. It is these same or similar capabilities that enabled firms to develop low cost and differentiation (including clean technology) strategies.

The genesis of this perspective was in the writings of Shrivastava (1995), Porter (1991), and Porter and van der Linde (1995) who argued that proactive environmental strategies would drive down operating costs by reducing waste, conserving energy, reusing materials, and reducing activities in the product life cycle. They also argued that ecological sustainability was a differentiating factor for a growing segment of consumers who wanted products with low or no packaging and a low environmental footprint in their operations. Firms could become first movers and environmental leaders in their industries via inimitable strategies and innovations. Proactive environmental practices would inoculate firms against the long-term risks of resource depletion (especially for firms that were dependent on natural resources), fluctuations in energy costs, product liabilities, and pollution regulations. Employee morale would be higher, especially for those who valued a healthy ecosystem and clean air and water. Finally, these firms would also reap reputational advantages and legitimacy that would place them in a better position to participate in shaping the regulatory environment and preempt regulations.

Empirical studies began to find linkages based on these arguments by going beyond direct correlations between broad measures of environmental practices and a firm's financial performance. Klassen and McLaughlin (1996) found a positive relationship between the environmental awards won by a firm and its stock prices. Judge and Douglas (1998) found a link between investments in emissions reductions by firms and above-average financial performance, partially explained by investments in emissions reductions that led to cost savings as a result of reduced material and energy use. However, such savings reached a plateau after the low hanging fruit of excessive and easy-to-eliminate waste was "harvested" (Hart and Ahuja, 1996). This was confirmed by Nehrt's (1996, 1998) findings that first movers into clean technologies were able to reap competitive advantage but late adopters were not.

Causal linkages between investments in environmental practices or environmental awards or other indicators of proactive environmental strategy and financial performance were not easy to establish without controlling for other internal and external variables that could affect financial performance and for lagged effects of investments and strategy implementation. Moreover, the payback from proactive and beyond-compliance strategies is often intangible, difficult to quantify, and slow to emerge. Some of these intangible benefits include employee morale and productivity, license to operate (Sharma and Vredenburg, 1998), and reputation. As a result, researchers began to open up the black box of the firm to understand the endogenous firm-level variables that may mediate the relationship between proactive sustainability strategy and financial performance. Proactive environmental strategy (Sharma and Vredenburg, 1998; Sharma, 2000) or pollution prevention environmental strategy (Russo and Fouts, 1997) include long-term patient investments in the redesign of processes and products to reduce material and energy use; adoption of cleaner technologies with lower or zero wastes and lower material and energy inputs; product stewardship for take-back, dismantling, recycling, and reuse of products; and, ultimately, the redefinition of the business model. An example is Interface's major organizational and business model redesign to lease services generated by a product rather than sell higher volumes of the product. Interface's servicization of its operations required switching from manufacturing and selling carpets made from virgin material to the leasing of "floor comfort" based on a closed-loop customer linkage and take-back of fully recyclable carpet tiles (Sharma, 2014).

Starting with Hart's (1995) theoretical development of the natural-resource-based view, this stream of research has become one of the dominant research perspectives examining the relationship between economic and environmental performance. Hart argued that organizations could develop capabilities that would help them not only develop environmental strategies of pollution prevention, clean technologies, product stewardship, and sustainable development but also achieve competitive advantage. Hart also proposed that environmental strategies based on capabilities of total quality management, cross-functional capability, and a shared vision of sustainability would contribute to competitive advantage. It is not surprising that such approaches resonated better with businesses and their managers seeking to understand how to incorporate the demands of multiple stakeholders for making their operations more sustainable, while delivering shareholder value, meeting the needs of consumers, and incorporating the objectives of other stakeholders such as employees and local communities.

A PES requires the inclusion of environmental and social criteria into decision-making, and the measurement, monitoring, and reporting of performance on these criteria, in addition to economic performance (Gladwin, Kennelly and Krause, 1995). These major changes in a firm's decision-making processes require investments in new organizational capabilities of stakeholder engagement or integration (Hart, 1995; Marcus and Geffen, 1998; Sharma and Vredenburg, 1998), continuous improvement (Hart, 1995), organizational learning (Russo and Fouts, 1997), higher-order learning (Sharma and Vredenburg, 1998), innovation (Christmann, 2000; Russo and Fouts, 1997; Sharma and Vredenburg, 1998), cross-functional integration (Russo and Fouts, 1997), technology portfolios (Klassen and Whybark, 1999), strategic proactivity (Aragón-Correa, 1998), and radical transactiveness (Hart and Sharma, 2004).

Indeed, subsequent research studies have shown that, as compared to regulatory compliance and pollution control via end-of-pipe clean-up of the wastes already generated, proactive environmental strategies that focus on preventing pollution at source are more likely to contribute to improved economic performance and competitive advantage. Empirical studies showed that environmental strategies focused on pollution prevention (Russo and Fouts, 1997) and proactive beyond compliance (Sharma and Vredenburg, 1998) were associated with above-average returns for firms (Russo and Fouts, 1997) and the development of competitively valuable organizational capabilities of stakeholder integration, organizational learning, and continuous innovation (Sharma and Vredenburg, 1998). Sharma and Vredenburg's (1998) pioneering study was the first to empirically find the relationship between proactive environmental strategy and the emergence of competitively valuable organizational capabilities. Moreover, this study developed a comprehensive measure for a firm's environmental strategy based on its activities rather than using simple proxies such as environmental awards, environmental fines, and toxic release data on chemical emissions.

Christmann's (2000) study showed that complementary capabilities of process innovation and implementation were required within firms for leveraging environmental practices in order to achieve cost reductions. This study applied the concept of complementary assets to show that best environmental management practices do not lead to cost advantage for all firms unless they possess complementary assets, in this case, the capabilities of process innovation and implementation. Similarly, Klassen and Whybark (1999) found that the allocation of a manufacturing facility's environmental technology portfolio (implying a set of complementary capabilities) toward pollution prevention technologies was significantly related to the reduction of hazardous pollutants emitted by it.

Adopting a governance lens, Darnall and Edwards (2006), in attempting to understand the factors that predict the cost of adopting Environmental Management Systems (EMS) by firms and how these costs vary for different ownership structures, found that a facility's internal capabilities and access to resources predicted its EMS adoption cost, found that manufacturing facilities with stronger internal capabilities prior to EMS adoption incurred lower EMS adoption costs and relied on external resources to a lesser extent, whereas facilities with fewer organizational capabilities incurred higher adoption costs and relied on external resources to a greater extent. The study supported the notions of complementarity and path dependence proposed by Christmann (2000) and Hart (1995). They found that publicly traded facilities incurred the lowest EMS adoption costs, had the strongest internal capabilities prior to EMS adoption, and were influenced the least by external resources. Government-owned facilities had the weakest internal capabilities, relied on external resources more frequently, and had the costliest EMS adoption process. Privately owned facilities fell in between the two extremes. The authors adopted the institutional logic to explain that firms tend to imitate the strategies of competitors in their field to gain legitimacy in the eyes of external stakeholders and thus reduce the uncertainty associated with developing specialized internal capabilities.

While causality between organizational capabilities and PES (i.e., which comes first) has not been satisfactorily established empirically, we know that these are correlated, perhaps via a dynamic process where one influences the other. Berchicci et al. (2012) showed that a firm's stock of environmental capabilities affects its strategy. That is, the acquisition choices of manufacturing firms are affected by both their own and their targets' degree of environmental capabilities. Firms may acquire capabilities externally or develop them in-house to develop a PES. Marcus and Geffen (1998) and McEvily and Marcus (2005) showed that firms acquire (and deploy) pollution prevention capabilities when they acquire information and knowledge during joint problem solving with lead suppliers. The suppliers also enable the firms to benchmark their practices against other firms in the industry. Moreover, information related to benchmarking of a firm's environmental practices against its competitors and industry standards allows performance to be monitored and improved whether the goal is to achieve industry standards or exceed them. Rondinelli and London

(2003) argued that, given the complementaryresources of for-profit firms and not-for-profit NGOs, forming cross-sector collaborations that more effectively use the knowledge and capabilities of each can create new opportunities to achieve both greater corporate profitability and stronger environmental protection.

Due to the significant importance of resources and capabilities in driving PES, we will explore the role of resources and capabilities applying the lens of family business.

The Development and Deployment of Capabilities for PES in Family Firms

Organizational capabilities are the coordinating mechanisms that enable the most efficient and competitive use of a firm's resources – whether tangible or intangible. For example, Amit and Schoemaker (1993) define capabilities as a firm's capacity to deploy its resources and McEvily and Marcus (2005: 1034) define capabilities as "the set of organizing processes and principles a firm uses to deploy its resources to achieve strategic objectives." Capabilities for sustainability are developed and deployed as a firm attempts to achieve optimal fit between the internal and external environments, especially where factors in the external environment have been increasingly pressuring the firm to act on sustainability concerns. In addition to its own survival, the firm develops and deploys capabilities that take into account the survival of systems, including natural ecosystems and societies, outside its technical core.

Proactive environmental sustainability (PES) strategies require investments not only in the *development* of new organizational capabilities (Hart, 1995; Marcus and Geffen, 1998; McEvily and Marcus, 2005; Sharma and Vredenburg, 1998) but also in the *deployment* of the new and existing capabilities (Christmann, 2000; Russo and Fouts, 1997). Firms have multiple strategic choices and opportunity costs for deploying an existing capability to undertake one strategy versus another. There are costs associated with deploying a specific capability relative to other available capabilities at a particular time (Zott, 2003).

Capability deployment facilitates decision-making via routines and processes that help overcome managerial bounded rationality (Gavetti, 2005). For that very reason, capability deployment is subject to intra-organizational conflicts and cognitive biases among managers due to their irrational risk aversion or risk-seeking (Amit and Schoemaker,

1993; Kahneman and Tversky, 1979). The biases can be reinforced as each decision to deploy a capability can potentially cause conflict by adding to the power base of one manager and negatively affecting another (Amit and Schoemaker, 1993). These biases affect managerial expectations of future strategic value of capabilities and therefore the investments made in their deployment (Barney, 1986). Empirical support for the relevance of managerial cognition in capability deployment (Adner and Helfat, 2003; Helfat and Peteraf, 2003) is provided by studies that show the influence of managerial interpretations of sustainability issues as opportunities rather than threats (Sharma, 2000), or managerial attitudes favoring environmental preservation (Cordano and Frieze, 2000), or managerial values in general (Bansal, 2003). To manage biases and conflicts, organizations need to design structures, rewards, and culture to channel capability deployment in desired directions (Amit and Schoemaker, 1993).

Studies have found influences of organization design on sustainable strategy. These include the legitimization of sustainability issues in corporate identity, employee empowerment via information exchange, control systems (Sharma, Pablo and Vredenburg, 1999), and the influence of supervisory roles (Ramus and Steger, 2000). Other drivers identified in empirical studies include strategic leadership (Egri and Herman, 2000) and the role of organizational champions (Andersson and Bateman, 2000). While family firms may be subject to a similar set of drivers, the introduction of family dynamics may change the nature and intensity of some of these internal drivers and may introduce some drivers unique to family firms.

As mentioned, the family business literature in this domain is very limited. Phenomena such as CSR and sustainability in family businesses have just begun to be examined by family business scholars. Dyer Jr. and Whetten's (2006) study focusing on CSR as philanthropic initiatives, found that family firms whose owners and managers personally identified with their firm were more likely to undertake corporate social practices. They concluded that having the family name on the building influenced the avoidance of any practices or actions that may damage the firm's reputation. It can be argued that avoiding damage to the family name is a reactive strategy and does not explain why a firm would adopt a PES involving long-term patient investments to make substantial changes to business strategy and operations.

In a study on environmental practices in family firms, Craig and Dibrell (2006) argued that, because family businesses have more flexible decision-making processes and longer strategic horizons (Sharma and Irving, 2005; Ward, 1987), they will exhibit higher levels of environmental innovations and economic performance as compared to non-family firms. However, the results of their study do not point to these conclusions. Finally, some scholars have argued for linking stewardship propensity as a characteristic of family firms (Anderson and Reeb, 2004) as a driver of their sustainability strategies. We will discuss the unique characteristics of family firms that will make them more likely to develop and deploy organizational capabilities for a PES: shared vision by members of the dominant coalition, stewardship orientation, long-term temporal orientation, familiness, and family identity.

Shared Family Sustainability Vision

The sustainability literature emphasizes the importance of a buy-in or diffusion of shared meaning of a sustainability vision across the organization. The shared meaning and buy-in is the starting point of a PES but is also essential for the development and deployment of organizational capabilities for such a strategy (Hart, 1995; Sharma, 2000; Sharma, Pablo and Vredenburg, 1999). As we discussed, individual capabilities affect the power base of individual managers and in nonfamily firms, this requires deep and costly integration, teamwork, organization design, and supervision. However, such shared vision for capability development and deployment is much easier in a family firm where the DC sings from the same hymnbook.

One of the widely accepted definitions of family business is "a business governed and/or managed with the intention to shape and pursue the vision of the business held by a dominant coalition controlled by members of the same family or a small number of families in a manner that is potentially sustainable across generations of the family or families" (Chua, Chrisman and Sharma, 1999: 25). This definition includes two relevant dimensions for the development of a sustainable vision: the vision of the business held by a DC, and the desire to ensure the sustainability (the word "sustainability" is used here to mean "uninterrupted survival and continuance over the long-term") of this vision across generations. Therefore, if the founder of the family business decides, or the DC agrees, to adopt and pursue a vision of a sustainable business, the ability to sustain this vision across time and generations is much more likely to be stronger in family firms versus non-family firms where values may not transmit intact across changes in top management teams or may be neutralized in internal power struggles for allocation of resources for specific projects and capabilities by managers.

The family has a central influence in shaping lifelong values as each subsequent generation adopts some of the parental values (Giddens, 1984). Studies in different contexts (e.g., customer service policies) have found that family firms emphasize personal values over corporate values in business (Lyman, 1991). It is not surprising, therefore, that these shape the family firm's vision, norms, and patterns of behavior (Pearson, Carr and Shaw, 2008). This vision is more stable because the ownership and control of family firms is more stable over time (Arregle et al., 2007; Pearson et al., 2008). A family vision of sustainability can emerge with the founder's vision of the firm or during times of succession when a family member with a strong vision of a sustainable business takes over. New values and norms are rarely introduced during the "working together" phase when the DC does not change (Gersick et al., 1997). This is because going against established norms creates conflict and adds risk to an established business model. A change toward a vision of sustainability may also happen when the family business growth matures and the firm faces saturated markets. At this stage, the family is more likely to seek major strategic rethinking and shift.

A shared vision held by a dominant family coalition rapidly infuses the family firm with meaning (Lansberg, 1999) and collective understanding of how to achieve long-term family goals (Pearson et al., 2008). Moreover, the power usually accorded to the family in decision-making facilitates diffusion of goals and norms (Arregle et al., 2007). This sharing of meaning and collective understanding of how to achieve long-term goals is based on resilient trust (based on binding reciprocal expectations embedded in social interaction versus fragile trust which is transactional; Leana and Van Buren, 1999) within families and is a key to the development and deployment of a firm's capabilities. Such resilient trust is difficult within top management teams of non-family firms consisting of professionals with personal agendas and goals.

This is illustrated in the following quotes from the winery industry. The quote from the winemaker of reactive Skyline in the Okanagan (a winery started by a father-and-daughter team and subsequently bought out by the corporate Peller group) provided in Chapter 3 is worth repeating here:

When we started the winery [as a family firm], we began with organic viticul-ture. When we were acquired by the Peller Group, the focus has been on product quality and production yields as per the group's policy of compliance with regulations and adopting the most efficient production practices. At the scale at which we operate across our several wineries, it is difficult to standar-dize organic practices across the Niagara and Okanagan regions.

Similarly, the CEO of Bird's Nest, a corporate winery in the Okanagan stated:

We have had quite a few changes in our top management. I joined six months ago and we are working on an entirely new strategic plan.

In contrast, the second-generation family member of Nirvana in the Okanagan reinforced how family values drove their strategy.

For us the winery is a realization of our family's values for the link between healthy ecosystems and human health.

The fourth-generation family member who is the vineyard manager for Viña De Martino in Chile stated:

The family constantly explores ways in which we can become better environ-mental stewards while producing the best wines possible.

For family firms with a vision of sustainable business, the deploy-ment of organizational capabilities for sustainability will be mediated by characteristics that are unique to family firms: familiness, commu-nity/stewardship orientation, time orientation, and family identity.

Familiness

Perhaps one of the most unique constructs in family business research is "familiness." The concept was introduced by Habbershon and Williams (1999) as a firm-level bundle of resources and capabilities unique to a family firm. While Habbershon and Williams saw these capabilities emerging as a result of systems interactions, Chrisman, Chua and Litz (2004) saw them as emerging from family involvement and interactions. Familiness is argued to contribute to competitive advantage for family firms (Tokarczyk et al., 2007) and to non-eco-nomic outcomes such as preservation of family ties or transgenera-tional value creation (Chrisman, Chua and Litz, 2004). This could well be extended to the social mission (Lansberg, 1999; Pearson et al., 2008) or sustainability vision of family firms. While familiness is a complex multi-layered construct, it needs to be noted that this construct has neither been reliably developed nor empirically measured/ tested in the family business literature. We view this as an opportunity to develop measures for this unique intangible feature of family firms.

The idiosyncrasy of familiness is based on the path dependency of a unique family history that is inimitable (Pearson et al., 2008). Familiness is also socially complex due to unique routines embedded in unique family dynamics (Pearson et al., 2008). It can be argued that the extent to which a vision is shared and diffused as collective understanding within the organization depends on the firm's degree of familiness. The higher the degree of familiness, the higher the degree of family social capital (Pearson et al., 2008), which facilitates information sharing and exchange in terms of quality, relevance, and timeliness (Adler and Kwon, 2002).

Levels of familiness may differ between founder–first-generation and sibling-run businesses (Gersick et al., 1997). Familiness can be dysfunctional and can have a negative valence due to internal family conflicts that could lead to conflicting visions and goals of family members. Similarly, a high degree of closeness in the family unit that shuts off outside influences can have a positive and negative valence. Closeness facilitates the development of norms, trust, and identity (Coleman, 1990; Pearson et al., 2008) and creates both social complexity and causal ambiguity of decision-making within the family unit that is critical for capability development and deployment. On the other hand, too much closeness in family dynamics could lead to closed-mindedness to new ideas (Adler and Kwon, 2002), such as sustainability, new technologies, and innovative business models. Therefore, familiness is a construct with negative and positive valence: a high degree of positive familiness being associated with an organizational competence to implement a strategy based on shared goals and meaning, and negative familiness representing conflicting goals and agendas.

Positive familiness fosters a high degree of family social capital and facilitates the development and deployment of organizational capabilities that are socially complex and require group interaction: higher-order learning (Sharma and Vredenburg, 1998), cross-functional integration (Russo and Fouts, 1997), and continuous innovation (Sharma and Vredenburg, 1998). Decisions within the family unit are often made via informal interactions versus recorded formal meetings with recorded minutes (in non-family firms) creating causal ambiguity. Mutual interdependence based on shared goals and interests is high in family firms and leads to collective action (Leana and Van Buren, 1999) in the form of capability deployment. Family interaction reflects the quantity, quality, and strength of those relationships (Pearson et al., 2008). Focus on non-economic goals such as sustainability can strengthen the shared meaning and interaction for collective action.

Some examples from the winery industry data point to the importance of positive familiness as reflected in the following quotes.

According to the founder of Landjoy in the Okanagan, a first-generation multiple family member business:

My wife manages the accounts, my son manages the marketing, my nephew manages the retailing to restaurants, my other son is studying organic wine-making which will complement my expertise in organic viticulture. We spend a part of our dinner every evening reflecting on the day and discussing how to become the leading organic wine producers in Canada.

The winemaker of Chateau Le Puy, a family member of the Amoreau family that has owned the winery for over 400 years stated:

We have managed to maintain our high quality and world class biodynamic practices due to close family oversight. We have decided to grow only as much as we can manage well based on the expertise of our family members.

Stewardship Orientation

The corporate sustainability literature generally does not consider the importance of localness or place, though these are important factors in developing a community and stewardship orientation among family members or managers. The exception is Shrivastava and Kennelly (2013) who argue that a firm's sense of place or rootedness influences its environmental strategy and that such firms are more likely than other enterprises to engage in environmentally sustainable performance. They argue that such firms are anchored in, and coupled to, particular places in rich and dense ways and have a greater motivation to adopt more sustainability strategies because of

• Local ownership and control. Capital invested in such enterprises will tend to be patient capital, invested for the longer term.

- Production activities that are interdependent with the place, relying on it for particular, unique, and inimitable resources, creating an enterprise identity that itself may be strongly related to place.
- Complex multilayered relationships with iterated meaning, where place creates enterprise and enterprises create place.
- A strong and holistic understanding that place is more than mere location, locality, or landscape, but is also socially created in a nexus of meaning.

Shrivasatava and Kennelly (2013) also argue that *family enterprises are more likely to have these characteristics*. Indeed, family-owned firms, particularly those with operations where the family lives, and concerns over the legacy they leave for future generations, are particularly sensitive to community pressures to be stewards of the community resources – social harmony and justice and the ecosystems – and perform in an environmentally acceptable and place-sensitive manner (Sharma and Sharma, 2011). These firms show a broad stakeholder orientation, in that they recognize the recursive effects of place on people and of people on place. They encompass both place attachment and community identity that can get closely tied to organizational identity and may hold lessons for all enterprises seeking stewardship-based sustainability.

The family business is the main asset of the family. Since family members have a major stake in this asset, they are likely to share goals for the business and participate in intergenerational decision-making and interdependence (Arregle et al., 2007). This is even more likely when the family shares a sense of place or localness that leads to a community and stewardship orientation. This is more pronounced when the family business is rooted to the land, e.g., for agro-processing businesses such as wineries or prestigious retail locations. A shared vision of corporate social responsibility may be reinforced by a sense of place or localness (Post, 1993).

As mentioned a couple of times in Chapters 3 and 4, the third generation of the Benziger Family Wineries in Sonoma County, California, explained how their connection to the land and the vision of future generations living on the same land led to their stewardship in developing biodynamic organic farming capabilities:

We lived on the land – the winery was our home – our children would continue live on this land. We owed it to the family and to our future generations and to the land that we lived on to work toward a sustainable ecosystem that would be healthy and productive forever.

Similarly, the winemaker of Chateau Le Puy in France, a member of the family that has owned the winery for over 400 years stated:

We have remained small to maintain our rootedness to this land and community of our ancestors. If we grew too big in too many locations and too many countries, we will lose that connection that motivates us to protect and preserve this land.

We argue that a family's sense of localness strengthens community and stewardship orientation and hence the development of a shared vision of sustainability and the development and deployment of capabilities for generating a sustainable strategy.

Long-Term Temporal Orientation

A family firm's time orientation in terms of directionality (past vs. present) and durationality (short term vs. long term) was discussed earlier in this chapter and we argued that DCs with a time orientation toward the future and the long term would be more likely to adopt a PES. We make a similar argument in regard to the development and deployment of capabilities for a PES. Strategic management research often includes discussions on the time orientation of strategies, where short-term plans are contrasted with long-term ones. Classic strategy works point to the importance of long-term coordinated strategies (Ackoff, 1970; Chandler, 1966). The theme of long-term strategies is also mirrored in the sustainability literature, which embeds the concern for the welfare of future generations and is positioned against the short-term performance approach delineated by short-term financial reporting (Hart, 1995; Kolk, 2008; Nieuwenhuys, 2006).

As we have argued, family firms are more likely than non-family firms to be focused on transgenerational survival rather than short term or quarterly performance. They are also more resilient in suffering short-term deprivation for long-term firm survival due to low overheads, flexible decision-making, and minimal bureaucratic process (Carney, 2005). Family firms are also more likely and able to make patient investments with longer-term outlook (Sirmon and Hitt, 2003). The ability of family firms to institute changes with less outside interference or control enables them to develop patient long-term strategies and relationships with stakeholders (Miller and Le Breton-Miller, 2005). Families can bring a level of commitment, long-range investment, and a love for the company that non-family businesses cannot (Gersick et al., 1997). Welfare of future generations creates the strategic bridge that allows family firms to undertake investments in proactive long-term sustainability strategies via the development and deployment of organizational capabilities. Hence, we argue that a family firm's long-term future-oriented time orientation will lead to a greater likelihood of the development and deployment of capabilities for developing a PES.

In the preceding discussion on familiness, the founder of Landjoy talked about his son pursuing an education program in organic winemaking to complement the founder's strengths in organic viticulture. This would strengthen the family goal of building the capabilities to become the leading organic wine producer in Canada. Similarly, Sunnyvale (Canada), Viña De Martino (Chile), and Chateau Fonroque (France) sent junior family members to New Zealand to apprentice in both the vineyards and the winery in order to learn the most advanced biodynamic practices. Usually, viticulturists and winemakers worldwide travel to Bordeaux in order to learn from over a thousand years of expertise in making the best wines in the world. It is remarkable that Chateau Fonroque sent a family member to New Zealand, a New World locale that is usually considered less advanced than the Old World.

Chateau Fonroque's general manager explained:

We have been experimenting with biodynamic viticulture for several years but no winery in Bordeaux has the level of expertise that has developed in New Zealand. This is the future.

Viña De Martino:

If we have to lead in biodynamic, we have to first learn from the best in the world, the New Zealand wineries.

Family Identity
We have argued that DCs in family firms are more likely to develop a PES because of the identification of family members with the business. We make a similar argument for the development and deployment of capabilities to adopt a PES.

Corporate identity is the central enduring characteristic of a firm (Albert and Whetten, 1985). Similarly, family firms whose family name is associated with the business are likely to share a strong family identity (Arregle et al., 2007). Since capabilities are embedded in people within firms, it is likely that DCs with a shared sustainability vision will select and promote employees and adopt compensation and human resource management practices that align with the family's sustainability goals and values (Arregle et al., 2007). Social interaction between family members outside work settings and at family gatherings reinforces social capital and identity (Arregle et al., 2007), leading to a more coherent, consistent, and unified strategic outlook.

Shared family identity leads to ease of information exchange and cooperation (Nahapiet and Ghoshal, 1998) and is a strong, enduring social force (Pearson et al., 2008). The desire to protect the family name associated with the business has been shown to influence CSR (Dyer and Whetten, 2006). Shared identity or identification with the family leads to shared interpretations. Shared managerial interpretations of sustainability issues as opportunities versus threats has been shown to positively influence capability development and deployment for generating a proactive sustainability strategy (Sharma and Vredenburg, 1998). Similarly, the legitimization of environmental issues within the corporate identity has been shown to influence the development of a proactive environmental strategy (Sharma, 2000). Hence, we argue that family members' identification with the business will make family firms more likely to develop and deploy capabilities for a PES.

This is illustrated in several quotes from the winery industry where the founders and family members talked about the importance of community and ecosystems because it was not only core to the family values but also to the family name (which happened to be on the winery). Even though we have anonymized several wineries, in more than 50 percent of the cases, the family name was the same as the name of the winery. As per a fourth-generation member of the DeMartino family:

We are proud of the quality and stewardship represented by the wines that carry our family name.

Based on the arguments presented above, we propose that

P17. *Family firms whose dominant coalition shares a vision of sustainability will be more likely to develop and deploy their organizational capabilities for a PES as compared to a non-family firm that has a leadership strategic vision that favors sustainable business.*

P18. *A family firm's stewardship orientation, long-term orientation, familiness, and family identity will have a positive mediating effect on the development and deployment of organizational capabilities for generating a PES.*

P19. *Family firms whose dominant coalition shares a vision of sustainability will be more likely to invest in patient capital to develop their organizational capabilities for a PES as compared to a non-family firm that has a leadership strategic vision that favors sustainable business.*

P20. *Family firms are more likely to adopt a PES strategy as compared to non-family firms when the family members in the dominant coalition identify with the family business.*

P21. *Family firms with disagreements within the dominant coalition regarding their goal to continue the firm over generations, and/or identification with the firm are less likely to adopt a PES as compared to non-family firms.*

P22. *A family firm's leadership comprising members of the controlling family will be more likely to successfully deploy patient capital for developing capabilities to implement a PES as compared to the leadership of a non-family firm, primarily due to longer tenures and the lack of need to convince multiple influential shareholders.*

P23. *Non-family firms effectively undertake a PES via the development of organizational capabilities of stakeholder integration, higher-order learning, and continuous innovation. Family firms are more likely to build these capabilities due to a patient strategic horizon (long-term temporal orientation), community engagement, and easier knowledge transmission within the organization (between family members, between generations, and between family members and managers via shorter channels of communication).*

The Contingent Natural-Resource-Based View

Before we close this chapter, it is relevant to discuss an extension of the dominant natural-resource-based paradigm in corporate sustainability research. The contingent perspective considers how exogenous factors moderate and/or mediate the role of capabilities in linking environmental strategy to competitive advantage. Aragón-Correa and Sharma (2003) developed the contingent natural-resource-based view arguing that a PES would lead to competitive advantage only under certain contingencies in the business environment. They argued that PES is a meta dynamic capability with a differential impact on competitive advantage of firms as moderated by certain contingencies in the general business environment as perceived by managers. Their theory proposed that the relationship between environmental strategy and competitive advantage will be strengthened by the perceived state uncertainty and munificence of the general business environment, and hindered by the perceived organizational effect and decision response uncertainties and the complexity of the business environment. Therefore, firms with similar characteristics in terms of capabilities, performance, and activities, may develop different approaches for managing the interface between their businesses and the natural environment.

Such studies began to contribute to the larger strategy literature in the resource-based view by answering calls to consider the influence of the general business environment on the value of resources and capabilities (Barney, 2001; Priem and Butler, 2001). Aragón-Correa and Sharma's (2003) theory integrated the contingency literature (e.g., Lawrence and Lorsch, 1967; Milliken, 1987) and the re-conceptualized dynamic capabilities literature (Eisenhardt and Martin, 2000) with work grounded in the natural-resource-based view of the firm (Hart, 1995; Marcus and Nichols, 1999; Russo and Fouts, 1997; Sharma and Vredenburg, 1998).

While this is an area that requires empirical research, it can be argued that family firms with a long-term future orientation will stay the course on the development and deployment of capabilities once they have undertaken a PES regardless of changes in the general business environment, unlike non-family firms that are subject to short-term market pressures. This is evident in many of the quotes from members of family firms that indicate that their PES is not driven by markets or consumers but by internal motivation for environmental stewardship.

In contrast, the corporate wineries often indicate the niche market for organic wines that is not worth the long-term patient investments.

Summary

This chapter draws on the literature in corporate sustainability, strategic management, and family business, and on case studies from wineries in Canada, France, and Chile to conclude that family firms are more likely than non-family firms to undertake a PES due to organizational factors such as the dominant coalition governance structure that fosters a long-term orientation and an identification of family members with the business; and unique family characteristics such as familiness, stewardship orientation, long-term temporal orientation, familiness, and family identity that are more likely to strengthen a shared vision for sustainability.

References

Ackoff, R. L. 1970. *A Concept of Corporate Planning*. New York: Wiley-Interscience.

Adler, P. S. and Kwon, S.-W. 2002. Social capital: Prospects for a new concept. *Academy of Management Review*, 27(1): 17–40.

Adner, R. and Helfat, C. E. 2003. Corporate effects and dynamic managerial capabilities. *Strategic Management Journal*, 24: 1011–1025.

Aguilera, R. V., Williams, C. A., Conley, J. M. and Rupp, D. E. 2006. Corporate governance and social responsibility: A comparative analysis of the UK and the US. *Corporate Governance*, 14(3): 147–158.

Albert, S. and Whetten, D. A. 1985. Organizational identity. In B. M. Staw and L.L. Cummings (eds.), *Research on Organizational Behavior*, pp. 263–295. Greenwich, CT: JAI Press.

Amit, R. and Schoemaker, P. J. H. 1993. Strategic assets and organizational rent. *Strategic Management Journal*, 14: 33–46.

Andersson, L. M. and Bateman, T. S. 2000. Individual environmental initiative: Championing natural environmental issues in U.S. business organizations. *Academy of Management Journal*, 43: 548–570.

Anderson, R. C. and Reeb, D. 2004. Board composition: Balancing family influence in S&P 500 firms. *Administrative Science Quarterly*, 49: 209–237.

Aragón-Correa, A. 1998. Strategic Proactivity and Firm Approach to the Natural Environment. *Academy of Management Journal*, 41(5): 556–567.

Aragon-Correa, J. A. and Sharma, S. 2003. A contingent natural-resource based view of proactive environmental strategy. *Academy of Management Review*, 28(1): 71–88.

Arregle, J., Hitt, M. A., Sirmon, D. G. and Very P. 2007. The development of organizational social capital: Attributes of family firms. *Journal of Management Studies*, 44(1): 73–95.

Balderjahn, I. 1988. Personality variables and environmental attitudes as predictors of ecologically responsible consumption patterns. *Journal of Business Research*, 17, 51–56.

Bansal, P. 2003. From issues to actions: The importance of individual concerns and organizational values in responding to natural environmental issues. *Organization Science*, 14(5): 510–527.

Barney, J. B. 1986. Strategic factor markets: Expectations, luck and business strategy. *Management Science*, 32: 1231–1241.

Barney, J. B. 1991. Firm resources and sustained competitive advantage. *Journal of Management*, 17(1): 99–120.

Barney, J. B. 2001. Is the resource based "view" a useful perspective for strategic management research? *Academy of Management Review*, 26: 41–56.

Basco, R. and Rodriguez, M. J. P. 2009. Studying the family enterprise holistically: Evidence for integrated family and business systems. *Family Business Review*, 22: 82–95.

Bear S., Rahman, N. and Post, C. 2010. The impact of board diversity and gender composition on corporate social responsibility and firm reputation. *Journal of Business Ethics*, 97: 207–221.

Berchicci, L., Dowell, G. and King, A. A. 2012. Environmental capabilities and corporate strategy: Exploring acquisitions among us manufacturing firms. *Strategic Management Journal*, 33: 1053–1071.

Berrone, P., Fosfuri, A., Gelabert, L. and Gomez-Mejia, L. R. 2013. Necessity as the mother of 'green' inventions: Institutional pressures and environmental innovations. *Strategic Management Journal*, 34: 891–909.

Berrone, P. and Gomez-Mejia, L. R. 2009. Environmental performance and executive compensation: An integrated agency-institutional perspective. *Academy of Management Journal*, 52(1): 103–126.

Berrone, P., Cruz, C. and Gomez-Mejia, L. R. 2012. Socioemotional wealth in family firms: Theoretical dimensions, assessment approaches, and agenda for future research. *Strategic Management Journal*, 25(3): 258–279.

Berrone, P., Cruz, C., Gomez-Mejia, L. R. and Larraza-Kintana, M. 2010. Socioemotional wealth and corporate responses to institutional pressures: Do family-controlled firms pollute less? *Administrative Science Quarterly*, 55(1): 82–113.

Bhat, V. N. 1992. Strategic planning for pollution reduction. *Long Range Planning*, 25: 54–61.

Bluedorn, A. C. 2000. Time and organizational culture. In N. M. Ashkanasy, C. P. M. Wilderom and M. F. Peterson (eds.), *Handbook of Organizational Culture* and *Climate*, 117–128. Thousand Oaks, CA: Sage.

Bluedorn, A. C. 2002. *The Human Organization of Time: Temporal Realities and Experiences*. Stanford, CA: Stanford University Press.

Brown, W. O., Helland, E. and Smith, J. K. 2006. Corporate philanthropic practices. *Journal of Corporate Finance*, 12(5): 855–877.

Buzzelli, D. 1991. Time to structure and environmental policy strategy. Journal of Business Strategy, March-April, 17–20.

Carney, M. 2005. Corporate governance and competitive advantage in family controlled firms. *Entrepreneurship Theory and Practice*, 29: 249–265.

Cennamo, C., Berrone, P., Cruz, C. and Gomez-Mejia, L. R. 2012. Socioemotional wealth and proactive stakeholder engagement: Why family-controlled firms care more about stakeholders. *Entrepreneurship Theory and Practice,* 2012 (November): 1153–1173.

Chandler, A. D. 1966. *Strategy and Structure: Chapters in the History of the Industrial Enterprise* (2nd ed.). Garden City, NY: Anchor Books.

Chrisman, J. J., Chua, J. H. and Litz, R. 2004. Comparing the agency costs of family and non-family firms: Conceptual issues and exploratory evidence. *Entrepreneurship Theory and Practice*, 28: 335–354.

Christmann, P. 2000. Effects of "best practices" of environmental management on cost advantage: The role of complementary assets. *Academy of Management Journal*, 43: 663–680.

Chua, J. H., Chrisman, J. J. and Sharma, P. 1999. Defining family business by behavior. *Entrepreneurship Theory and Practice*, 23(1): 19–39.

Chua, J. H., Chrisman, J. J., Steier, L .P. and Rau, S. 2012. Sources of heterogeneity of family firms. *Entrepreneurship Theory and Practice*, 36 (6): 1103–1113.

Coffey, B. S. and Fryxell, G. E. 1991. Institutional ownership of stock and dimensions of corporate social performance: an empirical examination. *Journal of Business Ethics*, 10(6): 437–444.

Coffey, B. S. and Wang, J. 1998. Board diversity and managerial control as predictors of corporate social performance. *Journal of Business Ethics*, 17 (14): 1595–1603.

Cohen, A. R. and Sharma, P. 2016. *Entrepreneurs in every generation: How successful family businesses develop their next leaders*. Oakland, CA: Berrett-Koehler.

Coleman, J. S. 1990. *Foundations of Social Theory*. Cambridge, MA: Harvard University Press.

Coombs, J. E. and Gilley, K. M. 2005. Stakeholder management as a predictor of CEO compensation: Main effects and interactions with financial performance. *Strategic Management Journal*, 26(9): 827–840.

Cordano, M. and Frieze, I. H. 2000. Pollution reduction preferences of U.S. environmental managers: Applying Ajzen's theory of planned behavior. *Academy of Management Journal*, 43: 627–641.

Craig, J. and Dibrell, C. 2006. The natural environment, innovation, and firm performance: A comparative study. *Family Business Review*, 19(4): 275–288.

Danes, S. M., Stafford, K., Haynes, G. and Amarapurkar, S. S. 2009. Family capital of family firms: Bridging human, social, and financial capital. *Family Business Review*, 22(3): 199–215.

Darnall, N. and Edwards Jr., D. 2006. Predicting the cost of environmental management system adoption: The role of capabilities, resources and ownership structure. *Strategic Management Journal*, 27: 301–320.

David, P., Bloom, M. and Hillman, A. J. 2007. Investor activism, managerial responsiveness, and corporate social performance. *Strategic Management Journal*, 28(1): 91–100.

Davis, P. S. and Harveston, P. D. 1999. In the founder's shadow: Conflict in the family firm. *Family Business Review*, 12(4): 311–323.

Dean, T. J. and Brown, R. L. 1995. Pollution regulation as a barrier to new firm entry: Initial evidence and implications for future research. *Academy of Management Journal*, 38(1): 288–303.

Deckop, J. R., Merriman, K. K. and Gupta, S. 2006. The effects of CEO pay structure on corporate social performance. *Journal of Management*, 32(3): 329–342.

Delmas, M. A. and Montes-Sancho, M. J. 2010. Voluntary agreements to improve environmental quality: Symbolic and substantive cooperation. *Strategic Management Journal*, 31: 575–601.

Delmas, M. A. and Toffel, M. W. 2008. Organizational responses to environmental demands: Opening the black box. *Strategic Management Journal*, 29: 1027–1055.

Desjardins, M. 2018. Under Pressure or Fairly Valued? The Effects of Security Analyst Coverage on Firm Investment Horizon. Paper presented at the *Eighth Gronen Research Conference*, Almeria, Spain, June 13th to 16th.

DiMaggio, P. J. and Powell, W. W. 1983. The iron cage revisited: Institutional isomorphism and collective rationality in organizational fields. *American Sociological Review*, 48(2): 147–160.

Dutton, J. E. and Dukerich, J. M. 1991. Keeping an eye on the mirror: Image and identity in organizational adaptation. *Academy of Management Journal*, 34(3): 517–554.

Dyer Jr., W. G. and Whetten, D. A. 2006. Family firms and social responsibility: Preliminary evidence from the S&P 500. *Entrepreneurship Theory and Practice*, November 30(6): 785–802.

Egri, C. P. and Herman, S. 2000. Leadership in the North American environmental sector: Values, leadership styles, and contexts of environmental leaders and their organizations. *Academy of Management Journal*, 43: 571–604.

Eisenhardt, K. M. and Martin, J. A. 2000. Dynamic capabilities: What are they? *Strategic Management Journal*, 21: 1105–1121.

Elkington, J. 1994. Towards the sustainable corporation: Win-win-win business strategies for sustainable development. California Management Review, Winter: 90–100.

Gavetti, G. 2005. Cognition and hierarchy: Rethinking the microfoundations of capabilities's development. *Organization Science*, 16(6): 599–617.

Gersick, K. E., Davis, J. A., Hampton, M. M. and Lansberg, I. 1997. *Generation to Generation: Life Cycles of the Family Business*. Boston, MA: Harvard Business School Press.

Giddens, A. 1984. *The Constitution of Society: Outline of the Theory of Structuration*. Berkeley, CA: University of California Press.

Gladwin, T. N., Kennelly, J. J. and Krause, T. S. 1995. Shifting paradigms for sustainable development: Implications for management theory and research. *Academy of Management Review*, 20: 874–907.

Gomez-Mejia, L. R., Takacs, K. H., Nunez-Nickel, M. and Jacobson, K. J. L. 2007. Socioemotional wealth and business risks in family-controlled firms: Evidence from Spanish olive oil mills. *Administrative Science Quarterly*, 52: 106–137.

Graves, S. B. and Waddock, S. A. 1994. Institutional Owners and Corporate Social Performance. *Academy of Management Journal*, 37(4): 1034–1046.

Greening, D. W. and Gray, B. 1994. Testing a model of organizational response to social and political issues. *Academy of Management Journal*, 37(3): 467–498.

Habbershon, T. G. and Williams, M. L. 1999. A resource-based framework for assessing the strategic advantages of family firms, *Family Business Review*, 12(1): 1–22

Hart, S. L. 1995. A natural-resource-based view of the firm. *Academy of Management Review*, 20: 874–907.

Hart, S. L. and Ahuja, G. 1996. Does it pay be green? An empirical examination of the relationship between emission reduction and firm performance. *Business Strategy and the Environment*, 5: 30–37.

Hart, S. L. and Sharma, S. 2004. Engaging fringe stakeholders for competitive imagination. *Academy of Management Executive*, 18(1): 7–18.

Helfat, C. E. and Peteraf, M. A. 2003. The dynamic resource-based view: Capability lifecycles. *Strategic Management Journal*, 24: 997–1010.

Hillman, A. J., Keim, G. D. and Luce, R. A. 2001. Board composition and stakeholder performance: Do stakeholder directors make a difference? *Business & Society*, 40(3): 295–314.

Hunt, C. B. and Auster, E. R. 1990. Proactive environmental management: Avoiding the toxic trap. *Sloan Management Review*, 31(2): 7–18.

Hoy, F. and Sharma, P. 2010. *Entrepreneurial Family Firms*. Upper Saddle River, NJ: Pearson Prentice Hall.

Ibrahim, N. A., Howard, D. P. and Angelidis, J. P. 2003. Board members in the service industry: An empirical examination of the relationship between corporate social responsibility orientation and directorial type. *Journal of Business Ethics*, 47(4): 393–401.

Jaffe, A. B., Peterson, S. R., Portney, P. R. and Stavins, R. N. 1995. Environmental regulation and the competitiveness of U.S. manufacturing: What does the evidence tell us? *Journal of Economic Literature*, 33: 132–163.

Johnson, R. A. and Greening, D. W. 1999. The effects of corporate governance and institutional ownership types on corporate social performance. *Academy of Management Journal*, 42(5): 564–576.

Judge, W. Q. and Douglas, T. J. 1998. Performance implications of incorporating natural environmental issues into the strategic planning process: An empirical assessment. *Journal of Management Studies*, 35: 241–262.

Kahneman, D. and Tversky, A. 1979. Prospect theory. *Econometrica*, 47(2): 263–292.

Kammerlander, N., Dessi, C., Bird, M., Floris, M. and Murru, A. 2015. The impact of shared stories on family firm innovation. *Family Business Review*, 28(4): 332–354.

Kassinis, G. and Vafeas, N. 2006. Stakeholder performance and environmental performance. *Academy of Management Journal*, 49(1): 145–159.

Kell G. and Lacy, P. 2010. Sustainability a priority for CEOs. *Business Week*, 25 June. www.businessweek.com/managing/content/jun2010/c a20100624_678038.ht (accessed September 16, 2015).

Kellermanns, F. W. and Eddleston, K. 2004. Feuding families: When conflict does a family firm good. *Entrepreneurship Theory and Practice*, 28(3): 209–228.

Kellermanns, F. W., and Eddleston, K. 2006. Corporate venturing in family firms: Does the family matter? *Entrepreneurship Theory and Practice*, 30 (6): 809–830.

Klassen, R. D. and McLaughlin, C. P. 1996. The impact of environmental management on firm performance. *Management Science*, 42: 1199–1214.

Klassen, R. D. and Whybark, D. C. 1999. The impact of environmental technologies on manufacturing performance. *Academy of Management Journal*, 42: 599–615.

Kolk, A. 2008. Sustainability, accountability and corporate governance: Exploring multinationals' reporting practices. *Business Strategy and Environment*, 17(1): 1–15.

Kolluru, R. V., ed. 1994. *Environmental Strategies Handbook*, New York: McGraw Hill.

Lansberg. I. 1999. *Succeeding Generations*. Boston, MA: Harvard Business School Press.

Lawrence, P. R. and Lorsch, J. W. 1967. *Organization and Environment: Managing Differentiation and Integration*. Boston, MA: Harvard Business School Press.

Leana, C. R. and Van Buren, H. J. 1999. Organizational social capital and employment practices. *Academy of Management Review*, 24: 538–555.

Levy, D. L. 1995. The environmental practices and performances of transnational corporations. *Transnational Corporations*, 4(1): 44–67.

Lumpkin, G. T., Martin, W. and Vaughn, M. 2008. Family orientation: Individual-level influences on family firm outcomes. *Family Business Review*, 21(2): 127–138.

Luoma, P. and Goodstein, J. 1999. Stakeholders and corporate boards: institutional influences on board composition and structure. *Academy of Management Journal*, 42(5): 553–563.

Lyman, A. R. 1991. Customer service: Does family ownership make a difference? *Family Business Review*, 4(3): 303–324.

Madsen, P. M. K. 2009. Does corporate investment drive a "race to the bottom" in environmental protection? A reexamination of the effect of environmental regulation on investment. *Academy of Management Journal*, 52(6): 1297–1318.

Magretta, J. 1997. Growth through global sustainability: An interview with Monsanto's CEO, Robert B. Shapiro. *Harvard Business Review*, 75(1): 78–88.

Mahoney, L. S. and Thorne, L. 2005. Corporate social responsibility and long-term compensation: Evidence from Canada. *Journal of Business Ethics*, 57: 241–253.

Marcus, A. A. and Geffen, D. 1998. The dialectics of competency acquisition: Pollution prevention in electric generation. *Strategic Management Journal*, 19: 1145–1168.

Marcus. A. A. and Nichols, M. L. 1999. On the edge: Heeding the warnings of unusual events. *Organization Science*, 10: 482–499.

McEvily, B. and Marcus, A. 2005. Embedded ties and the acquisition of competitive capabilities. *Strategic Management Journal*, 26: 1033–1055.

McKendall, M., Sanchez, C. and Sicilian, P. 1999. Corporate governance and corporate illegality: The effects of board structure on environmental violations. *International Journal of Organizational Analysis*, 7(3): 201–223.

Miles, R. E and Snow, C. C. 1978. *Organization Strategy, Structure, and Process*. New York: McGraw-Hill.

Miller, D. and Le Breton-Miller, I. 2005. *Managing for the Long Run: Lessons in Competitive Advantage from Great Family Businesses*. Boston, MA: Harvard Business School Press.

Milliken, F. J. 1987. Three types of perceived uncertainty about the environment: State, effect and response uncertainty. *Academy of Management Review*, 12: 133–143.

Nahapiet, J. and Ghoshal, S. 1998. Social capital, intellectual capital, and the organizational advantage. *Academy of Management Review*, 23(2): 242–266.

Nehrt, C. 1996. Timing and intensity effects of environmental investments. *Strategic Management Journal*, 17: 535–547.

Nehrt, C. 1998. Maintainability of first mover advantages when environmental regulations differ between countries. *Academy of Management Review*, 23: 77–97.

Neubaum, D. O. and Zahra, S. A. 2006. Institutional ownership and corporate social performance: the moderating effects of investment horizon, activism, and coordination. *Journal of Management*, 32(1): 108–131.

Pearson, A. W., Carr, J. C. and Shaw, J. C. 2008. Toward a theory of familiness: A social capital perspective. *Entrepreneurship Theory and Practice*, 32(6): 949–969.

Porter, M. E. 1980. *Competitive strategy: Techniques for analyzing industries and competitors*. New York: The Free Press.

Porter, M. E. 1991. America's green strategy. *Scientific American*, April: 168.

Porter, M.E. and van der Linde, C. 1995. Green and competitive. *Harvard Business Review*, Sept–Oct: 120–134, 196.

Post, J. E. 1991. Managing as if the Earth mattered. *Business Horizons*, 34 (4): 32–38.

Post, J. E. and Altman, B. W. 1992. Models of corporate greening: How corporate social policy and organizational learning inform leading-edge environmental management. In J. E. Post and I. E. Preston (eds.), *Research in Corporate Social Performance and Policy*, pp. 3–30. Greenwich, CT: JAI Press.

Priem, R. L. and Butler, J. E. 2001. Is the resource-based "view" a useful perspective for strategic management research? *Academy of Management Review*, 26(1): 22–40.

Purser, R. E., Park, C. and Montuori, A. 1995. Limits to anthropocentrims: Toward an ecocentric organization paradigms. *Academy of Management Review*, 20: 1053–1089.

Ramus, C. A. and Steger, U. 2000. The Roles of Supervisory Support Behaviors and Environmental Policy in Employee "Ecoinitiatives" at Leading-Edge European Companies. *Academy of Management Journal*, 43(4): 606–625.

Rondinelli, D. A. and London, T. 2003. How corporations and environmental groups cooperate: Assessing cross-sector alliances and collaborations. *Academy of Management Executive*, 17(1): 61–76.

Roome, N., 1992. Developing environmental management strategies. *Business Strategy and the Environment*, 1: 11–24.

Rugman, A. M. and Verbeke, A. 1998. Corporate strategies and environmental regulations: An organizing framework. *Strategic Management Journal*, 19(4): 363–375.

Russo, M. V. and Fouts, P. A. 1997. A resource-based perspective on corporate environmental performance and profitability. *Academy of Management Journal*, 40: 534–559.

Salvato, C., Chirico, F. and Sharma, P. 2010. A farewell to the business: Championing exit and continuity in entrepreneurial family firms. *Entrepreneurial and Regional Development*, 22: 321–348.

Schmidheiny, S. 1992. *Changing Course: A Global Business Perspective on Development and the Environment*. Cambridge, MA: MIT Press.

Sharfman, M. P. and Fernando, C. S. 2008. Environmental risk management and the cost of capital. *Strategic Management Journal*, 29: 569–592.

Sharma, P. and Irving, G. 2005. Four bases of family business successor commitment: Antecedents and consequences. *Entrepreneurship Theory and Practice*, 29(1): 13–33.

Sharma, P. and Sharma, S. 2011. Drivers of Proactive Environmental Strategy in Family Firms. *Business Ethics Quarterly*, 21(2): 309–332.

Sharma, S. 2014. *Competing for a Sustainable World: Building Capacity for Sustainable Innovation.* Greenleaf Publishing, UK.

Sharma, S. 2000. Managerial interpretations and organizational context as predictors of corporate choice of environmental strategy. *Academy of Management Journal*, 43: 681–697.

Sharma, S. and Henriques, I. 2005. Stakeholder influences on sustainability practices in the Canadian forest products industry. *Strategic Management Journal*, 26: 159–180.

Sharma, S, Pablo. A. and Vredenburg, H. 1999. Corporate environmental responsiveness strategies: The role of issue interpretation and organizational context. *Journal of Applied Behavioral Science*, 35(1): 87–109.

Sharma, S. and Vredenburg, H. 1998. Proactive corporate environmental strategy and the development of competitively valuable organizational capabilities. *Strategic Management Journal*, 19: 729–753.

Shrivastava, P. 1994. CASTRATED environment: GREENING organizational studies. *Organization Studies*, 15: 705–726.

Shrivastava, P. 1995a. Ecocentric management for a risk society. *Academy of Management Review*, 20: 118–137.

Shrivastava, P. 1995b. Environmental technologies and competitive advantage. *Strategic Management Journal*, 16: 183–200.

Shrivastava, P. 1995c. The role of corporations in achieving ecological sustainability. *Academy of Management Review*, 20(4): 936–960.

Shrivastava, P. and Kennelly, J. J. 2013. Sustainability and place based enterprise. *Organization & Environment*, 26(1): 83–101.

Sirmon, D. G. and Hitt, M. A. 2003. Managing resources: Linking unique resources, management and wealth creation in family firms. *Entrepreneurship Theory and Practice*, 27: 339–358.

Slawinski, N. and Bansal, P. 2012. A matter of time: The temporal perspectives of organizational responses to climate change. *Organization Studies*, 33(11): 1537–1563.

Sorenson, R. L. and Bierman, L. 2009. Family capital, family business, and free enterprise. *Family Business Review*, 22(3): 193–195.

Sorenson, R. L., Goodpaster, K. E., Hedberg, P. R. and Yu, A. 2009. The family point of view, family social capital, and firm performance. *Family Business Review*, 22(3): 239–253.

Stanwick, P. A. and Stanwick, S. D. 1998. The relationship between corporate social performance, and organizational size, financial performance and environmental performance: an empirical examination. *Journal of Business Ethics*, 17(2): 195–204.

Stanwick, P. A. and Stanwick, S. D. 2001. CEO compensation: Does it pay to be green? *Business Strategy and Environment*, 10: 176–182.

Tapies, J. and Ward, J. L. 2008. *Family Values and Value Creation: The Fostering of Enduring Values within Family-Owned Businesses*. New York: Palgrave Macmillan.

Tokarczyk, J., Hansen, E., Gree, M. and Down, J. 2007. A resource based view and market orientation theory examination of the role of "familiness" in family business success. *Family Business Review*, 20(1): 17–31.

Walley, N. and Whitehead, B. 1994. It's not easy being green. *Harvard Business Review*, May–June: 46–52.

Walls, J. L., Berrone, P. and Phan, P. H. 2012. Corporate governance and environmental performance: Is there really a link? *Strategic Management Journal*, 33: 885–913.

Wang, J. and Dewhirst, H. D. 1992. Boards of directors and stakeholder orientation. *Journal of Business Ethics*, 11: 115–123.

Ward, J. J. 1987. *Keeping the Family Business Healthy*. San Francisco: Jossey-Bass.

Ward, J. J. 1991. *Creating Effective Boards for Private Enterprises: Meeting the Challenges of Continuity and Competition*. San Francisco: Jossey-Bass.

Ward, J. L. 2005. *Unconventional Wisdom: Counterintuitive Insights for Family Business Success*. West Sussex, UK: John Wiley and Sons.

Webb, E. 2004. An examination of socially responsible board structure. *Journal of Management and Governance*, 8(3): 255–277.

Wernerfelt, B. 1984. A resource-based view of the firm. *Strategic Management Journal*, 5: 171–180.

Zott, C. 2003. Dynamic capabilities and the emergence of intraindustry differential firm performance: Insights from a simulation study. *Strategic Management Journal*, 24: 97–125.

5 | Managerial Drivers of Environmental Sustainability Strategy

A firm's managers and employees play a critical and central role in interpreting the exogenous and endogenous influences that were discussed in Chapters 3 and 4, and in implementing the firm's environmental sustainability strategy. Individuals, rather than organizations, interpret the external institutional forces and stakeholder pressures. Managers, individually or working in teams, implement the organizational strategy and their actions are influenced by organizational governance, structure, and leadership. Most critically, organizational capabilities reside within individuals and teams of organizational employees interacting with organizational processes and systems. An organization cannot change unless the behavior of its employees changes. Organizations cannot learn unless its employees learn and embed this learning, creating organizational memory, and, hence, sparking creative ideas and innovation.

Creative ideas for sustainable products, services, processes, and business models are generated by a firm's managers and not by the abstract legal entity, the firm. The firm can facilitate idea generation via leadership, culture, and the creation of appropriate organizational incentives and resources for innovation. A firm's managers have the most interaction with, and, hence, the most intimate understanding of, the firm's business, customers, processes, and capabilities. At the same time, the managers' decisions are influenced not only by institutional forces, stakeholders, and organizational governance and leadership but also by their personal values toward sustainability (Bansal, 2003), attitudes toward their roles in solving environmental sustainability challenges (Cordano and Frieze, 2000), cognitive frames as pragmatic or paradoxical (Hahn et al., 2014), interpretations of environmental issues as threats or opportunities (Sharma, 2000; Sharma, Pablo and Vredenburg, 1999), and risk propensity for undertaking creative sustainability strategies (Sharma and Nguan, 1999).

In their day-to-day work, managers tend to remain locked into everyday routines, patterns of thinking, and cognitive biases that may stifle creativity. Moreover, many firms do not unleash the creative potential of their employees and tend to compartmentalize and assign the creative process to a small group of people, often in the research and development function. Firms that are able to develop successful PES strategies are those that create the opportunities for all or most employees to apply fresh ideas and strategic thinking to address sustainability challenges and environmental and social impacts of their business by enabling them to overcome their biases and everyday routines. In such organizations, empirical research points to the role of leadership vision and values (Egri and Herman, 2000), supervisors (Ramus and Steger, 2000), and organizational design including legitimization of sustainability in corporate identity, incentives, and control systems, information availability, and cross-functional coordination (Sharma, 2000; Sharma, Pablo and Vredenburg, 1999).

While family business literature has yet to examine the organizational context for managerial decision-making for a sustainable strategy, the literature argues that family firms have some unique features that influence strategic decision-making by managers (which includes the family members) differently as compared to non-family firms. These unique features will undergird the discussions in this chapter about if, and how, will managers in family firms that aim for transgenerational continuity of their enterprise will make decisions differently when addressing environmental issues.

- First, decision-making is significantly influenced by the values, attitudes, and beliefs of the family members that control the firm, especially the members of the dominant coalition (DC). Firms with aligned values among members of the top management team are likely to make quicker decisions and progress on disruptive initiatives such as those needed to embrace proactive sustainability strategy (PES).
- Second, shared values, attitudes, and beliefs are imprinted in the firm at its founding, and transmitted from parents to children not only in the context of workplace but also in family and social situations. Thus, they are embedded deep in the mind-sets of family members, thereby influencing their interpretations of context and opportunity or risk (Cabrera-Suárez, De Saá-Pérez and García-Almeida, 2001).

- Third, family firms are interested in long-term survival of their business via succession to the next generation(s). Hence, they are willing to make decisions oriented toward patient long-term investments in new businesses, products, and capabilities (Miller and Le Breton-Miller, 2006).
- Fourth, while transmission of knowledge during succession may lead to the decision-making biases of one generation being passed on to another generation, it is less likely if a family firm maintains an entrepreneurial mind-set focused on the long-term development of the next generation's human capital resources, the interpersonal and network influences on that developmental process, and the social capital resources provided by the family firm (Cabrera-Suárez, García-Almeida and De Saá-Pérez, 2018; Cohen and Sharma, 2016).
- Fifth, the entrepreneurial mind-set facilitates the succeeding family generation's continuance of developing new networks and knowledge relevant for decision-making in the changing business and societal environment (Nordqvist et al., 2013). Hence, the innovative family firm enables a focus not only on exploitation of knowledge passed on from senior generations but also on fostering exploration of knowledge for innovations by the next generation (Cabrera-Suárez et al., 2018; Goel and Jones, 2016).

This chapter discusses how managerial values, attitudes, interpretations, and biases influence their decision-making to address sustainability challenges and how firms can create the context to enable managers to overcome their locked-in thought patterns, cognitive frames and biases, and habitual behavior to apply creative thinking in order to develop proactive sustainability practices and strategies (PES). In addition to implementing such strategies, managers can also act as catalysts of sustainability strategies by championing environmental initiatives (Andersson and Bateman, 2000). As champions, they sell environmental issues upward to the firm's leadership, laterally to their peers, and downward to their subordinates (Howard-Grenville, 2007; Sharma, 2000). In family firms, family members and managers have additional pathways and opportunities to influence others via family members not involved in the ownership or management of the business but with significant power within the family circle.

In this chapter, we begin by outlining empirical research in the corporate sustainability literature on the influence of managerial values and attitudes on decision-making to address sustainability challenges, the biases that inhibit motivations for sustainability initiatives, and strategies to be undertaken by managers. We then discuss how various leadership and organizational design variables can address these inhibitions. Similar research in the family business literature focused on sustainability issues is limited and hence we will draw on general strategic decision-making literature in family business and our primary data from the winery industry in Canada, France, and Chile, to illustrate how family firms differ in motivating managerial creativity for sustainable innovation.

The Influence of Managerial Values, Attitudes, and Interpretations

The corporate sustainability literature has long argued for the significant relationship between the values of a firm's decision-making coalition (TMT in a non-family firm or DC in a family firm) and its engagement in proactive environmental strategy (Hart, 1995). Moreover, if managers have personal values about social justice and environmental preservation, and if these values are matched by a firm's values or mission, then it is more likely that the managers will make decisions to view the firm as a vehicle to address the sustainability issues that interface with the firm's operations (Bansal, 2003).

Decision-making by managers is also influenced by their self-evaluations about their ability to influence sustainability practices (Sonenshein, DeCelles and Dutton, 2014). That is, managers need to believe that they can really make a difference via their decisions and actions. Sonenshein et al. (2014) found that managers' self-evaluations were shaped by cognitive, relational, and organizational challenges that individuals interpreted about a sustainability issue from the domain of work and also from personal domains of home or school. These authors found that even among the most dedicated sustainability supporters, self-doubts played an important role in their experiences. However, these self-doubts could be enabling or damaging, depending on the managers' individual experiences and domains.

Managerial values or belief systems are deeply ingrained and difficult to change. Often, rather than trying to change the embedded values of long-term employees, large non-family firms attempt major cultural changes through recruitment policies to develop intellectual capital with values that are congruent with their own. As compared to the leadership in non-family firms, the family's values and beliefs are likely to have a more enduring and tenacious influence on the shared vision and strategic direction of a firm. This is due to a combination of the firm's architecture (vision, structure, and processes) chosen at its inception, long tenures of leaders, and the alignment of ownership and management that facilitates the pursuit of values held by the controlling family. This influence is accentuated by the significant ties – at times extending over generations – of employees with the family (Miller and Le Breton-Miller, 2005). Taken together these factors create a ripe environment for an enduring influence of family values on the firm (Tapies and Ward, 2008).

The "family-of-origin" into which one is born or adopted at a young age offers unique opportunities, over several years and instances, to imbue parental values into family members (Cohen and Sharma, 2016; Hoy and Sharma, 2010). As the same family continues to control the business over generations, the unification of family values with the guiding policies of the firm become deeply rooted and resilient (Sorenson et al., 2009). Research has revealed the significant impact of family values on the nature of relationships of the family business with the community and its key stakeholders, as well as on multiple dimensions of success and performance of family firms (Basco and Rodriguez, 2009; Danes et al., 2009; Sorenson and Bierman, 2009). There is sufficient evidence that family members in the decision-making DC are significantly influenced by their personal values and family values via informal and social interactions outside the workplace (Cohen and Sharma, 2016; Hoy and Sharma, 2010). Hence, there is a greater likelihood that managers and family members in family firms will bring personal and family values and beliefs into their decision-making as compared to managers in non-family firms.

While employees of a family firm have a higher likelihood of value congruence with the DC and family beliefs and values are likely to have significantly stronger influence on the strategy of a family firm as compared to non-family firms, it is important to recognize that family business scholars have observed significant variation within family businesses in terms of their beliefs and values regarding the role of family in business and that of business in family (Basco and Rodriguez, 2009; Ward, 1987). Therefore, one can also expect family firms to vary regarding their core beliefs and values not only about the urgency to take action to preserve the environment, but also regarding the role of private business in such preservation efforts. Thus, family firms may vary in the type of environmental strategy they pursue.

The differences of values between family and non-family firms toward environmental preservation are illustrated via the following quotes from family members in all three regions we studied.

The head of the first generation of the multi-family firm environmentally proactive Nirvana winery in the Okanagan Valley, Canada:

No one is asking us to adopt organic or biodynamic practices ... Why do we do it? Because we care for the land and what we put into our bodies.

The second-generation family member who owns Sunnyvale winery in the Okanagan Valley in Canada:

My father always says that for our family co-existing with the land as a healthy ecosystem is as important as running a business.

The fourth generation family member of Viña De Martino in Chile:

The De Martino family have lived on this land for over 80 years. Our stewardship for the land is an integral part of our business operating philosophy.

The first-generation founder of Chateau Duvivier in La Provence, France:

Some wineries are trying to convert to organic or biodynamic practices after operating with a traditional chemical focused system for decades. For us, the winery business is not worth running unless we have a thriving and resilient ecosystem.

Among non-family firms that have adopted a PES, the winery manager of Vina Santa Rita in Chile did not reflect values or beliefs for environmental preservation but rather a market-oriented corporate philosophy:

Our company has a goal of becoming the largest seller of organic wines by 2025. We are in the process of adopting organic practices in our vineyards and are acquiring two more organic vineyards this year and are well on our way to achieving this goal

According to the Directeur Général of Chateau Soutard owned by the French insurance company La Mondiele, another non-family firm with a PES,

Many of the best award-winning wines from the Bordeaux region are coming from biodynamic vineyards. All three vineyards owned by the company are being converted to biodynamic viticulture to enhance our quality and market appeal.

These quotes provide a clear distinction between the values-driven approach toward a PES by family firms and a market-driven approach toward PES by a non-family firm. However, it is important to recognize that we conducted case studies within a convenience sample and we did examine family firms who did not have values favoring environmental preservation (e.g., Europa and Northshore in Nova Scotia, Canada, and Hannibal in the Okanagan Valley, among others) and there were also non-family firms that favored environmental preservation (e.g., Vina Indomita). While we agree, on the one hand, that there will be many more family firms that do not favor a PES, and, on the other, many non-family firms that will develop a PES, our hypothesis is that family firms will be more likely to have the long-term orientation necessary for sustainable innovation for a PES.

Cognitive Frames and Biases

Developing a proactive environmental sustainability strategy requires managers to creatively develop actions, tactics, practices, products, services, processes, and business models that deliver value on economic and environmental metrics. Therefore, managers have to incorporate environmental impacts and performance outcomes in addition to economic outcomes in their decisions, increasing the complexity of problem solving. Further, managers also lack complete information about the firm's environmental impacts and which organizational actions will affect these outcomes. This creates risk, complexity, ambiguity, and uncertainty in decision-making.

Hahn, Preuss, Pinkse, and Figge (2014) argued that, in making decisions to address the complexity and ambiguity presented by sustainability challenges, managers frame sustainability issues either pragmatically or paradoxically. Those who frame sustainability issues pragmatically attempt to reconcile conflicts and contradictions between economic and environmental outcomes. Those who frame sustainability issues paradoxically accept the complexity that sustainability poses for an organization and the tensions, conflicts, and tradeoffs between these three dimensions. Their theory argues that managers with a pragmatic business-focused frame or stance will favor responses of limited scope (e.g., eco-efficiency approaches of reducing wastes, energy use, recycling of packaging, or reducing inputs for pollution reduction) to sustainability challenges, based on established routines and practices. These managers will be more aware of the risks to economic performance of adopting sustainability practices. On the other hand, managers who adopt a paradoxical frame will favor more radical and bolder responses (e.g., reformulation of products, radical change of processes, or changing the business model for pollution prevention) to sustainability issues but may not follow through with corresponding decisions and practices because they may be hampered by ambivalence and prudence in the organizational context. Hahn et al. (2014) speculate that while managers with paradoxical frames may be better at pioneering thinking about actions to address sustainability challenges, these managers are unlikely to succeed without help from managers with pragmatic frames who can reduce the complexity of sustainability issues to enable successful implementation. They argue for mixed teams of managers with different cognitive frames to address sustainability challenges.

Along similar lines, family business researchers have noted the inherent need to incorporate the dualities and objectives of a family and an economic system in goal setting and decision-making (Kotlar and De Massis, 2013). Thus, paradoxical decision-making lies at the core of these firms, though not all family firms are able to successfully negotiate this decision-making frame, finding themselves tilted too much toward either economic or family decisions. Those that successfully do manage this duality enjoy higher performance on business and family dimensions (Basco and Rodriguez, 2009).

Facing increased complexity, ambiguity, and uncertainty, managers are more likely to default toward perceiving the need to balance difficult-to-measure environmental metrics with well-honed and developed economic metrics as a threat to their everyday operations rather than as an opportunity (Sharma, 2000; Sharma et al., 1999). The more rapidly the external business environment changes in terms of societal demands for greater responsiveness by business to environmental sustainability challenges, the more likely managers are to see this as a challenge and threat to their everyday routines and decision-making. Since innovation requires the quick and timely seizing of opportunities, managers who view external changes as threats will be less likely to develop any creative responses or solutions to sustainability challenges.

Being engaged in repetitious daily routines, managers often tend to default toward applying standard solutions and using rules of thumb to tackle emerging issues and problems. Their tendency is to resort to decision-making based on automatic responses that require limited concentration and effort. Thus, during day-to-day operations, managers make decisions based on established heuristics without giving enough thought to the uniqueness of the specific problem or issue (Tversky and Kahneman, 1974). Further, in such everyday decisions, managers tend to rely mainly on available and easily accessible information. They usually do not undertake the effort to conduct research to develop a full set of alternatives based on complete information. Thus, managers who are often pressed for time not only adopt rules of thumb but also extrapolate from personal experience and anecdotes, and overweigh dramatic and salient events while underweighing rare events. Hence, such automatic decisions do not lead to choices that managers need to evaluate in order to analyze different courses of action and the implications of these courses of action for a firm's sustainability performance.

Innovative thinking requires breaking out of routine everyday patterns for decisions that are effortful; based on exercising cognitive stress, focus, and concentration; and engaging of the mind. Such decisions lead to choices and evaluation of alternatives to determine the most effective actions rather than automatic responses that managers make every day (Tversky and Kahneman, 1974). When managers have to make decisions to simultaneously deliver environmental and economic value, significant cognitive stress is required. Kahneman and Tversky (1984) conducted several experiments to show how managers routinely make decisions without cognitive stress. In order for firms to make appropriate changes in their organizations to foster creative thinking and innovation, they must first understand why managers make biased decisions. Based on the work done by Kahneman and Tversky, the most common sources of managerial decision bias are the following.

Halo Effects

In the absence of cognitive stress that may lead to the generation of creative and new alternatives, it is common for managers to be influenced by first impressions, limiting debate and discussion. Managers' personal likes and dislikes often influence decisions for an opportunity. Influence by first impressions is known as halo effect or halo error (Thorndike, 1920). This effect has been shown in multiple contexts and situations in experiments over the past several decades. If managers have to exercise cognitive stress to develop deep understanding of how to apply sustainable logic to innovate products, services, processes, and business models that deliver value to customers, investors, society, and the environment, firms need to provide the space and opportunity for managers not only to develop but to evaluate complete information so that they do not make decisions based on first impressions or the most salient data. *The halo bias may be more pronounced in family businesses depending on the prevailing values (positive or negative) toward environmental preservation of the dominant coalition.* That is, if the dominant coalition of the family, particularly those senior in familial hierarchy, favor environmental protection, managers will automatically make decisions that will generate ideas and solutions for patient investments in projects that lead to a PES. If the DC has values and beliefs that do not favour environmental protection or the role of business in this protection, the halo effect will be related to the prevailing philosophy of short-term profit maximization or survival. The following quotes are illustrative:

A fourth -generation family member of Viña De Martino responsible for the biodynamic viticulture in the vineyards stated:

The consumer who buys and consumes our wine is not just drinking our wine, he is sharing in the DeMartino family passion for quality wine and ecosystem stewardship.

A second-generation family member of the Guillard family who is just entering the business explained:

Our family believes strongly that we must become stewards of the ecosystems and communities if we have to survive into the future.

In contrast, a halo effect was demonstrated by the reactive firms' managers as well, but this halo effect did not favour a PES. A quote from the winemaker of the Skyline winery, a part of a larger corporate non-family winery in the Okanagan Valley in Canada is repeated here:

[T]he focus has been on product quality and production yields as per the group's policy of compliance with regulations and adopting the most efficient production practices.

Similarly, the following quote repeated from Chapter 4 from the CEO of Bird's Nest, a Canadian corporate non-family winery in the Okanagan Valley:

Our focus on quality in order to generate consumer loyalty. We achieve this quality by complying with all regulations and being a responsible company. Producing organic wine is a personal preference that some wine owners have that I am sure they are willing to pay for in low grape yields and unpredictable quality. (underline added to show the dominant bias against organic practices)

As is evidenced by some of the other quotes earlier in this chapter, the halo effect that influences auto-pilot decision-making by managers is focused on ecosystem stewardship in other family firms such as Landjoy, Nirvana, and Chateau Duvivier.

Anchoring Effects
Anchoring bias occurs when individuals use an initial piece of information to make subsequent judgments. The initial information becomes the anchor around which other judgments are made by adjusting away from that anchor. There is then a bias in interpreting other information around the anchor. For example, the initial asking price for a used automobile sets the standard for the rest of the negotiations, so that prices lower than the initial price seem more reasonable even if they are still higher than what the auto is really worth. This decision bias, identified by Kahneman and Tversky (1979) found that individuals are overly reliant on a specific piece of information or a reference point to govern their thought process. Once the anchor or reference point is set, there is a bias toward adjusting or interpreting other information to reflect the anchored information. The anchor can affect future decision-making and information analysis.

In family firms, this bias may extend to the source of information. For example, if a successful incumbent leader holds a particular bias toward PES, other members of DC may choose to remain silent given their regard for contributions by this individual. Thus, decisions may be delayed not because some members of the DC are unaware or unconvinced but out of respect for those in power positions.

In making decisions on sustainability issues, managers may anchor decisions on widely differing notions of existence or extent of climate change, acceptable carbon dioxide emissions, extent of deforestation or endangered species, or the degree to which water resources are secure and clean. For example, in terms of water quality and availability for vineyards in Chile, managers have differing anchor points for decision-making.

The director of the non-family firm, Vina Santa Rita on water resources in the Maipo Valley, Chile:

We are blessed with water that will last hundreds of years. That has been the basis of rapid growth of the winery industry and fruit exports from Chile. Our abundant water resources will be the basis of our growth in the future.

The fourth-generation family member, vineyard manager of Viña De Martino, commenting on the same water resources in the Maipo Valley:

Chile has excellent water management and equitable distribution system. It is our responsibility to be vigilant and work with the government and local communities to make sure that this system does not break down so that we can be sustainable into the long-term future.

Clearly, the managers of the corporate winery Santa Rita operate with an anchoring bias that water resources are unlimited and they can grow without constraints. The managers of De Martino operate with an anchoring bias that water resources are well managed rather than unlimited and, hence, need stewardship and engagement with stakeholders to ensure long-term sustainability.

Loss Bias

Kahneman and Tversky are most well known for their work on prospect theory which relates to loss bias. Daniel Kahneman won the 2002 Nobel Prize for Economic Sciences primarily for this work. Prospect theory describes how individuals choose between alternatives that involve risk; that is, where the probabilities of outcomes are known. Kahneman and Tversky (1979) and Tversky and Kahneman (1986) argued that people make decisions based on the potential value of losses and gains rather than the final outcome. Their research confirmed in different contexts that, in general, possible losses loom twice as large as possible gains and managers usually tend to stick with the status quo to avoid potential loss. For example, people tended to overweigh the 10 percent probability of mortality a month after a surgery and underweigh the identical 90 percent probability of survival a month after that surgery.

This loss aversion is even more significant in family firms as leaders of these firms ascribe more value to the accumulated financial and affective endowments of their firms in the form of control and close identification with the firm. When such assets are at risk, they have been found to be willing to forgo significant financial gains to preserve their socioemotional wealth (Gomez-Mejia et al., 2007). Although the TMT of non-family firms might experience this as well, the intrinsic socioemotional value of a firm is not likely to be as intense (Gomez-Mejia et al., 2011).

In the context of developing an environmental strategy, it has been empirically shown that when managers interpreted environmental issues as a threat, their firm was likely to adopt a reactive environmental strategy that focused on minimum legal compliance and pollution control; and when managers interpreted environmental issues as opportunities, their firm was likely to adopt a proactive environmental strategy that included pollution prevention and clean technologies (Sharma, 2000). This research by Sharma (2000) also showed that when managers viewed environmental issues as threats, they also viewed them as negative, as a source of potential loss to their performance on the job and to their organizational performance, and as uncontrollable. On the other hand, when they viewed environmental issues as opportunities, they viewed them as positive, as a source of potential gain for their performance on the job and for their organizational performance, and as controllable (Sharma, 2000; Sharma et al., 1999).

Overweighing of losses also leads to the strengthening of sunk-cost bias by managers. Sunk costs are costs that have already been incurred and cannot be recovered. Rational decision-making would dictate that only prospective (future) costs are relevant to an investment decision. Rational managers should not allow sunk costs to influence their decisions. However, research has shown that such costs do influence managerial decision-making due to loss aversion.

For example, many individuals tend to hold on to equity stocks long after their values have fallen to irrecoverable levels, in the hope that prices will rise again.

Thus, as managers face the prospect of having to make more complex decisions that require consideration of not only economic but also social and environmental metrics, it is likely that they will view these decisions as negative, a source of loss, and uncontrollable. Left on their own and facing the demands of everyday routines, managers will be very unlikely to exercise cognitive stress (thinking differently as compared to routine everyday patterns) in decisions. Rather, firms have to create the white space (Maletz and Nohria, 2001), the opportunities, and the incentives for more effortful and thoughtful decision-making in everyday workflow to generate alternate choices.

Managerial interpretation of environmental issues as threats versus opportunities and the linkage of such interpretations to the firm's strategy was abundantly clear during our interviews in the winery industry. This adds to the empirical evidence in the corporate sustainability literature (Sharma, 2000; Sharma et al, 1999).

While Table 5.1 is based on a convenience sample of wineries, it supports extant rigorous empirical evidence that establishes the link between threat versus opportunity perception and reactive versus proactive environmental strategy. However, in our sample of firms, it was apparent that managers/owners in family firms had a greater longer-term opportunity interpretation that is necessary for patient long-term investments versus their counterparts in non-family firms.

As discussed, managers and members of the dominant coalition in family firms will tend to exhibit more pronounced cognitive biases in terms of halo effects, anchoring effects, and loss biases, whether as threats or opportunities, under the influence of the family's dominant biases. That is, family firms will exhibit both a higher level of negative, and a higher level of positive cognitive bias in interpreting environmental issues. Hence,

P24. As compared to non-family firms, managers of family firms will exhibit more pronounced cognitive biases in interpreting environmental issues, whether negative or positive, under the influence of the family's dominant cognitive biases.

In addition to cognitive biases associated with halo effects, anchoring effects, and loss-versus-gain perceptions, managers are also

Table 5.1 *Interpretation of Environmental Issues as Threats vs. Opportunities*

Environmental Strategy	Non-Family Firms	Family Firms
	Threat Interpretations	
Reactive	*Lascombs:* Several wineries in the Margaux (region) are adopting organic/biodynamic to varying degrees. We are not sure if it enhances the quality of the wine or brings premium prices. We are not sure if the market is ready or large enough for organic wines. *Bird's Nest:* Reducing packaging and energy saves costs and is a good environmental practice. Organic viticulture is risky and does not give us any better prices in the market. *Skyline:* Our parent company has standardized operations for productivity and efficiency. We cannot afford the unpredictability that organic practices add.	*Hannibal:* The wine business is a tough business. The vines grow wild and suffer from continuous insect infestations. We have to stay on top with application of expensive herbicides and chemicals. There are rocks everywhere in the soil that have to be blasted out. It is not easy making any money in this business. *Northshore:* If I could save money on chemicals, I would do so. If the vines become infested, you lose your crop and could lose your business. *Europa:* The customers care about the quality of the wine and the experience at the winery. You cannot experiment with risky organic techniques and jeopardize quality.

Opportunity Interpretations

Proactive	
Soutard: Many of the best award-winning wines from the Bordeaux region are coming from biodynamic vineyards. All three vineyards owned by the company are being converted to biodynamic viticulture to enhance our quality and market appeal.	*Landjoy:* Organic practices lead to a living and well-balanced soil composition that guarantees the health of the plant and the terroir expression of the wines. This leads to wine that is in harmony, healthy, and flavorful. Our wines win awards every year. People who drink our wine want to know more about the organic practices that led to the quality rather than the other way around. We spend a part of our dinner every evening reflecting on the day and discussing how to become the leading organic wine producers in Canada.
Santa Rita: Our company has a goal of becoming the largest seller of organic wines by 2025.	*Nirvana:* Why do we do it? Because we care for the land and what we put into our bodies. The side effect is the higher quality of our wine and the awards we win.
Indomita: It is important for us to be a part of the community and generate employment and preserve nature and land and that we intend to operate on for the long term.	*De Martino:* The consumer who buys and consumes our wine is not just drinking our wine, he is sharing in the DeMartino family passion for quality wine and ecosystem stewardship.

Table 5.1 (*cont.*)

Environmental Strategy	Non-Family Firms	Family Firms
		Dreamscape: Our commitment to organic produces very high-quality wines. We would not have it any other way.
		Duvivier: We do not think about threats or opportunities. Our mission is to run a business that operates in harmony with the ecosystem or not do it at all.
		Fonroque: The Chateau's leadership and expertise in organic viticulture and winemaking was already well known in Bordeaux. When the winery became available, we were ready to take over and carry forward the momentum to incorporate biodynamic practices and certification. Our family believes strongly that we must become stewards of the ecosystems and communities if we have to survive into the future.

influenced by regulatory and industry standards. As discussed in Chapter 3, managers operate in an environment with exogenous influences that include multiple and often conflicting environmental standards and regulations. Tenbrunsel, Wade-Benzioni, Messick, and Bazerman (2000) found that standards influence the managers in their evaluation of environmental investment proposals that may be independent of the degree of environmental protection offered by the proposals. These authors also found that standards distort managerial perceptions of environmental proposals so that they find proposals that conform to standards much more attractive than the proposals that do not conform to the standard, even if they have much greater positive environmental impact. Hence, conflicting standards, especially those imposed by regulators and industry associations may prevent opportunity seeking by managers to generate creative ideas and innovations to address sustainability challenges. Hence, wineries (mainly non-family firms) with a focus on compliance with regulations invoked the standards during the interviews while the firms with a PES (more likely family firms) talked about value-driven strategies focused on achieving the highest level of organic and/or biodynamic certifications. Hence,

P 25. Managers of family firms will be more likely to be driven by family values (whether pro or con environmental preservation) as compared to managers of non-family firms who will be more likely to be driven by regulatory compliance and industry standards.

Firms have the ability to exercise influence over managerial values, attitudes, and interpretations toward strategically important issues such as sustainability challenges. Next we discuss research indicating how organizations can foster cognitive stress and creative problem solving to address sustainability challenges. Managerial biases and decision-making can be influenced by leadership values and vision, supervisory behavior, and organizational design and context.

Opportunity Framing of Environmental Issues

Leadership

In a 2013 study conducted by Accenture in partnership with the United Nations Global Compact, of the 766 corporate CEOs polled worldwide, 93 percent said that sustainability issues will be critical to their firms' successes in the next ten years (Accenture, 2013). This was up from 72 percent three years ago. In terms of empirical evidence, Egri and Herman's (2000) study of leaders of non-profit environmental and for-profit environmental product and service organizations showed that these leaders' personal values were more eco-centric or oriented toward environmental preservation, open to change, and self-transcendent than those of leaders in other types of organizations. The authors concluded that while such eco-centric leaders have personality characteristics of other effective leaders, they also have values that include concern for the welfare of others and the environment and the desire to motivate change within the firm. Such leaders also focus on transforming the organization by inspiring managers in the firm to support their vision and exhibit both transformational and transactional leadership behaviors.

However, we do not have studies establishing clear causality between the values of the leaders and the successful motivation of managers to make the decisions to undertake change within the firm for the generation of a PES. There is a great deal of anecdotal evidence for the influence of leadership values in the popular business press such as *Fortune*, but limited empirical research. Egri and Herman's study (2000) found that that nonprofit environmentalist organizations were highly receptive contexts for transformational leadership, whereas for-profit environmental organizations were only moderately receptive in this regard. This finding may be obvious – not-for-profit environmental organizations are expected to be more receptive to eco-centric values and behavior of their leaders. The real challenge is for organizations that operate in the economic value maximization paradigm. Perhaps, top management leadership is more important at early stages of the emergence of sustainability issues and challenges when a firm's managers are looking for signals about appropriate action. Case studies examining the emergence of environmental strategies in North America identified top management as a driver at early stages of environmental strategy development (Portugal and Yukl, 1994; Winn, 1995). At early stages, leaders can drive sustainability innovation by managers by changing organizational structure, that is, formal functional areas and positions and departments to address sustainability challenges issues via fostering exchange of information and collaboration (King, 2000).

As sustainability challenges become complex, multi-faceted, and with multiple interfaces with the firm, top management does not have the capacity to keep up with and interpret the changing landscape and the role of managers at the middle and lower levels becomes increasingly important. Firms can shape managerial attitudes by creating the appropriate information availability and incentive systems. Cordano and Frieze (2000) found that communication barriers within firms may inhibit managerial decisions to address sustainability challenges. These authors found that most managers responsible for the environmental function within the firm (referred to in this book as environmental managers, regardless of their actual title) had positive attitudes about pollution prevention but did not feel the pressure from the top management to improve environmental performance beyond regulatory requirements. As a result, they were unable to communicate the economic benefits of pollution prevention to other operations managers using business logic. The authors suggested that if environmental managers focused on easy-to-implement pollution reduction practices, they would generate quick wins that would change the attitudes of business managers. Short-term wins can help reinforce the business logic of sustainability practices, undermine cynics and resisters, reward change agents, keep supervisors on board with a project, and build momentum (Kotter, 1996).

Supervisory Influences

While middle managers have been found to be critical for the development of an organization's sustainability strategy as the ones selling social and environmental issues to their superiors, peers, and subordinates; as issue interpreters for information input into decision-making; and as environmental champions (Andersson and Bateman, 2000; Bansal, 2003; Howard-Grenville, 2007; Sharma, 2000; Sharma et al., 1999), there is limited evidence as to whether middle managers in their supervisory roles influence environmental strategy. The study by Ramus and Steger (2000) examined the influence of organizational and supervisory encouragement in companies with leading environmental initiatives on employees' perceptions of their willingness to undertake and promote these environmental initiatives. They found that employees who perceived strong signals of organizational and supervisory encouragement were more likely to develop and implement creative ideas for environmental initiatives than employees who did not perceive such signals. The authors found that a strong organizational commitment to the environment was influential, as evidenced by the strong link between the existence of a published environmental policy and the willingness of employees to attempt self-described environmental initiatives. However, they found that even supervisors in firms with strong environmental commitment, used less supportive behaviors when managing environmental activities, as compared to general business activities.

Based on our discussions about the differences between family and non-family firms discussed at the beginning of this chapter, we argue that the level of commitment of the firm to environmental preservation will be more strongly transmitted to employees in family firms versus non-family firms. This is due to the greater likelihood of congruence rather than conflict in the DC (the strategic planning team) and the shorter lines of communication. Hence, there will be lower levels of confusion about the signals from top management and supervisors. Sharma (2000) found that in non-family firms in the oil and gas industry, managers expressed great frustration about the differing signals they received from their supervisors that their performance would be evaluated on profit and/or output metrics while being urged to contribute to the mission expressing environmental preservation and social responsibility. Such crossed signals discouraged any decision-making on a PES. In our wineries, the impact of leadership/supervisory influences was evident, whether positive or negative.

We repeat a quote from Chapter 3 here. The winemaker of reactive Skyline in the Okanagan Valley in Canada (a winery started by a father-and-daughter team and subsequently bought out by the corporate Peller group) said:

When we started the winery, we began with organic viticulture. When we were acquired by the Peller Group, the focus has been on product quality and production yields as per the group's policy of compliance with regulations and adopting the most efficient production practices.

In contrast, the winemaker at Nirvana in the Okanagan Valley Canada, who is not a family member of the second-generation winery business said:

I took a two-year sabbatical in New Zealand mastering biodynamic viticulture and organic winemaking. I could have stayed on in New Zealand but I came back because I knew all family members are committed to making the best biodynamic wines in the region.

The vineyard manager, a non-family member, of Chateau Duvivier, France:

The commitment of the family to environmental stewardship for a healthy and resilient ecosystem filters down to every employee.

A junior employee in the tasting room at the reactive founder owned Mountain winery in the Okanagan Valley, Canada:

Well, we market a small selection of our wines as estate grown organic because these command a premium price. However, we have grown so fast that our estate can only supply a very small quantity of grapes. Technically, we are blending grapes that we buy from several vineyards which we cannot dictate or monitor. What matters in the end is nose, body, and flavor and our wines are the best in the Okanagan.

The public relations manager of Chateau Fonroque, a family-owned biodynamic winery in Bordeaux:

I was skeptical about biodynamic practices until I joined Fonroque ... now I agree with the family's philosophy that this produces very high quality wines.

Based on these quotes, we propose:

P26. *As compared to non-family firms, the level of commitment of the firm to environmental preservation will be more strongly transmitted to employees in family firms due to the greater likelihood of congruence of values toward environmental preservation in the DC and the shorter lines of communication.*

Organizational Context and Design

Addressing sustainability challenges requires managers to balance short-term financial, social, and environmental performance while innovating to achieve future long-term financial, social, and environmental performance. This is much more complex than the focus that firms have traditionally had on optimum utilization of current assets to maximize financial performance in the short term. The need to balance short-term and long-term economic, social, and environmental performance leads to managers facing many more decision variables and factors that they have to consider in a business environment that is volatile, uncertain, complex, and ambiguous (VUCA). In such an environment, the decision rules of thumb that have been used by managers earlier are ineffective. Effective decisions in such a context require the generation of cognitive stress, search for information, experimentation, and innovation. This requires managerial sense making; that is, managers need to interpret and analyze how the several factors and variables in the environment will individually affect their business, and also how interactions among the factors will affect the firm (Sharma, 2000; 2014).

Innovations that enable the firm to balance short-term and long-term economic, social, and environmental performance require higher-order learning which goes beyond using existing skill sets and knowledge for problem solving to learning how to frame problems differently and seeking new knowledge to address unfamiliar challenges. This process involves harnessing information from a variety of external stakeholders, combining the external information with internal information and knowledge within the firm, generating new frames of decision-making reference, learning about potential solutions, and fostering a process of experimentation and continuous innovation (Sharma and Vredenburg, 1998).

As discussed above, busy managers tend to interpret major changes in their environment as threats to their perfected routines, and since threats generally loom twice as large as opportunities (Kahneman and Tversky, 1979), organizations that seek to generate innovative solutions to sustainability challenges need to transform managerial threat perceptions to opportunity perceptions. This is referred to as opportunity framing by Sharma (2000). Opportunity frames require changing managerial perceptions of sustainability challenges as a source of loss, as negative, and as uncontrollable to perceptions of solutions to these challenges as sources of gain, as positive, and as controllable. Sharma, Pablo, and Vredenburg (1999) found that firms fostered an opportunity frame for decision-making by making the following changes in their organizational design.

Legitimization of Environmental Sustainability in the Firm's Identity

Managers' perceptions of their company's identity have been shown to influence how they interpret strategic issues, and thus indirectly influence organizational actions and strategies (Albert and Whetten, 1985). When concern for the environment becomes an integral component of corporate identity, environmental issues become harder to disown (Weick, 1988). A change in the corporate identity that explicitly includes a concern for sustainability makes it more likely for the firm to send the appropriate signals to managers. It becomes easier and legitimate not only for the firm, but also for managers, to channel resources for the development of sustainability practices and innovations and justify further commitment and allocation of resources. When managers perceive their organization's identity as partially or wholly focused on addressing sustainability challenges, finding solutions to deliver triple bottom line performance will assume importance and lead to positive emotional linkages to sustainability practices.

Large non-family firms find it difficult to ensure the dissemination of shared values across employees spread over different operations, business units, and geographic locations. Such firms can affect the legitimization of environmental preservation by changing their mission or vision statement and signalling to their managers that action on sustainability is important for the organization. Some non-family firms achieve shared values for environmental stewardship by being founded with social and/or environmental sustainability enshrined in their mission statement. For example, firms such as Patagonia and The Body Shop were set up with a mission for environmental preservation and promoting social justice (Patagonia, 2015; The Body Shop, 2015). Ben and Jerry's mission statement comprehensively brings together the economic, social, and environmental elements of sustainability. Even though Ben and Jerry's is now owned by Unilever, it operates as an autonomous company with an independent mission. The firm converted in 2012 to a B-corp (benefit corporation registered in the United States as a non-profit that uses the power of business to solve social and environmental problems) so that it can focus on delivering value to multiple stakeholders instead of only to shareholders. The company now reports its performance on governance and impacts on workers, community, and the environment (Ben and Jerry's, 2015). Changing an existing corporate mission to drive managerial decisions requires extensive and repeated communication, widely across the organization. Recently Unilever, under its CEO Paul Polman, established a mission to double profits while halving environmental impact.

Polman has used every opportunity to publicize this as a part of Unilever's identity (Confino, 2013).

However, as mentioned above, family firms are able to achieve greater congruence of values amongst employees due to the influence of the DC and shorter channels of communication within the firm. If the DC favors environmental preservation, then legitimization is much easier, as compared to non-family firms, and there is less need of formal symbols and signalling, such as mission statements and slogans that are more relevant for large non-family firms. This is reflected in several of the quotes presented earlier in this chapter in the section on Influence of Managerial Values that reflect employees sharing the family firm's commitment for environmental stewardship without reference to a formal mission statement or policy.

At the same time, the fact that the family name is often also the same as the business name, makes it more likely that family values are reflected in the business values as represented by managers. A fourth-generation family member of Viña De Martino in Chile expressed this sentiment clearly:

The De Martino name has been on all our wineries for seven decades. The consumer who buys and consumes our wine is not just drinking our wine, he is sharing in the De Martino family passion for quality wine and ecosystem stewardship.

As per the winery manager (non-family member) of the biodynamic family firm, Chateau Duvivier in France:

I am not sure what our mission statement is but it does not matter … all of us who work here are committed to a resilient and healthy ecosystem.

Regardless of the extent to which legitimization needs embedding in the mission and operating policies, both family and non-family firms can reinforce sustainable thinking by finding avenues for their managers to experience environmental loss and social injustice first hand. The Tata Group of companies in India (while technically a family firm, it is a giant conglomerate with many professionally managed companies with oversight by a family-held trust) reinforce an identity for sustainability by requiring its managers to spend time in rural areas to experience how 70 percent of India's billion-plus people live. This has led to changed mind-sets toward finding sustainable solutions to business problems and has generated several sustainable product and business models. For example, the Tata-BP Solar joint venture's managers have learnt from such experiences to develop businesses to deliver energy to the rural poor, including solar home lighting systems, solar lanterns, solar cookers, and solar hot water systems. It is the first-hand experience in rural markets and a sustainability mission that enables Tata's managers to identify ideas for sustainable innovation (Sharma, 2014).

The greater the extent to which addressing sustainability challenges is central or core to the corporate identity, the greater the extent to which managers will view actions, decisions, and solutions to such challenges as positive rather than negative, changing this element of threat perception to an opportunity interpretation (Sharma, 2000). However, as we have argued, it will be easier to affect such changes in interpretations in family firms versus non-family firms. Hence,

P27. While non-family firms can foster an opportunity frame for their employees by legitimization of environmental preservation in their identity via embedding this into their mission, via extensive communication across the organization, and via policies and procedures designed to drive employee behavior, family firms are able to achieve such legitimization with a lower need for changing their mission and policies.

P28. Family firms often have the advantage of congruence between family identity and the firm identity, enabling family values of preserving the firm's reputation via stewardship to more easily influence managerial values for environmental preservation.

Integration of Environmental Metrics into Performance Evaluation

Managers searching for, and experimenting with, sustainability solutions that may require new inputs/materials, processes, product reformulations, logistics, and technologies face high outcome uncertainty. This means that managers are not sure how new innovations will impact the firm's economic performance and affect their own job performance. Innovative processes, products, business models, and technologies may yield positive economic performance and returns only over a long-term period and carry a threat of failure for managers. This increases the possibility of a negative impact on their performance and may jeopardize their job, enhancing threat perceptions. Firms need to address managerial interpretations of sustainability issues as potential losses by adding social and environmental criteria to their performance evaluation (Sharma, 2000; Sharma et al.,1999).

For experimental projects or radical new technologies, even the economic performance criteria usually require a lower rate of return initially, longer-term expectations for the start of payback (as also for new experimental technology firms), and a holistic evaluation of employee performance rather than a short-term and narrow focus on monthly and quarterly economic (sales, output, profits) performance. Balancing the long-term, output-based economic, social, and environmental performance criteria with short-term economic criteria in employee performance evaluation encourages managers to address sustainability challenges as an opportunity for gain rather than as a threat of loss. Rewarding managers for achieving long-term sustainability targets reduces the possibility that managers will associate the unpredictability and risk of their actions in the short term as a threat of loss (Sharma, 2000; 2014).

To illustrate, in 2010, Unilever established a goal to halve the environmental impact of each brand while doubling sales by 2020 (Pearce, 2013). Similarly, in 2001, DuPont set four specific goals to evaluate employees on their sustainability performance, each with a target date of 2010. The first was to derive 25 percent of its revenues from non-depletable resources such as agricultural feedstocks, up from about 10 percent in 2002 and up from 5 percent in its base year, 1998. The second was to reduce its global carbon-equivalent greenhouse gas emissions by 65 percent using 1990 as a base year. The third was to hold total energy use flat, using 1990 as a base year, thereby offsetting all production increases with corresponding improvements in energy efficiency. The fourth was to source 10 percent of its global energy use in the year 2010 from renewable resources (Holliday, 2001). Chad Holliday, the former chairman and CEO of Dupont, propagated SVA (shareholder value added) as a performance evaluation criterion. This was defined as the shareholder value created above the cost of capital (which typically is 10 to 12 percent for corporations in the United

States) based mainly on the addition of knowledge. As per DuPont's targets, the higher the SVA per pound of production, the greater the knowledge intensity in creating economic value. Along with more traditional financial measures like return on invested capital and cash flow, this metric provided a useful indicator of the long-term sustainability of different growth strategies (Holliday, 2001).

Paul Polman, chairman of Unilever, has eliminated quarterly reporting for Unilever (Confino, 2013) in order to invest in projects to address sustainability challenges with long-term paybacks. Unfortunately, it is rare for publicly listed dispersed-ownership firms to be able to take such bold steps. After Chad Holliday left DuPont, the new leadership did not maintain these goals and performance evaluation criteria. Based on our arguments, such change in values and strategy is less likely in family firms.

In the winery industry, family members and employees of organic and biodynamic firms never once mentioned compromising short-term profits or returns in order to undertake such practices. Excerpts from quotes in Table 5.1 from family firms are illustrative:

The founder of Landjoy, family firm winery in the Okanagan Valley, Canada:

Organic practices lead to a living and well-balanced soil composition that guarantees the health of the plant and the terroir expression of the wines. This leads to wine that is in harmony, healthy, and flavorful. Our wines win awards every year. People who drink our wine want to know more about the organic practices that led to the quality rather than the other way around.

The first generation founding family member of Nirvana in the Okanagan Valley, Canada:

Why do we do it? Because we care for the land and what we put into our bodies. The side effect is the higher quality of our wine and the awards we win.

The fourth-generation family member and vineyard manager of Viña De Martino winery in Chile:

The consumer who buys and consumes our wine is not just drinking our wine, he is sharing in the De Martino family passion for quality wine and ecosystem stewardship.

The first generation founding family member of Dreamscape in Nova Scotia, Canada:

Our commitment to organic produces very high-quality wines. We would not have it any other way.

The winery manager (non-family member) of Chateau Duvivier, France:

Our mission is to run a business that operates in harmony with the ecosystem or not do it at all.

The Directeur Général, second generation family member of Chateau Fonroque, France:

Our family believes strongly that we must become stewards of the ecosystems and communities if we have to survive into the future.

Unlike the managers of family firms, who did not mention any economic-environmental performance conflicts, the managers of non-family firms consistently mentioned the risks to profitability, yields, and wine quality as a result of the two- to three-year conversion process to organic or biodynamic.

A quote from the CEO of Bird's Nest, a Canadian corporate non-family winery, is repeated here:

Producing organic wine is a personal preference that some wine owners have that I am sure they are willing to pay for in low grape yields and unpredictable quality.

Organic viticulture is risky and does not give us any better prices in the market.

The vineyard manager of Chateau Lascombs, a corporate winery in France:

Several wineries in the Margaux (region) are adopting organic/biodynamic to varying degrees. We are not sure if it enhances the quality of the wine or brings premium prices. We are not sure if the market is ready or large enough for organic wines.

The winemaker of Skyline, Okanagan owned by a Canadian corporate group:

Our parent company has standardized operations for productivity and efficiency. We cannot afford the unpredictability that organic practices add.

Hence,

P29. *While non-family firms may be able to foster an opportunity frame for its employees by implementing metrics and project/investment/performance evaluation systems for projects, family firms are able to undertake and implement projects with long-term paybacks more easily than non-family firms due to less short-term scrutiny and reporting obligations and greater family commitment to long-term survival of the business family.*

As more managers within a firm interpret sustainability challenges as opportunities, these issues become increasingly legitimized as a component of their corporate identity and reinforce the organizational actions and practices that enable the successful management of these issues. This generates a virtuous cycle. If a firm's PES is considered successful in terms of achieving the desired sustainability metrics, and if it continues to balance economic, social, and ecological performance well, then managerial interpretations of sustainability issues as opportunities will be further reinforced. Conversely, continued failures to achieve the desired outcomes and economic/production losses may force a re-evaluation of corporate identity and the organizational design, and may reinforce negative managerial interpretations of sustainability challenges as potentially being an uncontrollable threat of loss (Sharma, 2000; Sharma et al., 1999).

Discretionary Slack

To manage the perceived threat associated with the unpredictability inherent in the search for, and adoption of, innovative sustainability solutions (technologies, products, services, business models) managers require a measure of discretionary resources and time. Discretion is the latitude of managerial action (Hambrick and Finkelstein, 1987) and slack is the "resource that enables an organization both to adjust to gross shifts in the external environment with minimal trauma, and to experiment with new postures in relation to that environment, either through new product introductions or through innovations in management style" (Bourgeois, 1981). Thus, discretionary slack is a combination of the time and resources that facilitate desired strategic or creative behavior within an organization and allow managers to adjust and respond to changes in the external environment.

Not all types of slack may help generate sustainable innovations. Only high discretion slack in the form of free time and resources can be applied to a wide variety of situations and problems and can facilitate problem-solving behavior. In contrast, low discretion slack, in the form of idle machines, excess production capacity, and idle personnel who are highly specialized in specific tasks, has very specific applications and may be difficult to adapt (Sharfman et al., 1988) for generating sustainable innovations. High discretion slack enables managers to increase their perceived sense of controllability to manage the threats associated with the unpredictability and risk of searching for, and adopting, innovative sustainability practices and technologies (Sharma, 2000).

A company well known for fostering innovation by providing its managers with discretionary slack is 3M (Goetz, 2011). 3M's goal is to generate one-third of its sales every year through new products. Correspondingly, it provides its senior managers with almost one-third of their budgets and time as discretionary. This enables them to experiment with, and develop, new products and services. The firm adopts a long-term approach to the new product development process by creating a culture of innovation that encourages risk-taking, tolerates mistakes made along the way, and rewards achievement. A culture of innovation means that senior management encourages employees to spend a significant portion of their time on experimentation and research that goes beyond their usual scope of responsibilities. This involves hosting ideation sessions in which the innovation champion creates an environment of trust and openness. Only by breaking out of their usual comfort zones can teams create truly disruptive technology. As part of the company's holistic innovation strategy, 3M aims to develop disruptive innovations outside the current existing portfolio. In 2008, 3M began strategically investing in start-ups with long-term benefit to the company, resulting in collaborations and increased technological development for sustainable innovations.

The greater the degree of discretionary slack provided to managers in managing sustainability challenges, the greater the likelihood that they will interpret these challenges as opportunities rather than as threats because they now have control over resources and time to experiment and innovate. The uncontrollability dimension in the threat perception changes to controllability in an opportunity perception (Sharma, 2000; Sharma et al., 1999).

Family-business scholars argue that family firms oriented toward long-term survival of the business family maintain an entrepreneurial mind-set focused on the long-term development of the next generation's human capital resources, the interpersonal and network influences on that developmental process, and the social capital resources provided by the family firm (Cabrera-Suárez et al., 2018; Cohen and Sharma, 2016). The entrepreneurial mind-set fostered by business families that take a long-term perspective, enables the next generation that is succeeding in the takeover of the business to focus on the changing societal and environmental issues and demands on business and motivates them to shape the firm to develop new networks and knowledge relevant for decision-making in such a changing business environment (Nordqvist et al., 2013), leading to the fostering of exploration of knowledge by the firm's employees (Cabrera-Suárez et al., 2018) to generate innovative responses to changing environments. Hence,

P30. *Family firms are more likely to have a long-term orientation as compared to non-family firms and will be more likely to foster an opportunity frame by creating discretionary slack to enable exploration for new ideas and innovations to undertake a PES in order to address sustainability challenges that are increasingly important to society and business in the future.*

Information Flow

In balancing short-term economic performance with long-term economic, social, and environmental metrics, managers face considerable uncertainties and ambiguities regarding the evolving regulations, societal expectations, and appropriate emerging technologies. There is a great deal of uncertainty about the relationship between organizational actions and performance outcomes. Even if managers know the right questions to ask, the information and knowledge necessary to answer these questions is not readily available. Without this information, the financial and technical implications of a decision are difficult to assess. When managers in for-profit firms have to deliver on social and environmental metrics, they still have to deliver on financial and technical metrics. Hence, managers experience a lack of control and a threat perception in managing sustainability challenges.

Firms deal with this uncertainty by developing detailed and specific measures of their sustainability footprint, developing detailed and specific performance targets, and undertaking detailed environmental audits using certified third parties to clearly benchmark the firm as compared to its peers and its goals (Sharma, 2014). Firms make this information publicly available to all employees and sometimes to other stakeholders via sustainability reports. While the staff-level legal and sustainability departments may be responsible for initial generation of this information, subsequent knowledge generation and solutions involve line managers at all levels, sparking a fast pace of learning.

Because line managers tend to emphasize economic and operational targets while staff managers tend to emphasize the interpretation and analysis of sustainability regulations, new technologies, and societal expectations, it is important to strike a balance of influence between line and staff units in formulating sustainability strategies. Companies with successful strategies achieve this via the use of such integrative devices as cross-functional committees, task forces, and rotation of staff officers to the business units (Haugh and Talwar, 2010; Sharma, Pablo and Vredenburg, 1999). This balancing of responsibilities for information support has the potential to catalyze processes of learning and knowledge generation for sustainable innovation. This alleviates the feeling of lack of control, and, armed with sufficient information about the technologies and best practices that can help the firm address sustainability challenges, managers now perceive these as opportunities (Sharma, 2000; Sharma et al., 1999).

As discussed, in family firms, information and knowledge is transferred between family members not only through formal organizational structure and across line and staff functions but also informally outside work situations and in family and social settings. Moreover, information sharing is quicker and more effective within a DC of a family firm as compared to the TMT of a non-family firm (Sharma and Sharma, 2011). The channels of communication are shorter in family firms and often employees are long term as compared to non-family firms and tend to be trusted and have closer information ties with the family. For example, family firms such as Hallmark, Timken, L.L. Bean, S.C. Johnson, W.L. Gore, and many others are known for their continuing and major investments in employee training, minimum-layoff policies, employee participation programs, painstaking staff selection, generous benefits, and extremely low turnover (Allouche and Amann, 1997; Miller and Le Breton-Miller, 2005). Hence,

P31. While non-family firms can foster an opportunity frame for their employees through formal structures for generating and sharing of information relevant for decision-making for sustainable innovations, family firms use both formal and informal channels of information sharing, have shorter channels of communication, and a higher level of trust between long-term employees and family members to foster information flow.

Championing and Selling Sustainable Ideas and Innovations

The desired outcome of creating an opportunity frame is to foster a bubbling of ideas from all over the firm, especially from the lower and middle levels, for sustainable innovations in products, services, and business models from the grassroots of the firm. At the same time, the top management team may have its own priorities for sustainable businesses. How does an idea rise to the top and have a chance of attracting resources for implementation? Which ideas are more likely to succeed? Research in multiple contexts has shown that pushing an idea down from the top management without laying groundwork at middle management levels has a low chance of success. Business ideas are implemented at the middle manager level. Therefore, ideas that are pushed down from top management without a champion(s) at the middle management level may stagnate, even though these ideas may be supported by the resources necessary for implementation. Such ideas are likely to enter the formal resource allocation process too soon, before a strong feasibility has been established and without buy-in by a critical mass of middle managers who are absolutely essential for effective implementation. In fact, innovations pushed down from the top without a support base at lower levels of the organization may have the effect that is opposite of the desired one. Managers who have not bought into these ideas may perceive them as a threat to their job and may not pour in their maximum effort to implement these ideas in innovative and effective ways (Dutton et al., 1997).

On the other hand, sustainable innovations initiated by middle managers can have the greatest possibility of success if they are carefully and effectively sold to peers and superiors. The successful ideas start at the middle of an organization that has created an opportunity frame to foster experimentation and research for sustainable innovation. Before resources are allocated, the sustainability champions use informal channels to build peer support and coalitions among other managers (Andersson and Bateman, 2000). The champions begin by using other managers as sounding boards for these ideas (Andersson and Bateman, 2000). Their peers also help them develop a strong feasibility and business case for the innovation (Sharma, 2014). The sustainability champions continuously monitor their progress against initial targets and may update their targets upward or downward depending on feedback. Success sustains a virtuous circle of sustainability practices and actions while repeated unsatisfactory performance may discourage the champion. The firm's leadership plays a role in sustaining the momentum of sustainability strategy by balancing feedback from individual champions and other managers on successive actions and outcomes (Branzei et al., 2004).

Similar principles apply for entrepreneurs seeking to sell sustainable innovations to investors and other stakeholders. They need to understand the decision biases of investors and venture capitalists and develop proposals that transfer threat perceptions of new innovations into opportunities to be supported.

Issue selling is one aspect of the championing of sustainability within organizations by managers. The championing process involves identifying sustainability issues that are relevant for the organization, framing them appropriately within the logic of the business, presenting them to colleagues, selling them, and timing the process (Andersson and Bateman, 2000). The appropriate timing of the issue selling has been found to be associated with greater success (Andersson and Bateman, 2000; Dutton et al., 1997). Andersson and Bateman (2000) found that champions attributed successful selling of ideas to framing of issues as simple, cutting edge, relevant to corporate values, good publicity, and as an opportunity. These authors argue that each successful championing manager must create a unique frame for his or her issue depending on the distinctive features of the issue and the context of the organization. They found that presenting an environmental issue using formal business logic rather than impassioned environmental or social rhetoric was more often associated with championing success.

Of course, it is important to be aware of the cultural contexts of family and non-family firms within which our arguments may be more or less predictive. We know from the international business literature that the cultural context within which managers operate affects their decision-making on sustainability challenges at the interface of their firm. There are major national and regional differences in values and attitudes toward, and understanding of, sustainability issues. For example, a study showed that for managers in Chinese firms, top-down influences from upper echelon managers were stronger than the bottom-up effects in the early stages of environmental strategy formation (Branzei et al., 2004). The authors attribute this to higher levels of power distance, higher status accorded to top executives, and an eagerness to follow upper-level directives. Hence, in both family and non-family firms, in countries with higher power distance, fostering an opportunity frame may be less effective because managers will be less likely to undertake initiatives from the bottom up without top-down direction.

The Family Business Advantage

As managers attempt to address sustainability challenges as opportunities, they gain practical experience about sustainability impacts of business and increase their knowledge of, interest in, and commitment to sustainability (Haugh and Talwar, 2010). Such action learning, in which employees have the opportunity to participate in practical sustainability projects, makes learning relevant for employees (Aragon-Correa and Sharma, 2003; Haugh and Talwar, 2010). Similar to social learning, learning about the interface of sustainability with business happens through observation, participation, and interaction in actual processes. Such managerial learning leads to organizational learning that is greater than the collective learning of individual managers, changing the knowledge base of the organization (Argyris and Schön, 1978).

Family business research argues that family firms have an advantage due to unique individual and organizational learning processes that are embedded in family relationships and social networks, and transmitted from one generation to another. This leads to knowledge that is firm specific and difficult to replicate by other firms, especially non-family firms (Cabrera-Suárez et al., 2001). Cabrera- Suárez et al. (2001) also argue that the family interactions and knowledge transmission leads to unique cognitive dimension of social capital that comprises a family's shared vision and purpose and its unique language, stories, and culture and the entrepreneurial legacy of the family (Jaskiewicz, Combs and Rau, 2015). Such shared vision and goal congruence between family members and their management team leads to an entrepreneurial orientation and innovation (De Clercq and Belausteguigoitia, 2015; Discua-Cruz, Howorth and Hamilton, 2013).

A critical component of the development of knowledge that is embedded in valuable, rare, inimitable, and firm-specific capabilities is the temporal dimension; that is, they take a long time to be developed and are path dependent on unique histories and actions within the firm (Dierickx and Cool, 1989). The uniqueness of the family firms in knowledge and capability creation lies in this temporal dimension as each succeeding generation is groomed over a long period of time via formal apprenticeship and informal discussions and interactions as the successor develops from student to manager to top executive over several years (Carter and Justis, 2009) developing deep business, product, market, and industry knowledge. Non-family-business scholars argue that such succession is not merit based and can lead to incompetent leadership. Family-business scholars counter that the long-term period of succession allows for adaptation, corrections, suitable education, appropriate training and apprenticeships in external firms, and appropriate mentorship with family and non-family experts (Giovannoni, Maraghini and Riccaboni, 2011). For example, firms such as Michelin and Motorola had multiple family members from different generations serving in an office of the CEO so that the younger generation could learn on the job by watching the veterans (Miller and Le Breton-Miller, 2005). Due to very long tenures and high-trust environments in family businesses, the older generation is willing not only to share wisdom but to discuss their own mistakes (Bubolz, 2001) versus non-family businesses where senior managers are often focused on protecting their own career and position.

The long process of succession fosters longer-term perspectives about the future of the business in the evolving societal environment and the opportunities that may be presented for future entrepreneurship and business. This enables the acquisition of new capabilities that can capitalize on the evolving opportunities that emerge in the changing environment, such as the addressing of sustainability challenges.

Woodfield and Husted (2017) argue that such a long succession process also can lead to reverse knowledge transfers as the succeeding generation gains new understanding of evolving social and environmental issues and their impacts on the future of business and can bring this knowledge to develop a PES in the business. We observed such reverse knowledge flows and capability in the winery industry as junior family members and managers were sent to other wineries (often New Zealand) to master biodynamic practices that could be implemented in the family winery. As the succeeding generation gains confidence over a period of time, the successor gains confidence and expertise and also respect from the older generation to be able to offer new knowledge and advise on developing a future-oriented PES (Cabrera-Suarez et al., 2018).

Miller and Le Breton-Miller (2005) argue that leaders of family firms are better stewards of the business and resources because they are intrinsically motivated to act for the collective good of their firm as compared to transient leaders of non-family firms. Davis, Schoorman, Mayer, and Tan (2000) find that leaders of family firms identify with the firm, embrace its objectives, and are committed to make it succeed, even at personal sacrifice, and are more likely to make farsighted investments, such as those in research and development, infrastructure, new business models, and capital investments in plant, equipment, and information technology. Moreover, family firms also reinvest a much higher percentage of their profits as compared to non-family firms by curtailing dividends (Anderson, Mansi and Reeb, 2003; Daily and Dollinger, 1992; Gallo and Vilaseca, 1996).

Family firms, especially when the family name is the same as the business name and when they are embedded in communities, are more concerned about the firm's reputation than non-family firms. The leadership often works to strengthen the reputation of the firm before the succession process to provide the successor a strong and healthy environment. Such investments may include image, branding, infrastructure, research and development, social capital, and environmental stewardship. Reputation and legitimacy for family firms more often than not involve community relationships including charitable investments in civic and social institutions and exceptionally generous political contributions (Morck and Yeung, 2003). Hence,

P32. Long-term succession processes; intangible knowledge creation and transfer; reputation building; and corporate culture that supports employee participation and long tenures, stewardship of firm, and community resources, all contribute to a greater likelihood of fostering an opportunity frame among employees, managers, and family members of family firms to adopt a PES.

However, we would like to also offer a note of caution. As we have argued, the dominant coalitions of family firms significantly benefit from the alignment of ownership and managerial control combined with long, steady tenures of key decision-makers easing the constraints to engage in pathbreaking innovations and make investments in PES-related initiatives with a longer harvest time. In their empirical study to understand the integration of discontinuous change in family and non-family firms, König, Kammerlander, and Enders (2013) found that emotional ties to existing assets, rigid mind-sets, and inertia to changing routines that have been successful in the past, slows down the recognition of opportunities for disruptive strategies. Thus, it is also possible that the DCs of family firms may tend to take longer to evaluate opportunities that require significant investments with unclear returns, as is the case with PES. Nevertheless, once a decision is made to undertake such strategic initiatives, implementation is likely to occur with greater speed and endurance in comparison to non-family firms. Thus, we can expect that:

P33. In comparison to non-family firms, family firms may take longer to develop a PES but once they do, they will be quicker and more efficient in implementing such strategies.

In Chapter 6, we will summarize the arguments we have put forward for the greater likelihood of exogenous and endogenous influences in family firms leading to their adoption of a PES as compared to non-family firms. We summarize our arguments via a framework and present research ideas and implications, as well as implications for practice and public policy.

References

Accenture. 2013. *The UN Global Compact-Accenture CEO Study on Sustainability 2013: Architects of a Better World.*

Albert, S. and Whetten, D. 1985. Organizational identity. *Research in Organizational Behavior.* 7: 263–295.

Allouche, J. and Amann, B. 1997. Le retour de capitalisme familiale. *L'expansion: Management Review*, 85: 92–99.

Anderson, R. C. and Reeb, D. 2004. Board composition: Balancing family influence in S&P 500 firms. *Administrative Science Quarterly*, 49: 209–237.

Aragon-Correa, A. and Sharma, S. 2003. A contingent natural-resource based view of proactive environmental strategy. *Academy of Management Review*, 28(1): 71–88.

Argyris, C. and Schön, D. A. 1978. *Organizational Learning: A Theory of Action Perspective.* Reading, MA: Addison-Wesley.

Arkes, H. and Blumer, C. 1985. The psychology of sunk cost. *Organizational Behavior and Human Decision Process*, 35: 124–140.

Anderson, R. C., Mansi, S. A. and Reeb, D. M. 2003. Founding family ownership and the agency cost of debt. Journal of Financial Economics, 68(2): 263–285.

Andersson, L. M. and Bateman, T.S. 2000. Individual environmental initiative: Championing natural environmental issues in U.S. business organizations. *Academy of Management Journal*, 43(4): 548–570.

Bansal. P. 2003. From issues to actions: The importance of individual concerns and organizational values in responding to natural environmental issues. *Organization Science*, 14(5): 510–527.

Basco, R. and Rodriguez, M. J. P. 2009. Studying the family enterprise holistically: Evidence for integrated family and business systems. *Family Business Review*, 22: 82–95.

Ben and Jerry's. 2015. www.benjerry.com/values (accessed October 7, 2015).

Bourgeois, L. J., III. 1981. On the Measurement of Organizational Slack. *Academy of Management Review*, 6: 29–39.

Branzei, O., Ursacki-Bryant, T. J., Vertinsky, I. and Zhang, W. 2004. The formation of green strategies in Chinese firms: matching corporate environmental responses and individual principles. *Strategic Management Journal*, 25: 1075–1095.

Bubolz, M. 2001. Family as a source, user and builder of social capital. *Journal of Socio-Economics*, 30: 129–131.

Cabrera-Suárez, K., De Saá-Pérez, P., García-Almeida, D. 2001. The succession process from a resource- and knowledge-based view of the family firm. *Family Business Review*, 14: 37–46.

Cabrera-Suárez, M. K., García-Almeida, D. J. and De Saá-Pérez. P. 2018. A dynamic network model of the successor's knowledge construction from the resource-and knowledge-based view of the family firm. *Family Business Review*, 31(2): 178–197.

Carter, J. and Justis, R. 2009. The development of successors from followers to leaders in small family firms: An exploratory study. *Family Business Review*, 22(2): 109–124.

Cohen, A. R. and Sharma, P. 2016. *Entrepreneurs in Every Generation: How Successful Family Businesses Develop Their Next Leaders*. Oakland, CA: Berrett-Koehler.

Confino, J. 2013. Interview: Unilever's Paul Polman on Diversity, Purpose and Profits. *The Guardian*, October 2, 2013. www.theguardian.com/sustainable-business/unilver-ceo-paul-polman-purpose-profits (accessed November 8, 2013).

Cordano, M. and Frieze, I. H. 2000. Pollution reduction preferences of U.S. environmental managers: Applying Ajzen's theory of planned behavior. *Academy of Management Journal*, 43(4): 627–641.

Daily, C. M. and Dollinger, M. 1992. An empirical examination of ownership structure in family and professional managed firms. *Family Business Review*, 5(2): 17–36.

Danes, S. M., Stafford, K., Haynes, G. and Amarapurkar, S. S. 2009. Family capital of family firms: Bridging human, social, and financial capital. *Family Business Review*, 22(3): 199–215.

Davis, J., Schoorman, R., Mayer, R. and Tan, H. 2000. The trusted general manager and business unit performance. *Strategic Management Journal*, 21: 563–576.

De Clercq, D. and Belausteguigoitia, I. 2015. Intergenerational strategy involvement and family firms' innovation pursuits: The critical roles of conflict management and social capital. *Journal of Family Business Strategy*, 6(3): 178–189.

Dierickx, I. and Cool, K. 1989. Asset stock accumulation and sustainability of competitive advantage. *Management Science*, 35(12): 1504–1511.

Discua Cruz, A., Howorth, C. and Hamilton, E. 2013. Inter-family entrepreneurship: The formation and membership of family entrepreneurial teams, *Entrepreneurship Theory & Practice*, 37(1): 17–46.

Dutton, J. E., Ashford, S. J., O'Neill, R. M., Hayes, E. and Wierba, E. E. 1997. Reading the wind: How middle managers assess the context for selling issues to top managers. *Strategic Management Journal*, 18(5): 407–415.

Egri, C. P. and Herman, S. 2000. Leadership in North American environmental sector: Values, leadership styles and contexts of environmental leaders and their organizations. *Academy of Management Journal*, 43(4): 571–604.

Gallo, M. and Vilaseca, A. 1996. Finance in family business. *Family Business Review*, 9: 387–401.

Giovannoni, E., Maraghini, M. P. and Riccaboni, A. 2011. transmitting knowledge across generations: The role of management accounting practices. *Family Business Review*, 24(2): 126–150.

Goel, S. and Jones, R.J., III. 2016. Entrepreneurial exploration and exploitation in family business: A systematic review and future directions. *Family Business Review*, 29(1): 94–120.

Goetz, K. 2011. How 3M Gave Everyone Days Off and Created an Innovation Dynamo. *Co-design*. www.fastcodesign.com/1663137/how-3m-gave-everyone-days-off-and-created-an-innovation-dynamo (accessed October 8, 2015).

Gomez-Mejia, L. R., Haynes, K., Nuñez-Nickel, M., Jacobson, K. J. L. and Moyano-Fuentes, J. 2007. Socioemotional wealth and business risks in family-controlled firms: Evidence from Spanish olive oil mills. *Administrative Science Quarterly*, 52: 106–137.

Gomez-Mejia, L. R Cruz, C., Berrone, P. and De Castro, J. 2011. The bind that ties: Socioemotional wealth preservation in family firms. *The Academy of Management Annals*, 5(1): 653–707.

Hahn, T., Preuss, L., Pinkse, J. and Figge, F. 2014. Cognitive frames in corporate sustainability: managerial sensemaking with paradoxical and business case frames. *Academy of Management Review*, 39(4): 463–487.

Hambrick, D. C. and Finkelstein, S. 1987. Managerial Discretion: A Bridge between the Polar Views of Organizational Outcomes. In B. M. Staw and L. L. Cummings (eds.), *Research in Organizational Behavior 4*, pp. 369–406. Greenwich, CT: JAI Press.

Hart, S. L. 1995. A natural-resource-based view of the firm. *Academy of Management Review*, 20: 874–907.

Haugh, H. M. and Talwar, A. 2010. How do corporations embed sustainability across the organization? *Academy of Management Learning and Education*, 9(3): 384–396.

Holliday, C. 2001. Sustainable Growth the DuPont Way. *Harvard Business Review* (September 2001): 129–34.

Howard-Grenville, J. A. 2007. Developing issue-selling effectiveness over time: Issue selling as resourcing. *Organization Science*, 18(4): 560–577.

Hoy, F. and Sharma, P. 2010. *Entrepreneurial Family Firms*. Upper Saddle River, NJ: Pearson Prentice Hall.

Jaskiewicz, P., Combs, JG. and Rau, S. B. 2015. Entrepreneurial legacy: Toward a theory of how some family firms nurture transgenerational entrepreneurship. *Journal of Business Venturing*, 30(1): 29–49.

Kahneman, D. and Tversky, A. 1979. Prospect theory: An analysis of decision under risk. *Econometrica*, 47(2): 263.

Kahneman, D. and Tversky, A. 1984. Choices, values, and frames. *American Psychologist*, 39(4): 341–350.

King, A. 2000. Organizational response to environmental regulation: Punctuated change or autogenesis? *Business Strategy and Environment*, 9: 224–238.

König, A., Kammerlander, N., and Enders, A. 2013. The family innovator's dilemma: How family influence affects the adoption of discontinuous technologies by incumbent firms. *Academy of Management Review*, 38(3): 418–41.

Kotlar, J. and De Massis, A. 2013. Goal setting in family firms: Goal diversity, social interactions, and collective commitment to family-centered goals. *Entrepreneurship Theory & Practice*, 37(6): 1263–1288.

Kotter, J. P. 1996. *Leading Change*. Boston, MA: Harvard Business School Press.

Maletz, M. C. and Nohria, N. 2001. Managing in the white space. *Harvard Business Review*, 79(2) February.

Miller, D. and Le Breton-Miller, I. 2006. Family governance and firm performance: Agency, stewardship, and capabilities. *Family Business Review*, 19: 73–87.

Miller, D. and Le Breton-Miller, I. 2005. *Managing for the Long-Run: Lessons in Competitive Advantage from Great Family Businesses*. Cambridge, MA: Harvard Business Press.

Morck, R., and Yeung, B. 2003. Agency problems in large family business groups. *Entrepreneurship Theory & Practice*, 27: 367–382.

Nordqvist, M., Wennberg, K., Bau, M. and Hellerstedt, K. 2013. An entrepreneurial process perspective on succession in family firms. *Small Business Economics*, 40: 1087–1122.

Patagonia. 2015. www.patagonia.com/us/patagonia.go?assetid=2047 (accessed October 5, 2015).

Pearce, F. 2013. Unilever Plans to Double its Turnover While Halving its Environmental Impact. *The Telegraph*, July 23. www.telegraph.co.uk/earth/environment/10188164/Unilever-plans-to-double-its-turnover-while-halving-its-environmental-impact.html (accessed October 7, 2015).

Portugal, E. and Yukl, G. 1994. Perspectives on environmental leadership. *Leadership Quarterly*, 5: 271–276.

Ramus, C. A. and Steger, U. 2000. The roles of supervisory support behaviors and environmental policy in employee "ecoinitiatives" at leading-edge european companies. *Academy of Management Journal*, 43 (4): 606–625.

Sharfman, M. P., Wolf, G., Chase, R. B. and Tansik, D. A. 1988. Antecedents of organizational slack. *Academy of Management Review*, 13(4): 601–14.

Sharma, P. and Sharma, S. 2011. Drivers of Proactive Environmental Strategy in Family Firms. *Business Ethics Quarterly*, 21(2): 309–332.

Sharma, S. 2000. Managerial interpretations and organizational context as predictors of corporate choice of environmental strategy. *Academy of Management Journal*, 43(4): 681–697.

Sharma, S. 2014. *Competing for a Sustainable World: Building Capacity for Sustainable Innovation*. UK: Greenleaf Publishing.

Sharma, S. and Nguan, O. 1999. The biotechnology industry and biodiversity conservation strategies: The influence of managerial interpretations and risk propensity. *Business Strategy and the Environment*, 8(Jan–Feb): 46–61.

Sharma, S., Pablo, A. and Vredenburg, H. 1999. Corporate environmental responsiveness strategies: The role of issue interpretation and organizational context. *Journal of Applied Behavioral Science*, 35(1): 87–109.

Sharma, S. and Vredenburg, H. 1998. Proactive corporate environmental strategy and the development of competitively valuable organizational capabilities. *Strategic Management Journal*, 19: 729–753.

Sonenshein, S., DeCelles, K. A. and Dutton, J. E. 2014. It's not easy being green: The role of self-evaluations in explaining support of environmental issues. *The Academy of Management Journal*, 57(1): 7–37.

Sorenson, R. L. and Bierman, L. 2009. Family capital, family business, and free enterprise. *Family Business Review*, 22(3): 193–195.

Sorenson, R. L., Goodpaster, K. E., Hedberg, P. R., and Yu, A. 2009. The family point of view, family social capital, and firm performance. *Family Business Review*, 22(3): 239–253.

Tapies, J. and Ward, J. L. 2008. *Family Values and Value Creation: The Fostering of Enduring Values within Family-Owned Businesses*. New York: Palgrave Macmillan.

Tenbrunsel, A. E., Wade-Benzoni, K. A., Messick, D. M. and Bazerman, M. H. 2000. Understanding the influence of environmental standards on judgments and choices. *Academy of Management Journal*, 43(5): 854–866.

The Body Shop. 2015. www.thebodyshop-usa.com/about-us/about_the bodyshop.aspx (accessed October 5, 2015).

Thorndike, E. L. 1920. A constant error in psychological ratings. *Journal of Applied Psychology*, 4(1): 25–29.

Tversky, A. and Kahneman, D. 1974. Judgment under uncertainty: Heuristics and biases. *Science*, 185(4157): 1124–1131.

Tversky, A. and Kahneman, D. 1986. Rational choice and the framing of decisions. *The Journal of Business*, 59(S4): S251.

Ward, J. L. 1987. *Keeping the Family Business Healthy: How to Plan for Continuing Growth, Profitability, and Family Leadership*. San Francisco: Jossey-Bass.

Weick, K. E. 1988. Enacted sensemaking in crisis situations. *Journal of Management Studies*, 24: 305–317.

Winn, M. 1995. Corporate leadership and politics for the natural environment. In D. Collins and M. Starik (eds.), *Sustaining the Natural Environment: Empirical Studies on the Interface between Nature and Organizations*, pp. 127–161. Greenwich, CT: JAI Press.

Woodfield, P. and Husted, K. 2017. Intergenerational knowledge sharing in family firms: Case-based evidence from the New Zealand wine industry. *Journal of Family Business Strategy*, 8(1): 57–69.

Zahra, S. 2018. Entrepreneurial risk taking in family firms: The wellspring of regenerative capability. *Family Business Review*, 31(2): 216–226.

6 Bringing the Family into the Corporate Environmental Sustainability Strategy: Implications for Research, Education, and Policy

Family firms are fundamentally different from non-family firms as they are controlled by individuals with kinship bonds and are often managed with an eye toward trans-generational continuity and longer time horizons than non-family firms (Chua, Chrisman and Sharma, 1999). As discussed in previous chapters, several business disciplines including management, strategy, finance, organizational theory, organizational behavior, and entrepreneurship, have examined family businesses using different theoretical lenses. This analysis identifies both a bright and a dark side of family enterprises that could provide them with a competitive advantage (or disadvantage) over non-family firms in making patient investments in long-term projects and businesses that are important for undertaking a proactive environmental strategy (PES). The positive characteristics include a long-term orientation (Brigham et al., 2014), stewardship mind-set in resource management (Davis, Schoorman and Donaldson, 1997; Sirmon and Hitt, 2003), engagement with local communities (Chirico et al., 2018), commitment to preserving the firm's reputation due to the identification of the family name with the business name (Dyer and Whetten, 2006), longer tenure of employees (McConaughy, 2000), and shorter lines of communication and greater levels of cohesion and shared vision among the members of the dominant coalition that facilitates quick decision-making including decisions to make long-term investments in innovative projects (König, Kammerlander and Enders, 2013).

On the other hand, scholars point to some negative characteristics, such as entitlement nepotism that leads to lower standards of meritocracy being applied during intra-family succession decisions (Jaskiewicz et al., 2013), preferential treatment of family versus non-family employees leading to a bifurcation bias (Verbeke and Kano, 2012), and family conflicts that may spill over into the business (Gordon and Nicholson, 2008). Families do not always operate with a shared vision in perfect harmony. When family relationship conflict is minimized in family firms, the kinship ties and shared history of the family and business can facilitate the development of shared norms and trust in family, leading to causally ambiguous decision-making mechanisms that are critical for competitively valuable organizational capability development and deployment (Coleman, 1990; Pearson, Carr and Shaw, 2008). Sometimes, family involvement in business can be dysfunctional as it adds complexity to business by intensifying the degree and tenacity of conflicts among family members who may have differences in their visions and goals (Eddleston and Kellermanns, 2007; Grote, 2003; Sorenson, 1999). In turn, such differences cause confusion in strategic direction and possible paralysis of action in the dominant coalition as divergent powerful family groups pursue competing objectives (Gersick et al., 1997).

Both the extent of family involvement in business and its consequences as reflected in the relationship conflicts within the controlling family, are likely to vary across family firms and within a family firm over time. Furthermore, the intensity of harmonious or conflictual relationships within the family group is generally higher both in positive and negative directions as compared to similar non-family groups. Because family firms are more likely than non-family firms to base their decisions on noneconomic criteria that relate to the creation and preservation of socioemotional wealth, family harmony or relational conflict are more likely to influence decision-making either *more* positively or *more* negatively, respectively, than non-family firms.

Of course, high-performing family firms that are managed for the long run (Miller and Le Breton-Miller, 2005) overcome the negatives by ensuring professional training and external apprenticeships of the succeeding generations, mechanisms and councils to generate and maintain harmony and cohesion among family members, and equal treatment of employees and family members (Ward, 2004). These characteristics of family firms may facilitate or inhibit their attention to societal issues and affect their economic and environmental performance.

Regardless of the positive or negative characteristics, it is a fact that family-owned businesses are important and dynamic participants in the world economy. The Family Firm Institute (FFI, 2018), an influential professional network of family business professionals, offers the following statistics about the impact and scope of family firms globally:

- Family firms account for two thirds of all businesses around the world.
- In most countries around the world, family businesses constitute between 70 and 95 percent of all business entities (European Family Businesses [EFB], 2012)
- An estimated 70–90 percent of global GDP annually is created by family businesses.
- Between 50 and 80 percent of jobs in the majority of countries worldwide are created by family businesses (EFB, 2012)
- Many of the world's largest firms are controlled by families or the State (La Porta, Lopez-De-Silanes and Shleifer, 1999).
- 85 percent of start-up companies are established with family money (EFB, 2012).
- 65 percent of family businesses are looking for steady income growth over the next five years (PWC, 2012)

Family businesses dominate the global economy and range in size from small partnerships to giant *Fortune 500* firms. Optimistic predictions are made for continued growth and dominance of these enterprises. For example, *McKinsey Quarterly* reports that, by 2025, family businesses will represent nearly 40 percent of the world's large enterprises, up from 15 percent in 2010 (Björnberg, Elstrodt and Pandit, 2014). Hence, family businesses need to be a critical and central player in addressing the environmental sustainability challenges of the world. Society cannot achieve its goal of a sustainable natural environment without engaging this important sector of the global economy. Hence, conducting research on the factors that make family firms undertake a PES is likely to generate new theoretical insights and frameworks.

While there exists over three decades of research in corporate sustainability in non-family controlled firms with dispersed ownership, family firms are significantly under-researched in this area of inquiry, largely due to the difficulty of obtaining data from closely held private family firms. On the other hand, amid growing concerns of aging population and the challenges associated with transitioning the leadership of an enterprise from one generation to another despite intentions of transgenerational sustainability of the firm, family business research has been focused on understanding the contributors and deterrents of successful succession in these firms (see review by Daspit et al., 2016) and on the next generation of businesses as avenues for the family entrepreneurship.

Since proactive environmental sustainability requires patient long-term investments in innovations in products, services, technologies, business models, and entering new emerging markets, our central motivating question for this monograph was *whether family firms, less subject to short-term financial reporting requirements and with a focus on transgenerational continuity of business, would be more likely to make patient long-term investments required for innovations in products, services, processes, technologies, and business models to address the environmental sustainability challenges of the world?*

As family business research points to heterogeneity within family firms based on how each firm balances its business and family-focused goals and performance in terms of short-term and long-term goals, the guiding sub-questions for the monograph were to understand:

(a) Whether family firms, which have longer-term strategic horizons and a more patient approach to investments, could be more motivated and engaged in addressing sustainability challenges?

(b) Whether family firms have unique characteristics and adopt different approaches and strategies, as compared to non-family firms, to manage the interface between their business and the natural environment?

(c) Whether there are lessons to be learnt from family firms for non-family firms seeking to undertake proactive environmental strategies?

(d) Whether family firms seeking to adopt a PES could learn from the considerable research in the context of non-family public dispersed ownership firms?

We began in Chapter 1 by clarifying our definitions of the key concepts in this monograph: family-controlled business, corporate governance, sustainable business, proactive versus reactive environmentally sustainable strategy, and patient capital. We distinguished between the three dimensions of the sustainability literature – profits, people, and planet – and clarified that we limit the scope of this monograph to the last dimension of corporate environmental sustainability. Combinations of ownership (concentrated vs. dispersed) and management (family vs. non-family dominated) were the basis for the discussion in the monograph. While research on the interface of family business and environmental sustainability is still in its infancy, our hope is that these different forms of governance will prove helpful in proposing topics for interesting and important research work.

In Chapter 2, we provided an overview of the cases in the winery industry in Canada, France, and Chile that were the basis of our primary and secondary data collection. The cases were used to supplement and illustrate the theoretical discussion in the monograph. While the cases in the Canadian winery industry followed a sampling logic of both family-controlled and non-family firms and those with reactive and proactive environmentally sustainable strategies, the cases from France and Chile are convenience samples based on availability of members of the domi-nant coalition for interviews during our short-duration overseas trips. The French cases provided insights from the Old World context of the winery industry with its hundreds of years of history, tradition, many generations of family engagement in the business, and viticulture and wine-making practices that had to conform to strict appellation stan-dards. The Chilean cases provided a New World context to contrast with the Canadian New World context with less tradition, history, and strictures on viticulture and wine-making practices. The influence of organizational and institutional level forces on proactive environmental strategies was evident in these regions. In Chile, we were fortunate to visit and study two of the most ambitious wineries, in which later-generation members of the founding family were leading the proactive sustainability strategies for their firms. Patient dedication and invest-ments in converting these wineries to organic practices are evident in these firms. In France, a major institutional change is underway as a 2016 ruling of the wine council of St. Émilion region ruled that, by 2019, every bottle of wine from this appellation region would be made from grapes grown following environmental strategies.

The next three chapters examined the drivers and barriers to firms adopting a proactive environmental strategy at three levels of analysis: exogenous influences, organizational influences, and individual/man-agerial influences. In Chapter 3, we examined the extant literature on two exogenous forces – institutional and stakeholder – on a firm's adoption of a proactive environmental strategy. We note that most of this literature is based on research in non-family firms with dispersed ownership and there is a paucity of literature in the family firm context. In family business literature, although institutional and stakeholder theoretical perspectives have been used to understand how the "family" variable influences, or is influenced by, these institutions or stakeholders, research on influences of these exogenous variables is virtually non-existent. This enabled us to propose some fresh insights for future scholarly investigations.

In Chapter 4, we examined endogenous organizational influences: institutional ownership, stakeholder activism, board of directors, top management team vs. dominant coalition, and the unique character- istics of family firms that may lead to a different impact of these influences on the development of a PES as compared to non-family firms. These characteristics of family firms include a longer temporal orientation and the identification of the family with the firm. Finally, this chapter examined the influence of market and competitiveness drivers – mainly generic business strategies – link to financial perfor- mance and the role of organization specific capabilities. In the devel- opment of unique capabilities that are valuable, rare, inimitable, and organization-specific enablers for the development of a PES, we exam- ined the uniqueness of family firms with regard to developing a shared vision for sustainability, family's control of the firm, community and stewardship orientation, longer-time orientation, and family identity.

Finally, in Chapter 5, we examined the unique role of individuals as employees and managers in making decisions, developing strategies, implementing strategies, and in developing and deploying capabilities. We examined how the behavior of managers within a firm is influenced by their individual values, attitudes, and interpretations in driving deci- sions, strategies, and actions, and how their decisions are influenced by cognitive biases such as halo effects, anchoring biases, and loss bias. We then examined how firms can create an opportunity frame to drive individual/managerial decisions, actions, and strategies toward a PES. These influences include leadership values and vision, supervisory influ- ences, and organization design. Organization design includes legitimiza- tion of environmental sustainability in the firm's identity, integration of social and environmental metrics into performance evaluation, discretion- ary slack, and information flow. We examined how and why family firms, due to their unique characteristics, may have an advantage in the devel- opment of capabilities that are valuable for the development of a PES. We concluded by discussing the potential family business advantage in cham- pioning and selling environmental issues within the firm.

In our analysis, we drew out differences between family and non- family firms in terms of unique characteristics of family firms that would make them more or less likely to undertake patient long-term and uncertain investments in proactive environmental strategies and practices. We discuss these next.

How Are Family Firms Different from Non-Family Firms?

While hard-and-fast boundaries between family-owned and-controlled firms and firms with dispersed ownership managed entirely by employees without kinship ties are not definitive in every case, there are certain characteristics that are *only* present in family firms and a few others that are *more likely* to be present in family firms as compared to non-family firms. These are summarized briefly in turn.

Characteristics Unique to Family Firms

- *Family as a Stakeholder.* This is a characteristic that is only present in family firms. In their role as controlling shareholders and active managers, the family is a critical stakeholder whose concerns and goals need to be balanced with those of other internal and external stakeholders (Sharma, 2001; Zellweger and Nason, 2008). Hence, the family's goal of survival for the long term through dynastic succession is paramount.
- *Preservation of Socioemotional Wealth.* The balancing of the goal of preserving and building the family's socioemotional wealth (SEW) with the goal of profit generation is central for family firms (Gomez-Mejia et al., 2007) and is a characteristic only present in family firms. SEW refers to "non-financial aspects of the firm that meet the family's affective needs, such as identity, the ability to exercise family influence, and the perpetuation of the family dynasty" (Gomez-Mejia et al., 2007: 106).
- *Identification of the Family with the Firm.* The family name is often embedded in the name of the business. While families still control some publicly listed firms that bear their name (e.g., the Ford family controls the Ford Motor Company voting rights and management through Class B shares and a minority ownership and the Waltons control Wal-Mart via majority stake in Wal-Mart), other families have lost control of businesses that bear their name (such as Dupont). Where family members are still engaged in managing and/or controlling businesses that bear their family name, there is

close identification with the business and the importance of preserving and building a positive reputation for the business. The family name often becomes synonymous with the firm's name leading to the amalgamation of the family's and the firm's identities (Miller and Le Breton-Miller, 2005).

- *Familiness.* Based on the resource-based view of the firm, Habbershon and Williams (1999) proposed the construct of familiness to refer to a firm-level bundle of resources and capabilities unique to a family firm emerging as result of interactions between the family system and the business system (Habbershon and Williams, 1999). Familiness is argued to contribute to competitive advantage for family firms (Tokarczyk et al., 2007) and to non-economic outcomes such as preservation of family ties or transgenerational value creation (Chrisman, Chua and Litz, 2004). On the other hand, familiness could be a disadvantage when there is conflict and nepotism in the family. Hence, there is a dark side as well as a positive side to familiness. In the absence of empirically verification, this construct is fairly abstract and merits further research.

Characteristics More Likely in Family Firms (but Also Could Be Present in Non-Family Firms)

- *Longer Temporal Orientation.* Connected to the preservation of SEW is the goal of long-term survival via succession to the next generation(s). The family business literature has not established causality in terms of whether the preservation of SEW is the motivation for the long-term orientation or vice-versa. Berrone, Cruz, and Gomez-Mejia (2012) propose that the long-term orientation is a dimension encompassed in the SEW construct. Hence, family firms are willing to undertake patient investments in the next generation businesses and long-term investments in new businesses, products, and capabilities (Miller and Le Breton-Miller, 2006). This is a characteristic more likely in family firms. However, there is also empirical evidence that a few dispersed-ownership public firms may also undertake long-term investments for different motivations, whether driven by leadership vision of continuous innovation as in the case of 3M, or saturated markets in current business, or first-mover advantage in new businesses and markets, or exploitation of new technologies (Sharma, 2014). However, family firms are more likely to have a long-term orientation while such an orientation in non-family firms has been found to be relatively rare.

- *Dominant Coalition.* The DC may comprise only family members or a mix of family members and professional managers. Just as decision-making in non-family firms is significantly influenced by the values, attitudes, and beliefs of the top management team (TMT), decision-making in family firms is influenced by the members of the DC. The differences between family and non-family firms on this dimension are:

  a) Family values and beliefs have a stronger role in the DC than personal beliefs and values of professional managers in the TMT in non-family firms;

  b) The beliefs and values of the family are more enduring and long term as compared to those of transient professional managers unless their tenures are much longer than the average tenures of CEOs and senior executives of typical *Fortune 500* firms (which average around 4.6 years);

  c) These values, attitudes, and beliefs are transferred between family members through interactions not only in the workplace but also outside since they are embedded in family relationships and take place in family and social situations and are transmitted from parents to children (Cabrera-Suárez, De Saá-Pérez, and García-Almeida, 2001).

- *Transmission of Knowledge across Generations.* Family firm leaders with intentions to retain the control of their business in their family have significantly more opportunities to transmit knowledge and values to next-generation members, and have been found to be motivated to engage in such behaviors (Zellweger et al., 2012). However, there could be both positive and negative aspects related to the such transmission of knowledge between family members as the decision-making biases of one generation could be passed on to the next generation or between family members. Not all family firms are adept at challenging assumptions of the past and embracing the new realities of business. Research based on sixteen cases of failing successions in family firms suggests that mindless acceptance and reverence of the past, wholesale rejection of it, or a wavering between the two is not conducive to successful continuity and success of a family firm (Miller, Steier and Le Breton-Miller, 2003). Such transmission of biases is much less likely in non-family firms as new leaders often bring fresh perspectives and ideas. Family firms that are more successful over the long run ensure that biases are not transmitted by maintaining an entrepreneurial mind-set focused on the long-term development of the next generation's human capital resources, the interpersonal and network influences on that developmental process, and the social capital resources provided by the family firm (Cabrera-Suárez, García-Almeida and De Saá-Pérez, 2018; Cohen and Sharma, 2016). This ensures an innovative forward-looking orientation by the succeeding generation that fosters the exploration of knowledge for new products, markets, and business models.

As we have pointed out, there is around three decades of extant research developing theories, frameworks, and empirical studies in the context of dispersed-ownership non-family firms (mainly due to the ease of obtaining public databases on listed companies) on drivers of a PES. Table 6.1 provides an overview of the differences between family and non-family firms in terms of institutional, organizational, and individual drivers for a PES. In terms of institutional influences, there are few arguments for differences of influence and response, other than the fact that family firm leaders with a long-term orientation are more likely to stimulate strategic and entrepreneurial responses to become institutional champions and entrepreneurs that help shape the organizational field and understanding of the business–natural-environment interface and acceptable responses by firms. We observed this in the Okanagan Valley, BC, winery industry where the founder of Landjoy helped catalyze the organic movement by personally sharing his expertise and time with many wineries to help them transition to organic viticulture and wine making. Another study in the same Okanagan Valley winery industry by Reay, Jaskiewicz, and Hinings (2015) found that several family-firm leaders became institutional champions to change regulations to enable wineries to sell their wine directly to restaurants and from the winery stores instead of having to go through the British Columbia Liquor Control Board stores. Generational family wineries were found to balance the market, family, and community logics in their decision-making and actions. In contrast, corporate wineries focused on the market logic for their decisions. The primacy of family and community logic over market logic at times is evident in long-lived larger family firms like Cargill, Fidelity, Hallmark, and Michelin (Miller and Le

Table 6.1 *Differences in Drivers for PES between Family Firms and Non-Family Firms (bold indicates unique features of family firms)*

	Non-Family Firms	Family Firms
Institutional Influences	Coercive Normative Mimetic	Coercive Normative Mimetic **Institutional Entrepreneurship**
Institutional Logic	Market	Market **Family** **Community**
Stakeholder Influences	External, Internal	External, Internal **Family**
Strategic Decision-Making Unit	TMT (professional managers not related by kinship)	DC (family members who may/may not be professionally trained)
Cognitive Influences on Decision-Making	Managerial Cognitive Biases, Values, Attitudes, and Interpretations	**Controlling Family's** Cognitive Biases, Values, Attitudes, and Interpretations
PES Opportunity Framing and Decision Criteria	Legitimization in Corporate Identity Performance Evaluation Discretionary Slack Information Flow	**Family's Identification with Firm** **Long-Term Orientation** Performance Evaluation Discretionary Slack Information Flow
PES Capabilities	Stakeholder Integration Higher-Order learning Continuous Innovation	**Community Stewardship and Engagement** **Knowledge Transmission** Continuous Innovation

Breton-Miller, 2005), as well as in smaller mills in the Spanish olive oil industry (Gomez-Mejia et al., 2007).

In terms of stakeholder influences, the main difference between non-family and family firms is the central role of family as a stakeholder. Hence, the goals and interests of the family (whether all family members are engaged in the business or not) have to be balanced with goals of the external (investors, customers, suppliers, regulators, communities, media, NGOs) and internal (employees) stakeholders that non-family firms have to balance. The strategic decision-making unit in the family firm is the dominant coalition (DC) that is controlled by members of one or more families that own the business. While the DC may also consist of professional managers, the strategic role of the family members is significant and dominates that of the non-family managers. In non-family firms, decision-making in the top management team, contrary to classical economic theory, is usually less rational and more likely to be based on a political process of issue selling and power brokerage (Chen, Ge and Song, 2010; Eisenhardt and Bourgeois, 1988). Due to the dominance of family members in the DC, the family values are an important input into the decision-making process. Hence, in family firms, decision-making reflects the importance of unique family goals and criteria of balancing socioemotional wealth with economic goals, the long-term orientation focused on the entrepreneurship of succeeding generations, the identification of the family name with the business name and, hence, the importance of preserving the family reputation via the business reputation, and the embedding of the family in the local community (Sharma and Sharma, 2018).

In motivating employees in non-family firms to interpret environmental issues and challenges as business opportunities, firms create an organizational context in which proactive environmental actions are legitimized in the corporate identity, performance evaluation metrics include environmental targets and goals and are balanced with economic goals, managers are provided discretionary slack to explore ideas and innovations, and appropriate and adequate information flows support the innovation process (Sharma, 2000; Sharma, Pablo and Vredenburg, 1999). Decisions and strategies in family firms are driven to a larger extent by family values and the goals of preserving socioemotional wealth, a long-term orientation on the investment horizons, stewardship of family and community resources that includes the natural environment, and the need to preserve the family name via the firm's reputation. Hence, while non-family firms have to create organizational control systems to regulate employee behavior, family firms function to a greater extent via the sharing of family values in the organizational culture. These values tend to drive more long-term patient investments in a PES.

The capabilities required to develop a PES as per the corporate sustainability literature are the engagement of, and integration of information and perspectives from, a wide range of primary and secondary stakeholders, to generate processes of higher-order learning, leading to continuous innovations in products, services, processes, systems, technologies, and business models to address sustainability challenges (Sharma and Vredenburg, 1998). While family firms need exactly the same capabilities as non-family firms, they have an advantage in terms of having the conditions and the building blocks for the development of such capabilities to a greater degree than non-family firms: patient strategic horizon (long-term temporal orientation), community stewardship and engagement, and easier and quicker knowledge transmission within the organization (between family members, between generations, and between family members and managers via shorter channels of communication). It is no wonder that, based on our primary data collection and secondary research, in the Canadian winery industry, we did not find a single non-family winery that had adopted a PES. While we did find non-family wineries with a PES in France, they were much fewer in number or as a percentage than the family firms with a PES. The French context is a unique institutional environment with the wineries having been acquired recently by large banks and insurance companies as many families have been unable to repay their loans due to generation-to-generation splintering of families over several hundred years without a corresponding growth of the business to accommodate all the members of the succeeding generations.

The discussions in the previous chapters lead to the following overarching research questions for empirical verification in comparing family and non-family firms:

• Do family firms have a greater propensity for community and, hence, environmental stewardship as compared to non-family firms?
• To what extent does the family name and identity drive strategic action to preserve and protect the firm's reputation via a PES?

- Do family firms have less need for legitimization of a sustainability mission in their identity as compared to non-family firms due to the melding of the family's and firm's identities?
- Do managers in family firms more easily share in the family vision for sustainability as compared to managers in non-family firms?
- Do family firms adopt different organizational communication and issue-selling processes as compared to non-family firms to bring professional managers on board with the adoption of a PES?
- Do family firms need different control systems in evaluating employee performance in balancing economic and environmental outcomes and goals?

Overall, based on our review of the sustainability and family-business literatures, and an examination of our primary and secondary data, we surmise that the governance systems in non-family firms are influenced by institutional ownership, shareholder activists, and top management teams of professional executives. In contrast, the governance systems of family-firms comprise dominant coalitions of family members who are bound by kinship ties and value systems. Hence, family firms are more likely to adopt a PES strategy due to a forward-looking and long-term temporal orientation, and due to the family members' identification with the family business. However, family firm leaders must balance the bright and dark side of familiness. Thus, we expect two clusters of family firms based on the values and attitudes of the DC toward PES, and intentions for continuity of the enterprise into future generations. The first cluster, with positive attitudes toward PES and long-term orientation is likely to be far more engaged in recognizing, implementing, and investing patient capital in pursuit of PES than non-family firms. In contrast, the other cluster with negative attitudes toward PES and/or short-term horizons that are aimed to exit from the family firm are likely to be less effective than non-family firms in investing capital toward PES.

Summary of Propositions

Below we also list the propositions emerging from our discussions in Chapters 3, 4 and 5 for empirical investigation. These are grouped on the basis of different drivers and influences: institutional and stakeholder (Ch. 3), organizational, competitive (Ch. 4), and managerial (Ch. 5).

Institutional Influences

P1. In the presence of weak and unclear coercive forces (regulations and laws), normative forces (familial or individual values and attitudes toward environmental issues) have a higher influence in strategic choices of environmental strategies of firms.

P2. Mimetic forces are stronger in the presence of an influential institutional champion shaping organizational fields. The intensity and impact of these champions is higher and more long lasting when they are members of the controlling family.

(Example: as in the case of the Landjoy founder as a passionate advisor for the diffusion of organic practices in several organic wineries in the Canadian Okanagan region).

P3. Family firms are more likely to make long-term patient investments in a proactive environmental sustainability strategy as compared to non-family firms in responding to institutional forces due to their central goal of survival of the business for future generation.

P4. Leaders of family firms are more likely than leaders of non-family firms to be driven by family values in responding to institutional influences in developing their environmental strategies.

P5. Leaders of family firms are more likely than leaders of non-family firms to play the role of institutional champion to shape organizational fields related to corporate environmental strategy due to their longer-term strategic horizons.

Stakeholder Influences

P6. Firms with significant influence of institutional investors with longer time horizons for returns (family firms with goals of transgenerational continuity or non-family firms with significant influence of pension funds on their operations) are more likely to adopt proactive environmental sustainability strategies.

P7. Firms with large and diverse boards that include owners (especially in family firms) are more likely to adopt proactive environmental sustainability strategies.

P8. Firms pursuing proactive environmental strategies are less likely to be influenced by either regulators or media as compared to firms with reactive environmental strategies.

P9. Firms pursuing proactive environmental strategies are more likely to work collaboratively with NGOs to find pragmatic solutions for environmental challenges being faced in their industry or community.

P10. Family firms with a goal to maintain control and influence over the firm, and/or preserve the dynasty and long-term reputation of the firm, are more likely to proactively engage with the internal stakeholders – family members and employees.

P11. Family firms with a goal of preserving the family's identity and core values, and/or the existence of strong social ties within the family group, and/or the principal owner's emotional attachment to the firm, will be more likely to engage both internal and external stakeholders.

P12. Family firms in which the principal owner's emotional attachments are paramount, are likely to engage stakeholders that are less distinct and remote and consider developing unique business models, for example such as markets at the base of the pyramid.

Organizational Influences

P13. Family firms whose dominant coalitions have transgenerational continuity intentions are more likely to undertake patient long-term investments in PES as compared to non-family firms.

P14. Institutional investors with a long-term orientation are more likely to encourage and support the pursuit of environmental sustainability strategies by the firms they invest in.

P15. Family firms are more likely to adopt a PES strategy as compared to non-family firms when the family members in the dominant coalition identify with the family business.

Market / Competitive Strategy

P16. Both family and non-family firms that continually search for product and market opportunities and engage in regular experimentation are better positioned to respond opportunistically to environmentally sustainability challenges.

Development and Deployment of Organizational Capabilities

P17. Family firms whose dominant coalition shares a vision of sustainability will be more likely to develop and deploy their organizational capabilities for a PES as compared to a non-family firm that has a leadership strategic vision that favors sustainable business.

P18. A family firm's stewardship orientation, long-term orientation, familiness, and family identity will have a positive mediating effect on the development and deployment of organizational capabilities for generating a PES.

P19. Family firms whose dominant coalition shares a vision of sustainability will be more likely to invest in patient capital to develop their organizational capabilities for a PES as compared to a non-family firm that has a leadership strategic vision that favors sustainable business.

P20. Family firms are more likely to adopt a PES strategy as compared to non-family firms when the family members in the dominant coalition identify with the family business.

P21. Family firms with disagreements within the dominant coalition regarding their goal to continue the firm over generations, and/or identification with the firm are less likely to adopt a PES as compared to non-family firms.

P22. A family firm's leadership comprising members of the controlling family will be more likely to successfully deploy patient capital for developing capabilities to implement a PES as compared to the leadership of a non-family firm, primarily due to longer tenures and the lack of need to convince multiple influential shareholders.

P23. Non-family firms effectively undertake a PES via the development of organizational capabilities of stakeholder integration, higher-order learning, and continuous innovation. Family firms are more likely to build these capabilities due to a patient strategic horizon (long-term temporal orientation), community engagement, and easier knowledge transmission within the organization (between family members, between generations, and between family members and managers via shorter channels of communication).

Individual / Managerial Influences

P24. As compared to non-family firms, managers of family firms will exhibit more pronounced cognitive biases in interpreting environmental issues, whether negative or positive, under the influence of the family's dominant cognitive biases.

P25. Managers of family firms will be more likely to be driven by family values (whether pro or con environmental preservation) as compared to managers of non-family firms who will be more likely to be driven by regulatory compliance and industry standards.

P26. As compared to non-family firms, the level of commitment of the firm to environmental preservation will be more strongly transmitted to employees in family firms due to the greater likelihood of congruence of values toward environmental preservation in the DC and the shorter lines of communication.

P27. While non-family firms can foster an opportunity frame for their employees by legitimization of environmental preservation in their identity via embedding this into their mission, via extensive communication across the organization, and via policies and procedures designed to drive employee behavior, family firms are able to achieve such legitimization with a lower need for changing their mission and policies.

P28. Family firms often have the advantage of congruence between family identity and the firm identity, enabling family values of preserving the firm's reputation via stewardship to more easily influence managerial values for environmental preservation.

P29. While non-family firms may be able to foster an opportunity frame for its employees by implementing metrics and project/investment/

performance evaluation systems for projects, family firms are able to undertake and implement projects with long-term paybacks more easily than non-family firms due to less short-term scrutiny and reporting obligations and greater family commitment to long-term survival of the business family.

P30. *Family firms are more likely to have a long-term orientation as compared to non-family firms and will be more likely to foster an opportunity frame by creating discretionary slack to enable exploration for new ideas and innovations to undertake a PES in order to address sustainability challenges that are increasingly important to society and business in the future.*

P31. *While non-family firms can foster an opportunity frame for their employees through formal structures for generating and sharing of information relevant for decision-making for sustainable innovations, family firms use both formal and informal channels of information sharing, have shorter channels of communication, and a higher level of trust between long-term employees and family members to foster information flow.*

P32. *Long-term succession processes; intangible knowledge creation and transfer; reputation building; and corporate culture that supports employee participation and long tenures, stewardship of firm, and community resources, all contribute to a greater likelihood of fostering an opportunity frame among employees, managers, and family members of family firms to adopt a PES.*

P33. *In comparison to non-family firms, family firms may take longer to develop a PES but once they do, they will be quicker and more efficient in implementing such strategies.*

Figure 6.1 represents a framework that shows the main drivers for a PES, based on the extant literature and knowledge from research in non-family firms with modifications and additions based on the discussions in this monograph about the drivers relevant for family firms. The modifications to the proposed framework of drivers of a PES relevant for family firms are indicated in italics. Our core argument is that family firms have a higher propensity and a higher likelihood of developing a PES.

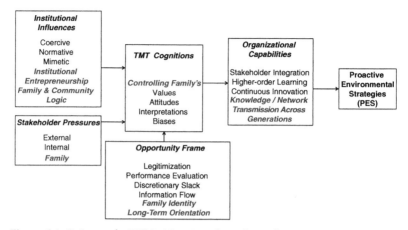

Figure 6.1 Drivers of a PES in Non-Family and Family Firms

Implications for Research

Overall, our research signals that family firms that have strong identification of the controlling family with their enterprise, longer tenures of dominant coalition, and a desire to continue the business for succeeding generations are more likely to undertake long-term patient investments to develop capabilities to pursue PES. In contrast, non-family firms managed by a top management team with short tenures (averaging around 4.6 years for *Fortune 500* firms), usually lack a similar patient long-term strategic horizon. The non-family firms are also responsive to quarterly financial reporting requirements and financial analyst pressure (Bansal and Desjardine, 2014), and have their compensation tied to stock options, which they would like an option to sell at short notice. Hence, they are reluctant to undertake such long-term investments in PES.

However, the higher propensity of family firms to undertake a PES does not necessarily mean that all family firms undertake a PES. Some may not be willing to undertake such strategies, and others unable to due to legacy and sunk costs and/or the inability to develop the capacity for action to address sustainability challenges (Chrisman et al., 2015). The willingness to take action is derived from family values regarding environmental stewardship as such values will open up the DCs to future business opportunities in areas of clean water, clean air, renewable energy, organic/biodynamic health and hygiene, etc. This motivates them to put into place the conditions to undertake long-term investments in a PES. Once the DC decides to undertake a PES, it is a much easier process as compared to a similar decision by the TMT of a non-family firm – the shared vision emerges much faster, the channels of communication are shorter and quicker, and, hence, the capability development and deployment for implementing the strategy is quicker and more effective (König et al., 2013). Nevertheless, factors such as dysfunctional and destructive family relationships, negative forms of nepotism, or an inability to fully engage talented non-family professionals (Eddleston and Kellermanns, 2007; Jaskiewicz et al., 2013; Verbeke and Kano, 2012) to recognize or implement PES, can dampen the best of aspirations to address sustainability challenges.

What implications does this have for research in corporate sustainability? Or for non-family firms seeking to undertake a PES? And for policy makers seeking to engage the power and resources of business to address global environmental sustainability challenges? We discuss each of these questions in turn.

PES in Different Industry Contexts

Our monograph is based on a theoretical analysis supported by exploratory case studies in an un- or under-researched, but critically important, sector of the global economy (family firms) within the context of addressing our planet's global sustainability challenges. The framework, arguments, and propositions that we present are based on extant literature in corporate sustainability, family business, deductive logic, and observations in a single industry sector – the winery industry. The framework and propositions will need be tested via rigorous empirical studies in single industries and also multiple-industry sectors with representative samples of family and non-family firms in each industrial sector matched on size, distribution of revenues, value chains, activities, products, markets, and institutional environments.

Undertaking a PES is easier in some industries than others. For example, while we did not survey the entire population of firms in Canada, France, and Chile, it was apparent during our research that all firms were compliant with environmental regulations on clean water, clean air, wastes, effluents, and packaging. Therefore, the variation in environmental strategies was driven more by endogenous organizational and individual/managerial drivers than exogenous institutional and stakeholder influences. However, the ease of undertaking a PES would vary in extractive industries, such as mineral and metal mining, oil and natural gas production, and forestry; and manufacturing industries, such as steel plants, metal finishing, paper and cardboard, machinery, furniture, auto parts, and processed foods. All these sectors have large numbers of family firms. For example, the world's largest steel manufacturer, Arcelor-Mittal, is publicly listed but family controlled through 40 percent ownership of shares coupled with ownership of shares via trusts and institutions. Many of these industries are marked by large environmental footprints. For example, mining and oil production uses massive quantities of water and the entails discharge of massive quantities of toxic tailings into water bodies. Vieri, a family-owned gold-mining company, has embedded sustainability in its entire value chain for a growing market that wants to buy sustainable gold from fair wages to fair trade to elimination of chemicals, etc. However, a comparison among large samples of family owned and non-family firms will determine if our frameworks apply in this industry sector. Similarly, forestry involves careful strategies for the sustainable management of forests and habitats, preservation of species, and preservation of the cleanliness of bodies of water and wetlands. Heavy manufacturing involves managing large air emissions. Furniture manufacture requires careful sourcing of sustainably grown and re-used wood. Coffee production requires managing global supply chains to ensure sustainably shade-grown coffee without clear-cutting of forests, damaging diverse habitats, etc.

It will also be very interesting to examine if their long-term strategic horizon enables family firms to be more proactive in investing patiently in a PES to clean up their current mining and manufacturing businesses or would they rather invest in greenfield new sustainable businesses of the future while continuing to run unchanged, their existing businesses with a large environmental footprints.

These studies could examine, in each industry sector, and in each institutional/country context, what proportion of family firms actually translate their family values to strategic action by using their firms as a vehicle to address sustainability challenges. Cross-industry comparisons can follow once an in-depth understanding of internal drivers is specified using controlled single-industry studies.

Measure Development

As we mentioned in Chapter 1, our focus was mainly on the two pure categories of firms: non-family firms with dispersed ownership with top management teams of professional managers not related by kinship; and family firms with concentrated ownership with a dominant coalition controlled by family members. While we acknowledge there will be other combinations with less intense influence of professional non-kin managers or family members on ownership and management dimensions of a firm, we need such finer-grained analysis to further theory building and empirical research. For this to happen, research in both fields of study will benefit from adding measures to gauge the extent of ownership held by family and non-family members, and the composition of the controlling management teams as a continuum rather than two discrete categories.

Chapter 5 focused on the attitudes, perceptions, and beliefs of TMTs and DCs, and how these are affected by, and affect, individual manager and family-member values respectively. These variables would necessitate comparative data collection from multiple individuals who form the TMTs and DCs in non-family and family firms. In the first instance, this would require the identification of these members. The measures would involve multiple respondents and a heuristic for aggregation of responses. Given the penchant for privacy in family firms, it is likely that multiple responses from dominant coalitions of family can be more effectively obtained via personal interviews rather than through mailed or electronic questionnaires. Thus, comparative case studies would be the first step toward empirically testing this framework. In addition to providing the preliminary test of the theoretical framework, such research could also be used to develop or refine measures for constructs in the study.

Measures for values regarding environmental preservation and the role of business in environmental sustainability have been developed in non-family-business contexts (e.g., Cordano and Freize, 2000), and in family-business contexts while examining family involvement in business, succession planning, stewardship climate, and financial and non-financial performance variables

(Holt et al., 2017; Klein, Astrachan and Smyrnios, 2005; Neubaum et al., 2017). The aggregated values and vision of the top management team of non-family firms, as a comparison point, could use the same measures. Although these can provide an important starting point, these measures will need to be further developed for empirical testing.

The corporate sustainability literature based on dispersed-ownership non-family firms has a rich theoretical (e.g., Hart, 1995) and empirical (e.g., Sharma and Vredenburg, 1998) research stream on the development of capabilities to undertake a PES. These capabilities, among others that have been empirically tested and proven, include stakeholder integration, higher-order learning, continuous innovation, and cross-functional integration (Russo and Fouts, 1997; Sharma and Vredenburg, 1998). We propose that family firms have parallel capabilities that facilitate the development of a PES: community engagement (stakeholder integration), knowledge transmission (higher-order learning and cross-functional integration), long-term strategic horizon (continuous innovation).

The corporate sustainability literature proposes that a proactive environmental strategy is itself a mega-capability that includes all the capabilities discussed above (Aragon-Correa and Sharma, 2003). Similarly, while the family business literature proposes the construct of familiness as a mega-capability that provides the firms with competitive advantage on multiple dimensions (Habbershon and Williams, 1999), this concept is still fuzzy and there is an opportunity to develop a robust measure and empirically examine if familiness enables and facilitates a PES.

The concept of socioemotional wealth has been discussed in the family business literature (Gomez-Mejia et al., 2007), but other than Berrone, Cruz, Gomez-Mejia, and Larraza-Kintana (2010), there is very little empirical work linking this concept to a firm's environmental strategy. Efforts are underway to unpack and examine the proposed dimensions of SEW (Hauck et al., 2016). How does each dimension in isolation and/or combination affect a firm's PES?

Proactive Environmental Strategy

For the main dependent variable of the study, proactive environmental strategy, the corporate sustainability or Organizations and the Natural

Environment literature has developed a wide variety of measures and instruments. These range from measures with high reliability but with a very narrow representation of environmental sustainability – e.g., pollution data in the form of toxic release inventories (King and Lennox, 2000) or pollution prevention registries – to measures with lower reliability that capture a wide range of environmental practices of firms (e.g., Sharma and Vredenburg, 1998). Thus, there are major opportunities to develop robust measures of corporate environmental strategy that capture a wide range of environmental practices and are reliable and replicable at the same time. Efforts are also underway to develop valid and reliable measures for sustainability performance variables in the family business literature (e.g., stewardship climate scale by Neubaum et al., 2017). However, sustainability remains an under-researched phenomenon in the family business domain, though researchers have measured the controlling family's influence on a business is multiple ways (e.g., Villalonga and Amit, 2010).

Generalizability

Family firms present a unique set of internal dynamics for strategic decision-making that motivate this research. Therefore, strategic management and family business scholars may find it worthwhile to explore if the theoretical ideas and framework presented here can be generalized to major strategic decisions by family firms other than the development of proactive environmental strategies. As the family business literature argues, family-controlled businesses represent a dominant segment of the global economy. Given the complexity and magnitude of environmental issues, research on how to motivate family firms to embrace sustainability strategy and to move toward a sustainable world becomes imperative.

While most of the literature on corporate sustainability has focused on large public firms, there are a few studies that examine the impact of the family firm on the community, society, and the environment. These include studies by Berrone et al. (2010), Dyer and Whetten (2006), and Sharma and Sharma (2011). Dyer and Whetten's (2006) study examining corporate social responsibility and citizenship as community and philanthropic initiatives found that family firms whose owners and managers personally identified with their firm were more likely to undertake corporate social practices, and concluded that having the family name on the business led them to avoid any practices or actions that might damage the firm's reputation.

Family-business scholars, e.g., Van Gils, Dibrell, Neubaum, and Craig (2014) argue that "family businesses are more attuned and attentive to social issues and stakeholders than nonfamily business. Noneconomic motivations (e.g., reputation, socioemotional wealth, and stewardship) appear particularly salient to family enterprises" (p. 193). They appeal to family business and strategy scholars to undertake studies to understand "how and *why* family firms make socially conscious decisions" (p. 202; emphasis added).

Temporal Perspective

Our monograph highlights the critical need to adopt a greater temporal perspective in both sustainability (e.g., Bansal and DesJardine, 2014) and family-business research (e.g., Sharma, Salvato and Reay, 2014). It is time that scholars and educators began to use the temporal lens to link the sustainability concept to the family firm context with a potential to bridge the gap between global-level multilateral agreements on sustainability challenges and organizational-level implementation to diffuse and adopt the concepts at the local level to generate innovations and solutions. This presents opportunities to examine how sustainability ideas are adopted and adapted by family firms to deliver a triple bottom line performance across generations, and build on these findings to improve integration of a proactive sustainability strategy in all types of firms, whether family or nonfamily business.

Agents of Institutional Change

In the Okanagan winery context, clearly the organic norms were driven by the owner of Landjoy, an expert in organic agriculture who became a catalyst for organic transformation of several vineyards. In the St. Émilion context, secondary data from website articles provides an indication that it could be a group of families that own the world's most prestigious wineries that are concerned about the image of the region's wines in a changing context where the world increasingly values ecosystem preservation and consumption of organic foods. Both examples point to interesting processes of institutional change and the role of agents as institutional champions in shaping organizational fields. We will elaborate on these two examples of institutional change.

During our data collection in the Bordeaux region in 2012, except for a few wineries, there was very little discussion about sustainable viticulture in this region. Since then, there has been a rapid institutional change. In some appellations, there is a move toward 100 percent universal organic or biodynamic practices. The local wine council for four Bordeaux appellations has passed a measure mandating sustainable farming. Any wine not farmed sustainably may only be bottled as a generic Bordeaux and not from the specific appellation that it is from. In 2016, the wine council of the St. Émilion region conducted a survey of its growers and found that 45 percent either had some sort of environmental certification or were working toward one. The Council ruled that, starting with the 2019 vintage, every wine bottle will have to be made from grapes grown with sustainable farming methods. As per secondary news articles, the impetus is partly driven by prominent family-owned wineries that produce some of the most expensive wines in the world and partly by attempts to recognize this region as a UNESCO World Heritage site. This decision impacts nearly 3.85 million cases of wine made annually by 973 grape growers in this appellation. Wineries can choose between state-approved certifications of organic, biodynamic or the HVE 3 (Haute Valeur Environmentale). St. Émilion is the first Bordeaux appellation to take this bold step toward sustainable practices. And the new rules are not legally binding until the national appellations authority has modified the specifications for each appellation. Nevertheless, other appellations have begun to discuss this example and start a movement that may convert the entire country's vineyards into organic or biodynamic. This could rapidly lead to 100 percent of the French wine regions and appellations producing and selling 100 percent organic or biodynamic wine. This would be a remarkable change for an industry that is hundreds of years old and steeped in tradition, culture, and history. Since French wines have a high reputation for quality and are high priced, if all regions (and especially Bordeaux) are able to produce high quality high priced red wines that increase in value with age as many Bordeaux wines do, the industry will be completely transformed. The other Old World and New World regions will have to follow since consumers will now have a new standard for quality as including sustainable viticulture and wine making.

How did this process of institutional change start in St. Émilion? Who were the change agents? Who were the institutional champions that catalyzed change in the organizational field? What were the dominant institutional logics during discussions and negotiations? The process of institutional change is still unfolding in St. Émilion and will unfold in the near future in all of Bordeaux and perhaps in the other regions in France and perhaps in other wine growing regions of the world. This would be a fascinating process of institutional change to document, study, and analyze. What role do family firms play in such change – as leaders or laggards as compared to non-family firms? What role do industry associations play? What role do members of families play in shaping collective action by industry associations? What role do NGOs and various stakeholders play in this change?

In the Okanagan Valley, we observed the role of an institutional champion – the founder of Landjoy's central role in championing and spreading organic practices among wineries in the region. As a champion, the founder has given freely of his time and expertise. His institutional role has shaped the organizational field in the Okanagan such that organic viticulture is widely accepted and implemented rather than biodynamic practices. This is due to the personal preferences, beliefs, and expertise of the founder of Landjoy. Would non-family firms play a similar role as institutional champions or is it more likely to be individuals and families?

Bringing the Family inside Non-Family Firms

In our research, the adoption of proactive environmental strategies via investments in longer-term patient innovation initiatives were much more evident in family firms that appeared to be driven mainly by family values rather than institutional forces or stakeholder pressures. The corporate wineries were driven mainly by production and market efficiencies. While the importance of market forces and the drive to gain competitive advantage and generate above-market returns for investors and shareholders is undeniable for business, non-family firms often struggle to create a culture where values and the vision of the business are shared. In many large non-family firms, employees are unable to visualize their own role and contribution to the strategic goals of business and how they can contribute to the long-term future competitive advantage of the firm.

Just as scholars who examine innovation develop frameworks to bring Silicon Valley inside a large firm (Hamel, 1999) – that is, the spirit of exploration, collaboration, idea generation, and creative innovation – scholars have the opportunity to develop frameworks for bringing the positive characteristics of an effective family inside a large non-family firm. Family members, DCs, and employees in non-family firms are more likely to share a sense of personal identity with the firm. How can non-family firms create a similar sharing of personal identity of employees with the firm? Family members, DCs, and employees are more likely to have a long-term strategic horizon. How can non-family firms motivate employees to undertake projects and strategies that require thinking beyond quarterly and annual goalposts and outcomes? Realizing the limitations of short-termism for undertaking patient investments in projects to generate products and businesses that address sustainability challenges such as clean water, elimination of packaging, non-toxic ingredients, and organic supply chains, Paul Polman, chairman of Unilever, made a corporate decision in 2009 (as soon as he became the CEO of Unilever) to scrap earnings guidance from quarterly reports in order to focus on creating long-term sustainable value (Feloni, 2018). Unilever is a publicly traded company with a long history and tradition. How is it not possible for the leaders of such giant, public, dispersed-ownership conglomerate companies to take a such a bold step as well to focus on creating long-term value for shareholders and institutional investors? Many investors do not invest in companies for the short term: institutional investors, mutual funds, index funds, and many shareholders, buy and hold patiently for dividends and capital appreciation for the long term. Why, then, do corporate leaders insist that they are unable to invest for the long term due to financial market and analyst pressures? These are interesting research questions that could generate interesting empirical studies.

How do non-family firms create a sense of place or local rootedness among employees? Family firms tend to be more engaged and stewards of their local communities because family members live in, and are embedded in, communities for generations and have a strong sense of localness and place. Family-owned firms, particularly those with operations where the family lives, and concerns over the legacy they leave for future generations, are particularly sensitive to community pressures to be stewards of the community resources – social harmony and justice and the ecosystems – and perform in an environmentally sensitive (also a place-sensitive) manner (Sharma and Sharma, 2011). These firms show a broader stakeholder orientation, in that they recognize the recursive effects of place on people and of people on place. They encompass both place attachment and community identity, which can get closely tied to organizational identity and may hold lessons for all enterprises seeking stewardship-based sustainability.

Shrivastava and Kennelly (2013) argue that firms (implying non-family firms) should create a sense of place or rootedness that motivates them to undertake a PES. The rootedness and sense of place will anchor and couple the firm to particular places in rich and dense ways and generate a greater motivation to adopt more sustainability strategies. This is because operations that are interdependent with the place and rely on it for particular, unique, and inimitable resources, and/or when an enterprise identity may be strongly related to the place, foster complex multilayered relationships with iterated meaning where place creates enterprise and enterprises create place and also a strong and holistic understanding that place is more than mere location, locality, or landscape, but is also socially created in a nexus of meaning.

Implications for Business Education

Given the need to unleash the ingenuity of both family and non-family business in addressing sustainability challenges, there is need for not only scholarship but also integrated academic programs that incorporate unique family business dynamics into business education while integrating sustainability as the driver of long-term competitive imagination and growth (Hart and Sharma, 2004). Executive education programs that bring together scholarship in family business and sustainability with practitioners from family and non-family firms have the potential to facilitate and catalyze knowledge building and adoption of corporate sustainability and transfer of knowledge from family to non-family controlled firms. Such programs would generate research and teaching cases to unleash the power of the dominant sector of the global economy (family business) to solve our sustainability challenges.

Implications for Policy

Policy makers need to recognize the power of family firms as major sectors in the world's economy, ranging from over 60 percent in the United States to almost 90 percent in many economies (FFI, 2018). Hence, policy in the form of environmental regulations and economic incentives needs to foster innovation and opportunity seeking among both family firms and non-family firms. For family firms, long-term survival, succession, and legacy is important. If incentives are created via taxation and regulations to motivate family firms to pursue business succession and legacy via forward-looking businesses to address sustainability challenges via long-term patient investments, family firms will be more motivated to undertake a PES.

Environmental regulations need to be based more on incentives to achieve positive environmental outcomes, such as clean air and water, which would spark innovations, rather than coercive prescriptions of technologies (which is often the case in many jurisdictions) that must be adopted to clean up certain toxic chemicals and emissions. Economic and investment incentives could also reward patient investments in blue ocean sustainable innovations and businesses that address global sustainability challenges by creating incentives for transgenerational succession in family firms.

Conclusion

Family businesses have an advantage due to unique individual and organizational learning processes that are embedded in family relationships and social networks, and transmitted from one generation to another. This leads to knowledge that is firm specific and difficult to replicate by other firms, especially non-family firms. Family interactions and knowledge transmission lead to unique cognitive dimensions of social capital that comprise a family's shared vision, and goal congruence between family members and their management team leads to an entrepreneurial orientation and innovation (Cabrera-Suárez et al., 2001; Jaskiewicz, Combs and Rau, 2015).

A patient long-term strategic horizon is central to the development of knowledge that is embedded in valuable, rare, inimitable, and firm-specific capabilities which take a long time to be developed and are path dependent on unique histories and actions within the firm (Dierickx and Cool, 1989). The uniqueness of the family firms in knowledge and capability creation lies in this temporal dimension as each succeeding generation is groomed over a long period of time via formal apprenticeship and informal discussions and interactions as the successor develops from student to manager to top executive over several years (Carter and Justis, 2009), developing deep business, product, market, and industry knowledge. Due to very long tenures and high-trust environments in family businesses, the older generation is willing to patiently groom the next generation and share wisdom versus non-family businesses where senior managers are often focused on protecting their own career and position. This facilitates patient long-term investments that may pay back and generate competitive advantage for the succeeding generation rather than the current generation.

The long process of succession fosters longer-term perspectives about the future of the business in the evolving societal environment and the opportunities that may be presented for future entrepreneurship and business. This enables the acquisition of new capabilities that can capitalize on the evolving opportunities that emerge in the changing environment, such as the addressing of sustainability challenges. Woodfield and Husted (2017) argue that such a long succession process also can lead to reverse knowledge transfers as the succeeding generation gains new understanding of evolving social and environmental issues and their impacts on the future of business, and can bring this knowledge to develop a PES in the business. As the succeeding generation gains confidence over time, the successor gains confidence and expertise and also respect from the older generation to be able to offer new knowledge and advise on developing a future oriented PES (Cabrera-Suarez et al., 2018).

Miller and Le Breton-Miller (2005) argue that leaders of family firms are better stewards of the business and resources because they are intrinsically motivated to act for the collective good of their firm as compared to transient leaders with increasingly shorter tenures in non-family firms. Davis, Schoorman, Mayer, and Tan (2000) find that leaders of family firms identify with the firm, embrace its objectives, and are committed to making it succeed, even at personal sacrifice, and are more likely to make farsighted investments such as those in research and development, infrastructure, new business models, and capital investments in plant, equipment, and information technology. Moreover, family firms also reinvest a much higher percentage of their profits in new businesses and technologies as compared to non-family firms by curtailing dividends (Anderson, Mansi, and Reeb, 2003).

Family firms, especially when the family name is the same as the business name and when they are embedded in communities, are more concerned about the firm's reputation than non-family firms. The leadership often works to strengthen the reputation of the firm before the succession process to provide the successor a strong and healthy environment. Such investments may include image, branding, infrastructure, research and development, social capital, and environmental stewardship. Reputation and legitimacy for family firms more often than not involve community relationships, including charitable investments in civic and social institutions (Morck and Yeung, 2003).

Long-term succession processes, intangible knowledge creation and transfer, reputation building, corporate culture that supports employee participation and long tenures, and stewardship of firm and community resources, all contribute to fostering an opportunity frame among employees, managers, and family members of family firms to adopt a PES. Unleashing the resources, motivations, and power of the millions of business families around the world as a force of good will have a positive impact on our planet's environmental sustainability via businesses undertaking more patient long-term investments to generate profitable businesses that also address global sustainability challenges.

References

Anderson, R. C. and Reeb, D. 2004. Board composition: Balancing family influence in S&P 500 firms. *Administrative Science Quarterly*, 49: 209–237.

Aragon-Correa, J. A. and Sharma, S. 2003. A contingent natural-resource based view of proactive environmental strategy. *Academy of Management Review*, 28(1): 71–88.

Bansal, P. and DesJardine, M. R. 2014. Business sustainability: It's about time. *Strategic Organization*, 12(1): 70–78.

Berrone, P., Fosfuri, A., Gelabert, L. and Gomez-Mejia, L. R. 2013. Necessity as the mother of 'green' inventions: Institutional pressures and environmental innovations. *Strategic Management Journal*, 34: 891–909.

Berrone, P., Cruz, C. and Gomez-Mejia, L. R. 2012. Socioemotional wealth in family firms: Theoretical dimensions, assessment approaches, and agenda for future research. *Strategic Management Journal*, 25(3): 258–279.

Berrone, P., Cruz, C., Gomez-Mejia, L .R. and Larraza-Kintana, M. 2010. Socioemotional wealth and corporate responses to institutional pressures: Do family-controlled firms pollute less? *Administrative Science Quarterly*, 55(1): 82–113.

Björnberg, Å., Elstrodt, H. and Pandit, V. 2014. The family-business factor in emerging markets. *McKinsey Quarterly*. December.

Brigham, K. H., Lumpkin, G. T., Payne, G. T. and Zachary, M. A. 2014. Researching long-term orientation: A validation study and recommendations for future research. *Family Business Review*, 27(1): 72–88.

Cabrera-Suárez, K., De Saá-Pérez, P. and García-Almeida, D. 2001. The succession process from a resource- and knowledge-based view of the family firm. *Family Business Review*, 14: 37–46.

Cabrera-Suárez, M. K., García-Almeida, D. J. and De Saá-Pérez. P. 2018. A dynamic network model of the successor's knowledge construction from the resource-and knowledge-based view of the family firm. *Family Business Review*, 31(2): 178–197.

Carter, J. and Justis, R. 2009. The development of successors from followers to leaders in small family firms: An exploratory study. *Family Business Review*, 22(2): 109–124.

Chen, Y., Ge, Y. and Song, Z. 2010. Power perspective: A new framework for top management team theory. *iBusiness*, 2: 274–281.

Chirico, F., Backman, M., Bau, M., Klaesson, J. and Pittino, D. 2018. Local embeddedness and rural-urban contexts for business growth in family versus Non-family firms. *Academy of Management Proceedings*.

Chrisman, J. J., Chua, J. H. and Litz, R. 2004. Comparing the agency costs of family and non-family firms: Conceptual issues and exploratory evidence. *Entrepreneurship Theory & Practice*, 28: 335–354.

Chrisman, J. J., Chua, J. H., De Massis, A., Frattini, F. and Wright, M. 2015. The ability and willingness paradox in family firm innovation. *The Journal of Product Innovation Management*, 32(3): 310–318.

Chua, J. H., Chrisman, J. J. and Sharma, P. 1999. Defining the family business by behavior. *Entrepreneurship Theory and Practice*, 23(4): 19–39.

Cohen, A. R. and Sharma, P. 2016. *Entrepreneurs in Every Generation: How Successful Family Businesses Develop Their Next Leaders*. Oakland, CA: Berrett-Koehler.

Coleman, J. S. 1990. *Foundations of Social Theory*. Cambridge, MA: Harvard University Press.

Cordano, M. and Frieze, I. H. 2000. Pollution reduction preferences of U.S. environmental managers: Applying Ajzen's theory of planned behavior. *Academy of Management Journal*, 43: 627–641.

Daspit, J. J., Holt, D. T., Chrisman, J. J. and Long, R. G. 2016. Examining family firm succession from a social exchange perspective: A multiphase, multi-stakeholder review. *Family Business Review*, 29(1): 44–64.

Davis, J. H., Schoorman, D. F. and Donaldson, L. 1997. Toward a stewardship theory of management. *Academy of Management Review*, 22(1): 20–47.

Davis, J., Schoorman, R., Mayer, R. and Tan, H. 2000. The trusted general manager and business unit performance. *Strategic Management Journal*, 21: 563–576.

Dierickx, I. and Cool, K. 1989. Asset stock accumulation and sustainability of competitive advantage. *Management Science*, 35(12): 1504–1511

Dyer, W. G. Jr. and Whetten, D. A. 2006. Family firms and social responsibility: Preliminary evidence from the S&P 500. *Entrepreneurship Theory & Practice* November 30(6): 785–802.

Eddleston, K. and Kellermanns, F. W. 2007. Destructive and productive family relationships: A stewardship theory perspective. *Journal of Business Venturing*, 22(4): 545–565.

Eisenhardt, K. M. and Bourgeois, J. 1988. Politics of decision-making in high velocity environments: Toward a midrange theory. *Academy of Management Journal*, 31(4): 737–770.

EFB. 2012. Family business statistics. *European Family Business*, EFB Position Paper, June 1st, 2012.

Feloni, R. 2018. Unilever's CEO says that in 9 years, no investor has asked him the questions he's waiting to hear. *Business Insider*, March 15. www .businessinsider.com/unilever-paul-polman-long-term-sustainability-dive rsity-2018-3.

FFI. 2018. www.ffi.org/page/globaldatapoints (accessed July 30, 2018).

Gersick, K. E., Davis, J. A., Hampton, M. M. and Lansberg, I. 1997. *Generation to Generation: Life Cycles of the Family Business*. Boston: Harvard Business School Press.

Gomez-Mejia, L. R., Cruz, C., Berrone, P. and DeCastro, J. 2012. The bind that ties: Socioemotional wealth preservation in family firms. *Academy of Management Annals*, 5(1): 1–79.

Gomez-Mejia, L. R., Takacs, K. H., Nunez-Nickel, M., Jacobson, K. J. L. and Moyano-Fuentes, J. 2007. Socioemotional wealth and business risks in family-controlled firms: Evidence from Spanish olive oil mills. *Administrative Science Quarterly*, 52: 106–137

Gordon, G. and Nicholson, N. 2008. *Family Wars: The Real Stories behind the Most Famous Family Business Feuds*. London, UK: Kogan Page Limited.

Grote, J. 2003. Conflicting generations: A new theory of family business rivalry. *Family Business Review*, 16(2): 113–124.

Habbershon, T. G. Y. and Williams, M. L. 1999. A resource-based framework for assessing the strategic advantages of family firms. *Family Business Review*, 12: 1–15.

Hamel, G. 1999. Bringing Silicon Valley inside. *Harvard Business Review*, September–October 1999.

Hart, S. L. 1995. A natural-resource-based view of the firm. *Academy of Management Review*, 20: 874–907.

Hart, S. L. and Sharma, S. 2004. Engaging fringe stakeholders for competitive imagination. *Academy of Management Executive*, 18(1): 7–18.

Hauck, J., Suess-Reyes, J., Prügl, R. and Frank, H. 2016. Measuring socioemotional wealth in family-owned and managed firms: A validation and short form of the FIBER scale. *Journal of Family Business Strategy*, 7 (3): 138–148.

Holt, D. T., Rutherford, M. W. and Kuratko, D. F. 2010. Advancing the field of family business research: Further testing the measurement properties of the F-PEC. *Family Business Review*, 23(1): 76–88.

Holt, D. T., Pearson, A. W., Carr, J. and Barnett, T. 2017. Family firm(s) outcomes model: Structuring financial and nonfinancial outcomes across the family and firm. *Family Business Review*, 30: 182–202.

Jaskiewicz, P., Uhlenbruck, K., Balkin, D. B. and Reay, T. 2013. Is nepotism good or bad? Types of nepotism and implications for knowledge management. *Family Business Review*, 26(2): 121–139.

Jasckiewicz, P., Combs, J. G. and Rau, S. B. 2015. Entrepreneurial legacy: Toward a theory of how some family firms nurture transgenerational entrepreneurship. *Journal of Business Venturing*, 30(1): 29–49.

King, A. and Lennox, M. 2000. Industry self-regulation without sanctions: The chemical industry's Responsible Care Program. *Academy of Management Journal*, 43(4): 698–716.

Klein, S. A., Astrachan, J. H. and Smyrnios, K. 2005. The F-PEC scale of family influence: Construction, validation, and further implications for theory. *Entrepreneurship Theory & Practice*, 29: 321–339.

König, A., Kammerlander, N. and Enders, A. 2013. The family innovator's dilemma: How family influence affects the adoption of discontinuous technologies by incumbent firms. *Academy of Management Review*, 38 (3): 418–41.

La Porta, R., Lopez-De-Silanes, F. and Shleifer, A. 1999. Corporate ownership around the world. *Journal of Finance*, 54(2): 471–517.

McConaughy, D. L. 2000. Family CEOs vs. nonfamily CEOs in family-controlled firms: An examination of the level and sensitivity of pay to performance. *Family Business Review*, 13(2): 121–131.

Miller, D. and Le Breton-Miller, I. 2005. *Managing for the Long-Run: Lessons in Competitive Advantage from Great Family Businesses.* Cambridge, MA: Harvard Business Press.

Miller, D. and Le Breton-Miller, I. 2006. Family governance and firm performance: Agency, stewardship, and capabilities. *Family Business Review*, 19: 73–87.

Miller, D., Steier, L. and Le Breton-Miller, I. 2003. Lost in time: Intergenerational succession, change, and failure in family business. *Journal of Business Venturing*, 18: 513–531.

Morck, R. and Yeung, B. 2003. Agency problems in large family business groups. *Entrepreneurship Theory & Practice*, 27: 367–382.

Neubaum, D. O., Thomas, C. H., Dibrell, C. and Craig, J. B. 2017. Stewardship climate scale: An assessment of reliability and validity. *Family Business Review*, 30(1): 37–60.

Pearson, A. W., Carr, J. C. and Shaw, J. C. 2008. Toward a theory of familiness: A social capital perspective. *Entrepreneurship Theory & Practice*, 32(6): 949–969.

PWC. 2012. *Family firm: A resilient model for the 21st century.* PWC Family Business Survey, October 2012.

Reay, T., Jaskiewicz, P. and Hinings, C. R. 2015. How family, business and community logics shape family firm behavior and "Rules of the Game" in an organizational field. *Family Business Review*, 28(4): 292–311.

Russo, M. V. and Fouts, P. A. 1997. A resource-based perspective on corporate environmental performance and profitability. *Academy of Management Journal*, 40(3): 534–559.

Sharma, P. 2001. Stakeholder management concepts in family firms. *Proceedings of the International Association of Business and Society Annual Meetings, Sedona AZ.*

Sharma, P., Chrisman, J. J. and Chua, J. H. 2003. Succession planning as planned behavior: Some empirical results. *Family Business Review*, 16(1): 1–15.

Sharma, P., Salvato, C. and Reay, T. 2014. Temporal dimensions of family enterprise research. *Family Business Review*, 27(1): 10–19.

Sharma, P. and Sharma, S. 2011. Drivers of Proactive Environmental Strategy in Family Firms. *Business Ethics Quarterly*, 21(2): 309–332.

Sharma, P. and Sharma, S. 2018. The role of family firms in corporate sustainability. In A. Sturdy, S. Huesinkveld, T. Reay and D. Strang (eds.), *The Oxford Handbook of Management Ideas.* Oxford, UK: Oxford University Press.

Sharma, S. 2000. Managerial interpretations and organizational context as predictors of corporate choice of environmental strategy. *Academy of Management Journal*, 43(4): 681–697.

Sharma, S. 2014. *Competing for a Sustainable World: Building Capacity for Sustainable Innovation*. UK: Greenleaf Publishing. ISBN: 13: 978–1–78353–224–7.

Sharma, S., Pablo, A. and Vredenburg, H. 1999. Corporate environmental responsiveness strategies: The role of issue interpretation and organizational context. *Journal of Applied Behavioral Science*, 35(1): 87–109.

Sharma, S. and Vredenburg, H. 1998. Proactive corporate environmental strategy and the development of competitively valuable organizational capabilities. *Strategic Management Journal*, 19: 729–753.

Shrivastava, P. and Kennelly, J. J. 2013. Sustainability and place based enterprise. *Organization and Environment*, 26(1): 83–101.

Sirmon, D. G. and Hitt, M. 2003. Managing resources: Linking unique resources, management, and wealth creation in family firms. *Entrepreneurship Theory & Practice*, 27(4): 339–358.

Sorenson, R. L. 1999. Conflict management strategies used in successful family businesses. *Family Business Review*,12(4): 325–339.

Tokarczyk, J., Hansen, E., Gree, M. and Down, J. 2007. A resource based view and market orientation theory examination of the role of "familiness" in family business success. *Family Business Review*, 20(1): 17–31.

Van Gils, A., Dibrell, C., Neubaum, D. O. and Craig, J. B. 2014. Social issues in the family enterprise. *Family Business Review*, 27(3): 193–205.

Verbeke, A. and Kano, L. 2012. The transaction cost economics theory of the family firm: Family-based human asset specificity and the bifurcation bias. *Entrepreneurship Theory & Practice*, 36(6): 1183–1205.

Villalonga, B. and Amit, R. 2010. Family control of firms and industries. *Financial Management*, 863–904.

Ward, J. L. 2004. *Perpetuating the Family Business: 50 Lessons Learned from Long Lasting, Successful Families in Business*. NY: Palgrave Macmillan.

Woodfield, P. and Husted, K. 2017. Intergenerational knowledge sharing in family firms: Case-based evidence from the New Zealand wine industry. *Journal of Family Business Strategy*, 8(1): 57–69.

Zellweger, T., Kellermanns, F., Chrisman, J. C. and Chua, J. H. 2012. Family control and family firm valuable by family CEOs: The importance of intentions for transgenerational control. *Organization Science*, 23(3): 851–868.

Zellweger, T. and Nason, R. 2008. A stakeholder perspective on family firm performance. *Family Business Review*, 21: 203–216.

Index